AF844428

The New-Wave Cinema

thinking|media

series editors:
bernd herzogenrath
patricia pisters

The New-Wave Cinema

Evolution of Society's Art System

Golnaz Sarkar-Farshi

BLOOMSBURY ACADEMIC
NEW YORK • LONDON • OXFORD • NEW DELHI • SYDNEY

BLOOMSBURY ACADEMIC
Bloomsbury Publishing Inc, 1359 Broadway, New York, NY 10018, USA
Bloomsbury Publishing Plc, 50 Bedford Square, London, WC1B 3DP, UK
Bloomsbury Publishing Ireland, 29 Earlsfort Terrace, Dublin 2, D02 AY28, Ireland

BLOOMSBURY, BLOOMSBURY ACADEMIC and the Diana logo are trademarks of Bloomsbury Publishing Plc

First published in the United States of America 2026

Copyright © Golnaz Sarkar-Farshi, 2026

For legal purposes the Acknowledgments on pp. xiv–xv constitute an extension of this copyright page.

Series design by Daniel Benneworth-Gray
Cover image © Paolo Sanfilippo

All rights reserved. No part of this publication may be: i) reproduced or transmitted in any form, electronic or mechanical, including photocopying, recording or by means of any information storage or retrieval system without prior permission in writing from the publishers; or ii) used or reproduced in any way for the training, development or operation of artificial intelligence (AI) technologies, including generative AI technologies. The rights holders expressly reserve this publication from the text and data mining exception as per Article 4(3) of the Digital Single Market Directive (EU) 2019/790.

Bloomsbury Publishing Inc does not have any control over, or responsibility for, any third-party websites referred to or in this book. All internet addresses given in this book were correct at the time of going to press. The author and publisher regret any inconvenience caused if addresses have changed or sites have ceased to exist, but can accept no responsibility for any such changes.

Library of Congress Cataloging-in-Publication Data
Names: Sarkar-Farshi, Golanz author
Title: The new-wave cinema : evolution of society's art system / Golnaz Sarkar-Farshi.
Description: New York : Bloomsbury Academic, 2026. |
Series: Thinking media | Includes bibliographical references and index.
Identifiers: LCCN 2026009176 | ISBN 9798765125106 hardback |
ISBN 9798765125113 paperback | ISBN 9798765125137 pdf |
ISBN 9798765125144 epub
Subjects: LCSH: Motion pictures–History–20th century |
Motion pictures–History–21st century | LCGFT: Film criticism
Classification: LCC PN1993.5.A1 S3675 2026
LC record available at https://lccn.loc.gov/2026009176

ISBN: HB: 979-8-7651-2510-6
ePDF: 979-8-7651-2513-7
eBook: 979-8-7651-2514-4

Series: Thinking Media

Typeset by Integra Software Services Pvt. Ltd.

For product safety related questions contact productsafety@bloomsbury.com.

To find out more about our authors and books visit www.bloomsbury.com and sign up for our newsletters.

Contents

Figures

Preface

During my undergraduate studies in Architecture, I often found myself drawn away from seminars and design workshops. Instead, I spent long hours sitting on the campus stairs, immersed in philosophy books and film magazines. The time at home that was intended for university assignments was frequently devoted to watching the "good" films—at the time we did not have a more differentiated term for describing them—that my friends and I were discovering together. In the late 1990s, when VHS cassettes and later DVDs were the dominant medium for watching videos and films, we would circulate copies among ourselves. I vividly remember watching the first two of these films, *Easy Rider* and *Zabriskie Point*, on a heavily worn VHS tape. Its poor visual quality only underscored how many hands it had passed through: those of young cinephile students, like ourselves, searching for art that felt rebellious, innovative, revolutionary, and liberating.

In addition to these at-home screenings of what I later learned were part of the New Hollywood movement, I recall waiting for hours in the cold to get tickets to film festival premieres. Many of these films would come to be associated with New Iranian Cinema. Likewise, the "mind-blowing" and "unconventional" films of Truffaut, Godard, Fassbinder, and Herzog—directors we came to admire over time—introduced us to the cinematic revolutions of the *Nouvelle Vague* and New German Cinema. I later learned that "new-wave cinema" was the term used in film scholarship for film art that we found "good," "mind-blowing," and "unconventional."

This passion for international new-wave cinema, coupled with an intense interest in philosophy, led me to pursue a master's degree in film and theater studies. It was during one seminar—serendipitously, as the course had nothing to do with the topic—that I first encountered Niklas Luhmann's systems theory of society. At the time—in the early 2000s—Luhmann's theory was practically absent from film and media studies, and it still is in academic circles globally.

Reading *Social Systems*—the first book by Luhmann I could get my hands on—was a revelation. His theory offered seemingly boundless possibilities for analyzing social phenomena—be it literature, cinema, politics, science, or philosophy. My interest quickly grew into a commitment. Over the past fifteen years, I have explored international new-wave cinemas through the lens of systems theory and have taught this approach in various academic settings, hoping to share both my passion and the insights I have gained with students. This book is the product of that sustained interest and the many years devoted to its development.

While many studies of national new waves of cinema—which I will address in the Introduction chapter—provide valuable insights, they frequently approach their subjects from multiple perspectives simultaneously, without clearly distinguishing among these viewpoints or elucidating the dynamics that connect them: viewpoints engaging with aesthetic elements, narrative structures, production conditions, and funding frameworks. One of the aims of this book is to propose a more differentiated methodology for the study of film—and ultimately new-wave cinema—by examining the distinctions among these aspects while also investigating their interrelations. As I will demonstrate, Luhmann's systems theory of society, combined with film theory, has the potential to offer such a methodology.

Despite the richness of this body of scholarship on new-wave films, a theoretical gap remains besides the methodological one addressed above: new waves of cinema are seldom examined as a coherent, transnational phenomenon, even though my research suggests that they consistently function in this way. A key observation supporting this perspective is that new waves of cinema tend to emerge during periods of significant social turbulence. This recurring pattern, which I have identified through my dual engagement with new-wave cinema and Niklas Luhmann's systems theory of society, became another central motivation for writing this book.

When I began my doctoral research in 2015, many colleagues half-jokingly questioned my sanity: "Why burden yourself with Luhmann's notoriously dense and abstract theory, especially to apply it to film?" These exchanges often evolved into productive conversations about the accessibility of complex theories. Like many others, Luhmann's ideas have become more approachable thanks to scholars who have taken the time to write critical introductions, teach them, and develop companion texts. Writers such as Dirk Baecker, Elena Esposito, and Peter Fuchs made Luhmann's theory more accessible to me, and I hope this book will extend that accessibility. To achieve this, I have dedicated the first part of the book to introducing key terms from Luhmann's theory that I use in my arguments, addressing readers who I assume are primarily film students, film scholars, or cinephile laypeople like I was during my undergraduate years.

These said, this book may still prove challenging for readers more familiar with conventional film scholarship. However, I consider that part of its strength and, hopefully, its appeal. The challenge lies in the book bringing together familiar concepts from film theory with those from Luhmann's systems theory—terms like *communication*, *information*, *understanding*, *form*, *observation*, and *meaning*. While these words may seem intuitive at first glance, their meaning within systems theory is more abstract than expected and it often diverges considerably from everyday usage. I have introduced these key terms in simple language in Part One of the book and encourage readers to refer back to these explanations when reading Part Two, particularly if they find certain formulations difficult to understand.

Another aspect of the book that might require more attention than usual while reading is the transliteration of Farsi names in the chapter on New Iranian Cinema. In this chapter, I have transliterated the Farsi names of political organizations, films, film characters, and most individuals according to the guidelines of the US Library of Congress.[1] However, I have retained the widely used Latin spellings for the names of contemporary Iranian directors, as these are often the versions they themselves use and promote in international settings.

This book is intended not only for students and scholars of film studies or laypeople curious about film but also for scholars of Luhmann's work who have criticized his theory for being too abstract to apply to concrete case studies. Although this specific investigation into new waves of cinema may not seem directly relevant to the sociological research projects I am familiar with that are grounded in Luhmann's theory, I believe it can nonetheless offer valuable methodological insights. It demonstrates how systems theory of society can be applied to concrete scientific observations—provided that such observations are equipped, both theoretically and methodologically, to engage with the inherent unobservability of certain processes, such as thinking, understanding, irritation, and resonance, as put forward by Luhmann.

To examine my original observation that new waves of cinema emerge simultaneously with major social changes in their context, and to provide concrete examples of how Luhmann's theory can be applied to the analysis of new waves from this perspective while addressing the thematic and methodological gaps mentioned above, I have selected three movements for my case study: New German Cinema, New Hollywood, and New Iranian Cinema. They were chosen for two major reasons. First, they reflect a broad range of social, linguistic, and cultural contexts, spanning three different continents. Second, they are bodies of work with which I have both linguistic fluency and significant contextual familiarity, through personal experience and extensive research.

It is my hope that this book not only presents the value of the synthesis between media studies—particularly the study of new-wave cinema—and

Luhmann's systems theory of society but also instills in its readers a sense of enthusiasm for this interdisciplinary approach comparable to my own. More importantly, I hope it encourages them to actively apply the resulting theoretical framework to their own work in film and media studies, thereby critically complementing and expanding it.

Acknowledgments

Writing this book has by no means been a solitary endeavor, despite the countless hours spent immersed in reading and writing in solitude at my desk or watching and rewatching numerous films. I owe a deep debt of appreciation to the many individuals and institutions whose support made this project possible.

First and foremost, I wish to express my sincere thanks to Professor Dirk Baecker for his invaluable academic guidance and for generously engaging in thoughtful, in-depth discussions on Luhmann's systems theory of society. I am equally indebted to Professor Lorenz Engell, whose insightful film-philosophical feedback significantly enriched my reflections on the evolution of new waves of cinema. The development of this book was greatly shaped by the detailed critical feedback of my dear friend and colleague Dr. Christina Weiss. Our extensive discussions helped refine the ideas and arguments formulated in the early sketches of this book, allowing them to mature into the present form. The high quality of the film screenshots presented in the book is thanks to the generous time and remarkable expertise that my dear friend Moritz Wehrmann devoted to enhancing their resolution and sharpness.

The research upon which this book is based was made possible by two distinguished sources of funding: a four-year doctoral scholarship from the DAAD (*Deutscher Akademischer Austauschdienst*; German Academic Exchange Service), which supported my research between October 2014 and September 2018, and the *Abschlussstipendium* (Graduation Scholarship) awarded by Bauhaus University Weimar from July to September 2019.

I extend heartfelt thanks to the dedicated and courteous staff at the Bauhaus University Weimar Library and Berlin State Library, who provided seamless assistance in accessing essential resources—especially during the challenges posed by the pandemic. This research could not have progressed without access to the many films cited and analyzed throughout the book. I am particularly appreciative of Dr. Peter Stettner, director of *Filminstitut Hannover* (Film Institute of Hannover), and the staff and colleagues at the *Deutsche Kinemathek* (German Cinematheque) in Berlin, who facilitated access to films produced in Germany between 1933 and 1949. I am also profoundly appreciative of Eberhard Baier, who generously shared his remarkable archive of New German Films with me. Discovering such a rich collection of films and film magazines in a small German town was both unexpected and deeply rewarding.

Finally, this project would not have come to fruition without the unwavering emotional support of my parents. The strength and perseverance they instilled in me sustained my efforts through the most demanding phases of this work. My heartfelt appreciation goes to my dear partner, Afshin, for his humor, compassion, and loving understanding, particularly on the days when my workload made long-distance communication difficult. And last but not least, I owe special thanks to little Iris, my niece, whose radiant smiles gave me the encouragement to keep going.

Introduction

To cultivate a comprehensive understanding of the conceptual framework underpinning this book, it is beneficial to employ the metaphor of ocean waves. Envision how these waves are an inherent part of the ocean, or more precisely, how they are the ocean itself, yet are in resonance with the wind; how they initially manifest as minuscule ripples and, as the wind persists, they evolve into more substantial and robust waves. While a wave may be perceived as a single entity, distinct from the calmer surface of the ocean, it is impossible to pinpoint its beginning or end. There is no clear line or plane that can demarcate these extreme points and distinguish the wave from the rest of the ocean. Finally, it is worthwhile to consider the movement of a wave in its entirety: its genesis and approach to the shore, its breaking upon the shoreline, and its return to the ocean followed by its eventual dissipation in the backwash.

The metaphor of wave has been used, in film critique and scholarship, for certain movements or phases in film history or for certain categories of films. These distinctions rhetorically follow the critics of the film magazine, *Cahiers du Cinéma* (Cinema Notebooks), who labeled a "certain" aesthetic and narrative "tendency"—as Truffaut (2022) has called it—in French filmmaking in the 1950s and 1960s *Nouvelle Vague*, which translates to *new wave*. For the subsequent film theorists and historians, new wave transformed from a title for a certain group of French films dating from a limited period into a category or a tendency that could be observed in other societies as well, such as in Germany, Iran, Czechoslovakia, India, Hong Kong, Japan, Italy, Brazil, Argentina, the United States, England, and the sub-Saharan African countries, mainly between the 1950s and 1980s. In this sense, Frisch uses the term in plural and speaks of different "*Nouvelle Vagues*" (2007, 14). Hence, many different innovative film movements that were respectively called New German Cinema, New Iranian Cinema, New Hollywood, *Cinema Novo*, etc., fall under the umbrella of new-wave cinema.

Reading research that engages with any of the new waves of cinema—whether mentioned here or not—one realizes that such studies often analyze a certain canon considered to constitute a new wave within a specific national society, drawing out a collection of common characteristics that distinguish that new wave from other films produced in the same society at the same time.[1] However, now that the term *new wave* is used to describe a multitude of global filmic movements that have emerged in different societies at different times with diverging characteristics, its global application requires justifications that go beyond defining categories based on a set of common traits. This is because, when observing films associated with different new waves of cinema, one realizes that their forms, narratives, and production contexts are extremely diverse and have very little in common. Furthermore, relying on canons and categories shifts the analysis away from understanding the organic nature of how a new wave of cinema emerges and declines—a quality that the metaphor of the ocean wave aptly captures. The search for the common quality of these very diverse global new waves, and for a concept and methodology that can account for their organic development and decline, has motivated the writing of this book.

Having studied multiple new waves of cinema, I have realized that, despite their differing formal approaches, narrative strategies, and production contexts, all these new waves share one common property: they all emerged simultaneously with significant, often problematic changes of some kind in the societal order and structure of their creation context. In this sense, there may have been a correlation between the new wave of cinema in Czechoslovakia and the Prague Spring of 1968, which was characterized by reforms introduced by the Communist Party (Hames 2006, 69). In 1950s India, the young, decolonized society was struggling to build a national identity, while the new wave of cinema in this society—also known as Parallel Cinema—was beginning to react to the dominant Bollywood film tradition (Gupta 1974, 23–4). The conflict-laden construction of a postcolonial identity also accompanied the New African Cinema south of the Sahara (Pfaff 1997, 58–9). In Hong Kong in the 1980s, film critics discovered a new aesthetic trend that they called Hong Kong New Wave Cinema. These films emerged in a society that had only recently freed itself from colonialism and was affected by the Vietnam War, as well as by student and labor movements (Kar 2001, 31). New Iranian Cinema emerged at a time when Iranian society was grappling with the foreshocks of the 1979 revolution. New German Cinema emerged parallel to the Student Movement in West Germany, followed by the emergence of the *Rote Armee Fraktion* (Red Army Fraction; *RAF*), while France, parallel to the emergence of *Nouvelle Vague*, was not only struggling with the Algerian War abroad in the late 1950s and the early 1960s but also experienced a student uprising at home a few years later. The situation was no different in the United States: the equal rights movements at home overlapped with the Vietnam War abroad when the first New Hollywood films were made.

This intriguing co-occurrence has been mentioned in passing by Naficy, who sees "periods of major social turmoil and transition" as the context that gives rise to "innovative cineastes and cinematic movements" (2012, 115). However, he does not explicitly label these cinematic movements as new waves of cinema, nor does he underscore the universality of this co-occurrence as a singular phenomenon. Beyond this, the co-occurrence has not been the subject of substantial research on the development of new-wave cinema as a borderless progression. Hence the question arises: could the common simultaneity to periods of major societal turmoil and transition explain and justify the existence of an overarching concept of new wave? If so, how should the correlation between the newly emerging formal and narrative structures of new-wave films and their contemporary social developments be studied?

This book aims to answer the above questions. It argues that complex but similar dynamics exist between radical social developments and the emergence of new-wave films that unfold in parallel, regardless of the geopolitical region in which these changes occur. Methodologically, in tracing the evolution of new waves in cinema, the book employs the metaphor of the organic formation of ocean waves and deliberately avoids treating new-wave cinema as a fixed category—a practice that inevitably leads to the construction of canons, deeming some films part of the new wave while dismissing others as irrelevant. Instead, it opts for a close analysis of the films that were made around the same time as major social events were unfolding. It studies these films' formal and narrative development to identify an organic pattern in the rise and fall of different new waves corresponding with specific social developments. To do so, the book focuses on three different new-wave cinemas from three different continents: New German Cinema, New Hollywood, and New Iranian Cinema. In this way, it ensures that its observations are sufficiently diverse and that the results of these observations are as generalizable as possible.

Answering the question of new-wave cinema as a universal phenomenon that emerges parallel to important social transitions opens a novel narrative about this film-scholarly concept, which has until now remained vague and not clearly articulated in film theory and history. Furthermore, if sufficiently grounded and substantiated, this new, universal concept challenges the common belief that new-wave cinemas merely followed the French *Nouvelle Vague* and adopted its aesthetic and narrative strategies. Rather, from this new perspective, German Expressionist Cinema (between the 1920s and 1930s), Italian Neorealist Cinema (between the 1940s and 1950s), and New Indian Cinema (between the 1950s and 1960s) may also be considered as new waves, even though they preceded *Nouvelle Vague*.

Film and Society

Viewed from an abstract perspective, studying the relationship of new waves of cinema and their formal and narrative characteristics with social developments requires a multifaceted theoretical gadget—something similar to a Swiss knife with at least two different but interconnected tools: a film-theoretical blade to cut through, analyze, and explain filmic developments, and a tool representing a theory of society that can link theoretical and analytical observations of films to concrete events in their social context. Before embarking on the analytical observation of new waves of cinema, this theoretical tool must first be constructed. To achieve this, I will employ an existing theory of society and integrate it with established theories of film to build a unique theoretical framework—one that functions like a Swiss knife—rather than relying on existing sociologies of film.

Sociologies of film treat films and society as two mutually exclusive realms with either or both of the following relationships. First, a causal relationship between film and society is assumed, meaning that films can directly affect individuals and institutions within society. For film sociologies with this approach, films can, for example, influence the way specific social groups behave, or they can undermine or reconfirm specific institutional relations, thereby strengthening or challenging them. Film sociologies based on the tradition of cultural studies, with Stuart Hall (1996) being their pioneer, also explore the ways in which individual viewers can react back to the hegemony that film, as an operator of the capitalist system, imposes on them.[2]

The second approach focuses on a mimetic relationship between film and society, meaning that films represent and reflect society. In this approach, film can, for instance, represent power relations, gender roles, or labor circumstances in a certain national society, thereby holding a mirror in front of society, reflecting its structure and dynamics back to it.

When it comes to observing and analyzing films, both approaches merely focus either on production circumstances or on characterization, plot, and diegesis—in other words, on narrative aspects of films—as representations of or influential factors on members of the audience, their actions in everyday life and the bigger context of the societal system they live in. Books and edited volumes on film sociology take either one of the above approaches or combine both to observe the causal and mimetic dynamics between films and the audience.[3]

While these approaches have made important contributions to sociology, they are not helpful for this book and its focus on the simultaneity of new-wave cinema and social upheavals. This is because some of the most significant features of new-wave films—as will be demonstrated later—lie in their formal components, such as camera movements and angles, shot compositions, editing, the relationship between sound and image, and other formal and technical aspects. These components and the complexity resulting from their coexistence within a single film cannot be addressed by existing film sociologies, which focus solely on diegesis and narrative. Furthermore, seeking a causal or mimetic relationship between new-wave film aesthetics and radical social events—as existing film sociologies could potentially do, though they have not yet—cannot be fruitful. On the one hand, not all new-wave films mimetically reproduce images of events unfolding in society at the time of their production. On the other hand, causation itself is subject to criticism, as causal relations are reliant on the observer's point of view and intention. Moreover, they can neither be affirmed nor rejected, either theoretically or empirically.[4]

Given these limitations, I will create a novel synthesis in this book and sketch a hybrid theory for the sake of the observations I will perform here—a theory that can address filmic forms and techniques and the complexity of society simultaneously. To do so, I will introduce Niklas Luhmann's systems theory of society to film studies. Luhmann's theory will be used as a catalyst to establish a conceptual bond between several existing theories of film, enabling them to serve as an innovative method for observing not film *and* society but rather film *as* society.

Luhmann's Systems Theory of Society

Niklas Luhmann was a German social theorist who lived from 1927 to 1998. He is the founder of systems theory of society, which serves as the theoretical backbone of this book. I am consciously avoiding the term *sociology* for Luhmann's theory, because he himself did not view his contribution as a continuation of the sociological theories and approaches of his time but rather as a reaction to their insufficiencies. In a lecture series held in 1991 and 1992, Luhmann stated that sociology in his era was "in a profound theoretical crisis," because the classical theories developed by Max Weber, Karl Marx, Georg Simmel, and Émile Durkheim were unable to address the problems that modern society was facing (2013, 1). Luhmann sought to develop an abstract and encompassing theory of modern society, inspired by his former teacher at Harvard, Talcott Parsons.

Luhmann began developing his theory of society based on Parsons' action system theory. However, he rejected Parsons' notion of society as an open system operating within an input-output schema (Knodt 1995, xxiii). Instead, he borrowed the concept of *autopoiesis* (or self-organization) from biology. Biologists Humberto R. Maturana and Francisco J. Varela originally coined this term to describe the "circular organization" that characterizes living beings (1980, xvii). Autopoietic living systems, as defined by Maturana and Varela, are self-producing and self-maintaining systems marked by organizational closure.

But the concept of autopoiesis was not enough for Luhmann's purposes either. While this concept offered a solution to the limitations of Parsons' open systems, it carried an inherent "biological reductionism" that Luhmann needed to overcome in order to employ it within his meta theory of society (Gilgen 2013, ix). Luhmann found the solution to this limitation in George Spencer-Brown's second-order cybernetics. A philosopher and mathematician, Spencer-Brown (1972) developed a formal calculus based on the act of drawing a distinction as the fundamental operation that enables observation. Through second-order cybernetics, Luhmann was able to conceptualize society as a self-referential system, meaning that it, as an autopoietic system, can draw a distinction between itself and its environment and thereby observe itself.

This brief excursion demonstrates how complex and multifaceted Luhmann's systems theory of society is. Unlike normative or applied sociology, this theory is grounded more in philosophical and logical concepts, providing a broad and abstract framework that applies to society as a self-referential, autopoietic, and all-encompassing system with specific evolutionary patterns, internal distinctions, and functions, despite local differences in national societies. This high degree of complexity and versatile applicability explain why I find Luhmann's theory suitable for observing the phenomenon of new-wave cinema as an apparently universal occurrence that consistently coincides with certain contradictions and conflicts in society.

Niklas Luhmann's systems theory of society can easily be mistaken for a grand narrative in the "postmodern age," which Lyotard (1984) famously declared as the end of grand narratives. However, there is a crucial difference between Luhmann's theory and the grand narratives that Lyotard criticizes for attempting to offer a cohesive, ideological, and all-encompassing truth. Luhmann's theory does not claim to discover an ontological truth about society and its evolution. Rather, it recognizes that its objects are constructed through the specific distinctions it draws in order to observe society's evolution. In other words, it is an auto-reflexive theory, meaning it is aware that its objects are not "ontologically autonomous" from its observations (Jahraus 2012, 432). In this sense, Jahraus refers to it as a "meta theory" or a "super theory," rather than a grand narrative (Jahraus 2012, 432).

Luhmann's systems theory can navigate highly abstract theoretical levels while maintaining concrete scholarly observations. Its broad scope allows for the analysis of micro units that construct society, such as communication units, alongside the simultaneous examination of broader social and societal phenomena like conflict and evolution. In this way, Luhmann's theory, as will be demonstrated, can provide a complex and coherent link between the formal aspects of new-wave films, explored as communication units, and the social crises in which these films were embedded.

Systems Theory and Film

It must have become evident by now that this book takes an unconventional theoretical and methodological approach compared to most works in film and media studies. It seeks to establish a connection between an artistic phenomenon and a socio-dynamic one—namely, between new-wave cinema and radical changes in society—through Luhmann's theory, which has so far remained almost entirely unfamiliar to film scholarship.[5] However, there is a gap in Luhmann's theory that poses a challenge for studying the evolution of films, namely its limited coverage of art. Luhmann (2000a) addresses art as a functional subsystem of modern society only toward the end of his life and career. In doing so, he focuses primarily on a limited number of art forms, without explicitly naming them—that is, the visual arts. Other art forms such as literature, music, dance, theater, and film—as well as their unique medial complexities—remain unaddressed within Luhmann's systems theory. This book endeavors to make film, as a subsystem of art, accessible to students and scholars working with Luhmann's systems theory.

To achieve this collateral aim—namely, to make Luhmann's systems theory accessible to film studies and to render film thinkable within the scope of systems theory—I dedicate Part One of this book to developing a novel theory of filmic communication and reception based on Luhmann's framework. In the first chapter of this part, I explain the key concepts of Luhmann's theory applied in this book to make them accessible to a film-scholarly audience—concepts including observation, medium and form, autopoiesis, communication, self-reference and other-reference, meaning, dissemination media and success media, functional differentiation, the system–environment relationship, memory, contradiction and conflict, and evolution.

In the second chapter of Part One, I focus on the formal structure and communicative process of films. I address key questions previously posed by psychoanalytical and phenomenological film theories and offer a novel response using Luhmann's theories of communication and observation. In doing so, I outline a new theoretical framework for understanding filmic communication through the lens of systems theory. This framework serves as the analytical basis for the concrete observations presented in the book's second part.

In Part Two, I apply the filmic communication model developed in Part One, based on Luhmann's systems theory, to analyze distinct new-wave cinemas across three continents to ensure both diversity and universality: New German Cinema, New Hollywood, and New Iranian Cinema. Each chapter in this section, dedicated to one of these new-wave movements, begins with a brief analysis of the crisis that had already begun in the respective national society shortly before the emergence of new-wave films. After providing this overview of the social context, each chapter delves into the narrative and formal analysis of specific films representing the respective new waves, examining their forms as shaped by the medium of filmic communication. Additionally, the role of three other communications within the environment of filmic communication is examined—specifically, economic communication in the forms of production funding and box-office sales; mass media, concretized as film review magazines; and the role of politics in enacting laws related to film funding and censoring specific forms and topics within filmic communication—in influencing the evolution of film within the framework of a new wave.

The first chapter of Part Two, dedicated to New German Cinema, is almost twice as long as the other two chapters in this part. This is because, as you will see, this particular new wave demonstrates a higher degree of complexity compared to the other two and can therefore serve as a seminal case against the background of which other new waves of cinema can be studied. On the one hand, New German Cinema was not only accompanied by a magazine—namely *Filmkritik* (Film Critique)—and multiple manifestos but also encompassed a Feminist New Wave with its own magazine, *Frauen und Film* (Women and Film). On the other hand, New German Cinema clearly demonstrates three distinct evolutional stages of film art—denoted by the neologisms *venture*, *rupture*, and *departure*—which are not present to the same extent or detail in the other selected new waves. Having distinguished these three tendencies in New German Cinema by means of thorough film analyses, I will then examine whether they were also present in New Hollywood and New Iranian Cinema in the subsequent chapters.

Summing up the theoretical endeavors in Part One, which enable the concrete observations of social contradictions and conflicts and the parallel evolution of film art in Part Two, the concluding chapter presents the key findings of this study. It outlines a universal schema for the evolution of film art in the form of a new wave and clarifies the relationship between this specific evolutionary path and the contradictions and conflicts within its social context. Finally, this chapter highlights significant questions raised in the analytical sections, encouraging future research on the evolution of film and other arts using Luhmann's systems theory of society.

Part One

A Systems-Theoretical Perspective on Film

1.1

Introduction to Systems Theory of Society

Observation and Form

Understanding the basics of George Spencer-Brown's *Laws of Form*—developed in a book of the same title—is crucial for comprehending the logic behind Luhmann's systems theory of society. In his endeavor to introduce a new mathematical notation system for writing logical statements, Spencer-Brown presents the ideas of *distinction* and *indication* (1972, 1). For him, in order to indicate something, it is necessary to draw a distinction between that object and everything else, thereby pointing to the side of the distinction that contains the object meant to be indicated. To visually demonstrate the combination of distinction and indication, Spencer-Brown introduces a new notation *mark*, namely a cross, as depicted below:

$$\overline{A\;}\big|\; B$$

The vertical line in the cross depicted above represents the distinction between *A* and *B*, whereas the horizontal line extends toward the side of the distinction that is being indicated here, namely toward *A*. Spencer-Brown calls *A*, or the indicated side of the cross, the *marked state*, with *B* being the *unmarked state* (1972, 5). He calls the unity of the mark, the marked state and the unmarked state, *form*. In other words, form is the unity of distinction and indication (1972, 1 ff.).

Note that I have been using the term *distinction*, and not *difference*, here. The reason is that Spencer-Brown and Luhmann, following his logic, are not developing ontological theories that assume inherent differences between objects, but rather rely on the operational concept of distinction, meaning that distinctions are actively made by an instance, whether it be human consciousness or a unit of communication (Luhmann 1993, 199). The one who draws the distinction is the *observer* (Baecker 2015). Observation in this context is an abstract term. It does not refer to visual observation but rather to drawing a distinction and indicating one side of the distinction. In this sense, although observation can materialize while looking at objects in the world—when looking at the chair in the room, we distinguish and indicate it as a chair by not looking at other objects in the room that are not the chair—it can also, and more importantly, take place while thinking about something or, as we will see later, in the process of communication.

The observer who generates the form, that is, the one who draws a distinction and thereby indicates one side of the distinction, can neither observe the unmarked state during the observation process nor observe himself as the observer who is making that distinction. Observing these two positions is only possible under one of the following conditions. One way to do so is for the observer to take time to also observe the unmarked state of his primary observation and thereby observe his own primary observation. In other words, he can observe what the unmarked state of his primary observation has been and what he has thereby distinguished the marked state from. In this sense, he can observe his own primary observation. Another way of observing the observer's primary observation is through a second observer who, also having taken time, can observe both the marked and unmarked states created by the primary observer. Luhmann calls the primary observation *first-order observation*. The observation of the first-order observation, be it through the primary observer himself or through a different instance, is called *second-order observation* by him (Luhmann 1990, 15–16). With the same logic, one can also speak of third- and fourth-order observations.

Autopoietic Systems and Their Environment

Drawing on Spencer-Brown's concept of form, Luhmann defines the concepts of *system* and *environment*. Theories of systems have already existed before Luhmann. These theories gained considerable complexity by defining a system as a collection of elements with certain relations under specific conditions, and then examining these elements, relations, and the conditions of their sustainability in detail.[1] However, just as Spencer-Brown sought to reduce the entire notation system of logic to one cross sign that could reproduce the complexity of logical thinking without relying on a complex notation system, Luhmann proposes that different social systems, at an abstract level, can be defined similarly to forms, namely as distinctions in the sense introduced above (Luhmann 2006, 46–7). There is, however, a major difference between forms and social systems. Whereas singular forms are created through a single observational operation and then disappear immediately, social systems are the sum of operations that draw the same kind of distinction continuously. These distinctions are made between the system, that is, the marked state of the form, and the unmarked state that Luhmann calls *environment* (Luhmann 2006, 44–5).

The systems that Luhmann engages with are social systems, not biological ones. However, to explain the relationship between social systems and their environment, Luhmann borrows the biological concept of *autopoiesis*, or self-reproduction, from Humberto Maturana and Francisco Varela. They conceptualize living organisms as autopoietic systems because they are composed of elements produced by and within the system itself. Although autopoietic systems rely on the environment as the source of energy and raw materials, their internal processes are not determined by the environment but rather by these processes themselves (Maturana and Varela 1980). Take, for example, the regeneration of cells within a living organism's body as an autopoietic system. The organism requires oxygen and food from the environment, which are processed within its body to nurture existing cells. However, new cells are not created through the direct transformation of oxygen and food into living cells but rather through processes of cell division. Hence, new cells can only be produced from the existing cells, despite this process's reliance on the intake of oxygen and food from the environment. In this sense, autopoietic systems are operationally closed, but their existence is only possible within and in reliance on their environment (Luhmann 2012a, 32–3).

For Luhmann, the operation that distinguishes society from its environment is *communication*. Communication, when produced continuously, draws a distinction between society and everything else that is not society—such as the organic bodies and the consciousnesses, or *psychic systems*, of the human beings involved in communication. This concept of society is highly abstract and differs from other sociological theories that view individuals as the basic building blocks of society.[2] In systems theory of society, although communication relies on human consciousness, which itself relies on the human body, it remains an operationally closed system, just as the body and consciousness are operationally closed in their own rights. Hence, consciousness and the body belong to the environment of communication and society.

Communication

The autopoietic operation that Luhmann conceives as communication is the synthesis of three distinctions: *information*, *utterance*, and *understanding*. Although communication is operationally closed to the psychic systems of the parties involved, it is worth considering these systems in the explanations that follow, for the sake of better understanding. Luhmann identifies these parties as *ego*, who plays a role similar to that of the receiver of communication in semiotics, and *alter ego*, who is "someone like oneself" (Luhmann 1995, 80), as the one who initiates and directs communication toward ego. I will refer to alter ego, as Luhmann himself does, simply as *alter*.

In this model, utterance is the only concrete, perceivable, and performative part of communication. It can occur through speech, text, visual or auditive media such as shapes or sounds, or even through actions and gestures such as whistling, frowning, or giving someone a high five. In order to understand alter's utterance, ego must draw a distinction between the specific form of utterance that alter has chosen and the information he might have intended to express through it. An example inspired by Esposito (2002, 15) clarifies these processes further: if alter verbally utters the sentence: "it's eleven o'clock," ego might distinguish different pieces of information from it, such as: "it's time to go home," or "let's turn on the TV to watch the soccer game." In either case, ego knows that alter had different choices of utterance to express the same piece of information, and that through his current utterance he might have meant different things (Baecker 1996a, 86–7). Given this contingency of information and forms of utterance, and also with ego being able to distinguish many different pieces of information from alter's utterance, both information and utterance are distinctions and selections made by alter and ego. It is in this sense that Luhmann conceptualizes all three components of communication, namely information, utterance, and understanding, as distinctions.

Ego, as a human being, must couple his consciousness or psychic system—a system with *thinking* as its main operation—with communication, thereby differentiating information from alter's utterance and understanding alter's intention. But there is no guarantee that alter is understood in the way he intended. Communication is often also *misunderstood*. Since alter has no access to ego's consciousness, he can only know whether his intention was properly understood or misunderstood when ego thematizes his understanding of alter's primary utterance in a subsequent utterance addressed to alter. Without this subsequent utterance, no one can know whether and how ego has (mis)understood alter, and whether communication has taken place as the synthesis of information, utterance, and understanding through the distinction between the former two.

For an external observer of the communication between alter and ego, who counts as a second-order observer of the communication, only the utterances exchanged between the two parties, which take the form of concrete actions, are perceivable. However, it is important not to reduce a chain of communication to the perceivable utterances that apparently "trigger each other," but rather to also heed the selectivity of information and understanding that are integrated into these utterances (Luhmann 1995, 164).

Self-Reference and Other-Reference

If a set of ongoing communications can differentiate society as an autopoietic—that is, operationally closed—system from the environment, then every single unit of communication must be operationally closed as well. As mentioned above, this means that communication cannot be directly influenced by the environment—that is, by anything other than information, utterance, and understanding. At the same time, its existence depends on the environment, just as the existence of an organism depends on receiving food and oxygen from its environment. Systems in the environment of communication that are necessary for its occurrence include the psychic systems of ego and alter, which themselves rely on the biological bodies of ego and alter in their own environment, which again depend on material resources from their environment to survive.

Although the environment cannot directly influence communication, it can be thematized by it. In other words, the information in the synthesis of information, utterance, and understanding can be about the environment—that is, about something other than the communication itself. For example, communication can be about alter's thoughts and feelings, the backache he recently had, the upcoming election, the film that ego and alter watched an hour ago, or the meal they are having right now—all of which belong to the environment of the communication taking place between them. Referring to the environment through information counts as communication's *other-reference.*

At the same time, operational closure means that communication is *self-referential*, indicating that understanding occurs only by distinguishing information from utterance. In other words, no factor outside the triad can directly influence or determine communication. Regardless of ego's current mood or physical condition, and regardless of the weather or global warming, ego can always understand alter's intention by distinguishing information from his utterance, and through no other means. This level of self-reference is called *basal self-reference* by Luhmann. The differentiation of autopoietic systems from the environment presupposes basal self-reference since their elements can only be reproduced in reference to themselves.

Luhmann identifies two additional levels of self-reference: *reflexivity* and *reflection*. Reflexivity arises when a communication process becomes the topic of itself. Consider the expression, "our talk in the past hour has been very fruitful, because we have been addressing the major problems in the company." In this example, one of the communication units within the ongoing chain thematizes the chain itself, marking a case of reflexivity (Luhmann 1995, 443). Reflection, by contrast, occurs when the difference between the system and its environment becomes part of the system's processes (Luhmann 1995, 444; 455 ff.). For instance, reflection takes place when a communication unit within a social system, such as art, thematizes the question: "what is art?" or engages with what art should be. Like reflexivity, reflection can also occur within the psychic system, as when someone thinks: "what is thinking?" Luhmann considers the reflection of autopoietic systems to be a form of *self-observation*, as the system thereby observes the distinction between its operations and its environment (Luhmann 1995, 456 ff.).

Medium, Form, and Meaning

Earlier, I brought up the example of alter uttering a sentence and ego being able to understand it in multiple ways. However, as Luhmann points out, it is not obvious that ego understands alter at all, which means that communication, as the synthesis of information, utterance, and understanding, is improbable unless a certain condition is met. To overcome the improbability of communication, ego and alter must both have access to the primary *medium* that makes the most fundamental type of communication—that is, verbal communication—possible. This medium is language, and understanding becomes possible only because both alter and ego have access to the same medium, in this case: the same language (Luhmann 2012a, 113 ff.).

In Luhmann's theory, medium is not merely something that mediates between alter and ego, nor can it be reduced to language. Rather, in a broader and more abstract sense, Luhmann conceptualizes medium as a collection of *loosely coupled* elements, whereas any *form* created from it consists of some of the same elements that are *strictly coupled* with each other (Luhmann 2012a, 117–18). This terminology, which might at first glance appear unintuitive and overly abstract, becomes more tangible when considered in Saussure's terms. In the case of language, Luhmann's concept of medium corresponds to Saussure's *langue*, whereas any form created based on it is an instance of *parole* (Saussure 2011). In Saussure's theory, *langue* consists of the vocabulary and grammar of a language. With Luhmann, these elements are understood as loosely coupled, meaning that vocabulary items can potentially combine in numerous ways according to grammatical rules to form concrete, meaningful expressions. Any such specific combination of these words, whether spoken or written, is considered *parole*, or form in systems-theoretical terms. In *parole* as form, certain words are strictly coupled based on a concrete set of grammatical rules.

The initial improbability of communication is overcome when both alter and ego learn the same language as their shared communication medium. Thereby, they understand which words carry which meanings in that language and how those words can be combined into larger meaningful units. When alter utters something, he creates a form out of the medium of language, which in turn potentially allows for the creation of countless other forms from its loosely coupled elements. In light of the concepts of medium and form, the previously introduced concept of the contingency of utterance in the context of verbal communication can be rendered more vividly. This refers to the contingency of alter choosing different forms from the medium of language to convey the same information. Ego, in turn, understands alter because he can trace the form of the utterance back to the medium of the language they both share.

By observing the distinction between the actualized form and other forms that were potentially possible within the context shared by alter and ego, ego distinguishes information from alter's utterance. The difference between the *actual* and the *potential* in communication represents another distinction between medium and form, with the medium here being *meaning*. The medium of meaning is constituted by the totality of potential utterances that could be made in a given communicative context. When a concrete utterance is made by alter, it only makes sense when ego observes it against the medium of meaning—that is, against the backdrop of all other utterances that could have been made instead in that specific context. This concept of meaning closely aligns with that established by Edmund Husserl in phenomenology as "the horizon of choices." As Peter Fuchs puts it, "meaning is—in phenomenological terms—given when events are observed as selections, for the understanding of which the horizon of choices is co-present" (2012, 247; my translation).

Media and forms abound in the world, depending on the observer who identifies them as such. For example, there are material medium/form distinctions such as sand/footprints or wood/chair, but these are not coupled with the medium of meaning. Meaning is not constituted by simply drawing a distinction between any form and its corresponding medium but only through the operations of social and psychic systems—namely, through communication and thinking. According to Luhmann, this is because human consciousness and society have "evolved together," and the shared medium of meaning ensures they have a means of structural coupling (1995, 59).

It is noteworthy that, while communication relies on the medium of meaning as well as other media—such as primary communication media or dissemination and success media, which will be discussed below—these media do not constitute information, utterance, or understanding, but rather only facilitate utterance and contribute to understanding. Thus, they can be considered as belonging to the environment of communication.

Dissemination Media and Success Media

Thinking about society as a complex system composed of communication, one realizes that overcoming the initial improbability of communication through spoken language is not sufficient for forming a society. Rather, Luhmann realizes that society creates additional media to address various problems related to communication (2012a, 120). One such problem is reaching larger groups of people and expanding the circle of information recipients. Society has addressed this second improbability of communication by developing so-called *dissemination media*. These media consist in "copying technologies to disseminate communication" (Luhmann 2000b, 2). They range from the products of the printing press—such as books, newspapers, and magazines—to electronic mass media (Luhmann 2012a, 121 ff.; 2000b, 2). In this case, the medium consists of the various contents and different styles in which these contents are presented through newspapers, books, radio and television programs, etc., with the concrete instances of each serving as form.[3]

Although dissemination media solve the problem of reaching those who are not present at a specific time and place, thereby extending communication beyond the limits of face-to-face verbal interaction, there are still challenges regarding certain communication types that they cannot overcome. These are forms of communication whose acceptance plays a crucial role in maintaining the continuity of communication and the sustainability of the system of society. For example, in the context of paying taxes to the government or complying with traffic rules in a complex, modern society, it is impractical to have a government representative present with every individual citizen, persuading them in face-to-face conversation to hand over a portion of their income to the government or to wait at a red light despite being in a hurry. It would be even less helpful to ask citizens through dissemination media—e.g., in newspapers or television—to please comply with traffic rules and pay their taxes.

This is where *symbolically generalized communication media*, or *success media*, are developed to increase the likelihood of acceptance for certain communications (Luhmann 2012a, 121–2). These media are symbolic in that they condense complex meaning into recognizable symbols. They are also generalized, as they can be applied to an unlimited number of communication units involving these symbols, regardless of the specific context or the parties involved. Luhmann distinguishes several symbolically generalized communication media in modern society, including truth and values, love, money, art, and power[4] (Luhmann 2012a, 203, 206, 208, 209, 212).

The function of symbolically generalized communication media lies in establishing a connection between *selection* and *motivation* (Luhmann 2012a, 199). Since all such media equally aim at connecting selection and motivation, they are "functionally equivalent" regardless of their varying use cases (Luhmann 2012a, 199). As discussed earlier, communication for Luhmann is a process involving selection—selecting what information to convey and how to utter it on alter's part, and what information ego ultimately selects to distinguish from alter's utterance. If alter chooses to couple his utterance with a symbolically generalized medium of communication, this in itself motivates ego to accept the communication. However, this acceptance is only motivated when both ego and alter recognize that their choices are shaped by such a medium.

Baraldi (2021c, 230) provides two examples to clarify the connection between selection and motivation established through symbolically generalized communication media, which I will elaborate on further here. In the first example, if alter is a random person who orders ego to stop while ego is riding a motorbike, it is highly unlikely that ego would comply. However, if alter is a police officer and thus his selection of giving a stop order is coupled with the symbolically generalized media of legal values and power, then ego—who is also familiar with those values and power relations—is motivated to comply to avoid having to pay a fine later. Another example is when ego accepts alter's claim about the earth orbiting the sun. This is because alter has selected to communicate this claim in an academic paper using the medium of scientific truth based on evidence and logic. Ego, who is also familiar with scientific methods and arguments for discovering the truth, gets motivated to find alter's claim valid.

Acceptance of communication that relies on symbolically generalized communication media implies that ego prioritizes doing something over not doing it. For example, in the case of communication involving the success medium of money, a transaction counts as acceptance of the communication, whereas no transaction counts as its rejection. In the case of communication involving the success medium of legal values, compliance with these values constitutes acceptance, while non-compliance signifies rejection. When it comes to art, accepting an object, a performance, an event, or a sensory input in general as an artistic utterance is contrasted with rejecting it as such. Luhmann refers to these binary schemata—being payment/non-payment, legal/illegal, and artistic/non-artistic in the above examples—as *codes*. According to Esposito, in explaining Luhmann's concept of code, "this binarity is expressed in logic through the principle of excluded middle (*tertium non datur*): a scientific communication is either true or false, and no other option exists" (2021a, 41; emphasis added). The same applies to communications involving the success media of money, legal values, and art: an incentive to payment is either accepted or rejected, law is either complied with or resisted, and certain sensory inputs are either artistic utterances or they are not.

Success media and their codes alone cannot guarantee the acceptance of communications that implement them, that is, ego favoring the positive rather than the negative side of the code. This is because success media are highly abstract and require a way to relate to concrete use cases, making them comprehensible and applicable for both alter and ego, ultimately motivating ego to rather accept than reject the communication. Take money as the success medium of the economic system, for example. Spending or receiving money—which is materially nothing more than worthless metal and paper and is increasingly losing its material form with online banking and the rise of cryptocurrencies—cannot be motivating unless a set of rules exists to regulate and assign value to money, and to define under which circumstances a transaction is meaningful and beneficial. The same applies to the law: unless there are rules explaining how law should be interpreted and implemented in concrete situations, and what the consequences are for noncompliance, the law alone cannot motivate citizens to accept communications paired with it. Even art depends on such rules, which make it possible to accept certain artefacts as meaningful artworks rather than as random objects in the world. These rules, for example, turn a urinal displayed by Marcel Duchamp in a gallery and titled *Fountain* (1917) into a work of art that conveys an artistic statement, rather than just being a urinal.

Hence, alongside the success media and the codes that guide the acts of accepting or rejecting them, society also develops instructions on what accepting or rejecting communications relying on a given success medium means and what benefits or consequences these decisions have for ego. These instructions are called *programs* in Luhmann's systems theory. According to him, "a program is a complex of conditions for the correctness (and thus the social acceptability) of behavior" (1995, 317). For example, pricing mechanisms, market regulations, and financial plans are programs that connect payment/nonpayment with the medium of money; programs of ruling parties in democracies (Baraldi 2021b, 172) or decisions of individuals in hierarchical societies determine how the code government/opposition can be coupled with the medium of power; and artistic schools of thought and manifestos define what should be perceived as art and what is non-artistic.

Whereas codes remain strict and abstract binary schemata that do not allow for third options, programs continuously evolve to incorporate newly introduced conditions into the code, thereby influencing what is considered the positive and what is considered the negative side of the code. Returning to the example of Duchamp's readymades, which marked a significant shift in the history of European art, it is notable how these objects—previously unrecognizable as artworks in the nineteenth century—entered galleries through Duchamp's exhibition of a *Bicycle Wheel* (1913), a shovel (*In Advance of the Broken Arm* (1915)), a urinal (*Fountain* (1917)), and other items. Duchamp's choice transformed the program of art by redefining the exhibition of readymades as a form of artistic communication.

Another example of the evolution and adaptation of the program of art is the *Futurist Manifesto*, published in 1909, which advocates for the inclusion of technological manifestations—including speed, the noise of machines operating in a factory, as well as images and mechanical components of the machines themselves—into the medium of art, thereby expanding the program of art and contributing to its complexity (Marinetti 1973).

Functional Differentiation

Symbolically generalized media of communication, along with the binary codes that guide the processes implementing them and the programs that define the meaning of each side of the code, lead to the differentiation of functional systems within the overarching system of society. As their name suggests, each of these systems fulfills a specific function—and no other—within society. For example, the function of the legal system is "to maintain stable expectations even if they are disappointed. Such expectations are norms that remain stable regardless of their potential contravention" (Corsi 2021b, 125). The function of the economic system is to "resolve scarcity through gaining access to goods" (Esposito 2021b, 79). And the function of the political system is "to guarantee the capacity to make collectively binding decisions" (Baraldi 2021b, 171).

When it comes to art as a functional system, it becomes problematic for Luhmann to assign a function to it. Although art possesses its specific code and programs, which have enabled it to differentiate itself from other communications in its environment, its exact function remains unclear. Luhmann acknowledges this difficulty and nevertheless attempts to propose possible functions for art (2000a, 143). I am not going to go into detail about these suggestions, because the function of art does not directly play a role in the discussions of this book. It is sufficient to briefly mention two of them that have been more extensively cited and elaborated on by Luhmann scholars.

According to Luhmann, the first function of art would be to build a bridge between perception, which is inherently incommunicable, and the broader communicative structures of society. Unlike language, which imposes clear distinctions between acceptance and rejection, art allows for open-ended interpretation and restores perceptual freedom for its audience. This ensures that perception remains a subjective experience within society, protected from the rigid constraints of linguistic consensus (Luhmann 2000a, 141).

Another function that Luhmann suggests for art is its ability to create a distinct relationship to reality by differentiating between the real and the fictional. Art can imitate, critique, or affirm reality, but it can also place the observer in a unique position to reflect on reality and himself in ways that everyday life does not permit (Luhmann 2000a, 143). In sum, both functions point to the way art, as communication, can influence the psychic system in its processes of thinking and perception. The dynamics between artistic communication through film and the operations of the psychic systems perceiving this communication will be revisited from a different perspective in Part Two of this book, where I will discuss the audience's expectations of film art.

Functional systems, like the societal system itself, consist of communication and are operationally closed. However, they differ from other forms of communication within the societal system in that their communications rely on success media and the binary codes associated with them. As Esposito declares, through binary codes, functional systems can observe the world and distinguish between communications that belong to them and those that do not, which are therefore part of their environment (2021a, 43). For instance, the economy, as the functional system that uses money as its success medium and payment/nonpayment of money as its binary code, treats anything that cannot be accepted or rejected through this code as part of its environment. Thus, communications belonging to other functional systems, such as science or politics, or interactions like neighbors greeting each other in the stairway or children playing in the schoolyard, are considered part of the economy's environment, since they neither motivate nor discourage the payment of money.

Later in this book, I will return to the codes and programs of three functional systems—economy, art, and politics—to examine the correlation between social crises and the emergence of new-wave cinema. As previously mentioned, these codes and programs are: payment/nonpayment as the code and market regulations and pricing strategies as the program for the functional system of economy; and government/opposition as the code and the programs of the ruling party, group, or individual as the program of politics. The case of art is more complex than that of the other two functional systems. While the economic and political systems exert major influence over society and therefore have a longer history of being studied sociologically, this is not the case for art. This is why, in Luhmann's latest work, *Theory of Society*, art refers both to a symbolically generalized communication medium and to the functional system differentiated on that basis (2012a, 209 ff.). I propose a minor correction to eliminate this ambiguity by defining the code as artistic/not-artistic and reserving the term art for the functional system differentiated according to this code.

As Luhmann argues, art does not possess a fixed symbolically generalized communication medium like economy and politics, but instead creates its specific, system-differentiating medium anew each time a concrete work of art is produced (2012a, 211). As a result, the symbolically generalized medium of art is a *second-order medium* for Luhmann, meaning that art first generates forms from material media—such as wood, stone, paint, paper, language, sound, or the human body. These forms can then function as media of artistic communication and differentiate themselves from non-artistic communication. In this way, the communication medium of art is a material medium that has been transformed into a communication medium through artistic formation, and this transformation serves as the success medium, or the system-differentiating medium, of art (Luhmann 1986).

I argue for an additional key difference between art and other functional systems beyond art's specific success medium: the programs that define the two sides of the code of art are less rigid and concrete, and more fluid than those of the economy or politics. Determining whether a communication is artistic is often considered a matter of taste, suggesting that the program of art can vary depending on the school of art to which the defining instances belong. Programs of art are therefore more diverse and they evolve more rapidly than those in the economy, politics, or science. Despite the heterogeneity and speedy evolution of art's program, the code artistic/not-artistic remains the sole criterion for differentiating the functional system of art.

Although art, power, science, law, and economic relations have existed in society for thousands of years, their autonomy through functional differentiation marks a condition that Luhmann identifies as *modern.* In contrast to earlier societies, where each social group served multiple functions, modern society is characterized by the clear differentiation of functional systems. This separation ensures that no single system can assume the role of another (Luhmann 1989, 48–9). Hence, functional systems in modern society operate independently and cannot replace or substitute for one another. Each functional system operates according to its own specific code and program.

While functional differentiation is, for Luhmann, the most recent and most complex form of system–environment distinction that society has achieved, earlier forms with different characteristics have also existed. As discussed earlier, society becomes differentiated from its environment as soon as communications begin to follow one another. This marks the initial system–environment distinction brought about by the formation of society. However, such distinctions do not end there. Societies also differentiate other systems within their internal environment to manage complexity. Complexity here means that "there are always more possibilities for experience and action than can actually be realized" (Luhmann 1985b, 32; my translation). With functional differentiation being the most recent form, Luhmann identifies three earlier forms of internal differentiation within society: segmentary, center/periphery, and stratified differentiation.

As Luhmann explains, and Baraldie further clarifies, segmentary differentiation characterizes archaic societies, where social subsystems are divided based on descent (e.g., tribes, clans, families) or residence (e.g., villages, households), often forming nested structures of similar groups. Center/periphery differentiation, in turn, introduces a hierarchical structure based on the distinction between a dominant, "civilized" center and a marginalized periphery, with social inequality shaped by geographical location. Finally, stratified differentiation organizes society through ranked hierarchies, where higher strata determine social order, while internal equality prevails within each rank, such as among aristocratic families (Luhmann 2012b, 27 ff.; Baraldi 2021a). Drawing on Luhmann's account of intra-societal system–environment differentiations, I assume that the three national societies discussed in this book—namely West German, American, and Iranian societies—are modern societies manifesting functional differentiation.

The System–Environment Relationship

We learned earlier that, for Luhmann, communication—and society by the same rule—cannot be directly determined by the environment. Luhmann calls this circumstance the operational closure of the system of society in relation to its environment. The same principle of operational closure also applies to functional systems in modern society. These systems treat not only the psychic systems and physiological bodies of individuals engaged in communication as their environment but also any other communication that cannot be coded using their binary codes. Since the binary codes of functional systems are mutually exclusive, these systems are operationally closed against each other and none of them can directly intervene in the operations of the others.

This is while the overarching societal system, as the sum of ongoing communications, relies on the psychic systems of the individuals involved in communication, even though communication and consciousness are both operationally closed and belong to each other's environment. The same applies to the relationship between the psychic system and the physiological system of an individual. Similarly, despite operational closure, functional systems in modern society are also mutually reliant on each other, just as they all depend on the overarching societal system for their existence. This mutual reliance becomes concrete when, for example, a work of art is sold at an auction or when the parliament passes laws regarding the import and export of certain goods. In these examples, it may appear as if the codes of art and economy, or those of politics and economy, overlap— which is not the case.

For Luhmann, these relations between autopoietic systems and their environments do not negate the systems' self-referentiality and operational closure. Instead, communication as an autopoietic system can—and indeed must—maintain a two-way relationship with its environment. We already learned that if communication takes the initiative to refer to its environment, it does so through other-reference, meaning that it thematizes the environment as information. But if the influence comes from the other side, namely from the environment, and the system becomes aware of it, this influence is called *irritation*. According to Krause, "irritation refers to noise in the environment of an autopoietic system that is perceived by the system but has not yet been specified as information according to its own operational code" (2005, 169; my translation). This definition emphasizes the active role of the system in sensing the noise. Irritation cannot be forcefully imposed on the system by the environment. Rather, it is a construct of the system itself, meaning that the system can autonomously and actively choose to treat irritation as noise and ignore it, or to treat it as information and thematize it in its communicative operations (Luhmann 2012a, 66–7).

If the system chooses to treat environmental irritation as information and modifies its structure to correspond to that information, it means that it has allowed the environment to *resonate* with its own operations. For Luhmann, the term *resonance* in this context is used in the same sense as in physics: the system is insulated from its environment and can only be set into vibration by environmental impacts at its own natural frequencies (Luhmann 1985a, 416–17).

Through irritation, the system forms a *structural coupling* with other systems in its environment. A system's structural coupling with another does not imply that the system and its environment are unified, or that their operations are intertwined. Rather, for Luhmann, structural coupling is enabled through "certain mutual irritation channels" between the systems involved (2012b, 110). In the structural couplings of functional systems in modern society, these channels may be stronger or weaker, depending on how frequently and intensely the systems involved have irritated each other throughout their evolution.

I argue that these channels are created when one system codes specific operations of another system as its own, or when it adapts the programs of another system to a certain subset of its own operations—without the codes and programs of both systems fully merging. In the example of an artwork sold at auction, the artwork is treated as merchandise and thus coded by the economic system. Here, artistic communication plays no role because no one at the auction is reflecting on the artwork, attempting to understand the utterance made by the artist through it.

In the other example mentioned above, where politics imposes regulations on import and export, both the application of one system's code to the operations of another system and the adaptation of another system's program occur. When the government develops regulations on import and export, it thematizes economic transactions—which belong to its environment—as information in its own communicative operations, assigning them to the positive side of the code government/opposition. In doing so, the government treats these transactions as a legitimate target for its medium of power by subjecting them to a new set of regulations. These regulations are programs developed by the political system and delegated to the economy. The economic system, in turn, complies with this political decision—which it experiences as irritation from the environment—allowing its operations to resonate with it. The economy continues to function with the medium money and the code payment/nonpayment, but it adopts the program provided by the political system that regulates payment/nonpayment in trade with other national societies through import and export.[5]

Memory

Earlier in this chapter, I discussed how a single communication unit is an event that occurs in an instant and then disappears. I also noted that society cannot be differentiated from its environment through isolated communications that quickly appear and then vanish. Rather, it is the ongoing sequence of communication units that follow and refer to one another that differentiates the system of society. Communication not only persists but also becomes increasingly complex over time, leading to the differentiation of various media and functional systems that extend and simultaneously manage this complexity. But how can communication, as a fleeting event, sustain continuity and keep getting more complex without repeating all the information that was previously thematized or all the schemata used in past communications in order to add something new to them? Luhmann's answer to this question is: through *memory*.

It is important to distinguish Luhmann's concept of memory, which applies to communication and the social systems based on it, from theories of collective memory that treat memory, (a) as equivalent to the memories of individuals and collectives; and (b) as an information reservoir.[6] For Luhmann, memory is a function of communication rather than a reservoir located in an individual human's brain or consciousness that stores information. Just as communication and the psychic systems of the individuals involved in it are operationally closed and structurally coupled at the same time, so too are the memories of individuals and the memory of communication.

Memory, for Luhmann, has the dual function of *remembering* and *forgetting*. Forgetting prevents the system from "blocking itself by congealing the results of earlier observations" (Luhmann 2012a, 349). For example, the economic system cannot retain all past transactions, their contexts, and the amounts of money exchanged in order for new transactions to occur. The same applies to science: when a new theory of physics or art is developed, it cannot cite every relevant theory from the beginning to the present to make a new contribution in the field. Thus, every communication system must forget most of the information, topics, and schemata produced and applied in its past to create capacity for new information, topics, and schemata. In this way, forgetting becomes the condition through which memory enables *variety* in communication.

However, not every aspect of past communications can be forgotten by the system. In the examples of economic and scientific communications, the transaction taking place now must retain certain schemata and pieces of information while discarding other details from the past. It must remember that there is a medium called money, which has replaced valuable metals, and whose value is determined based on certain programs accepted by all participants in economic communication. It must also remember that it is, for instance, taking place in the context of a governmental support program as a monthly payment to an NGO whose goal is to protect nature from industrial pollution. Similarly, a new scientific paper does not need to cite every existing source in the field, but it must nevertheless remember a limited number of books and articles on which it bases its argument through citing them. It must also remember the accepted format of a scientific paper within the community, the proper way to refer to others' work, and the rules governing the peer-review process. The memory's decision on which information, topics, and schemata to forget and which to remember in current communication is not random but follows a certain logic. As Esposito notes, schemata and topics that recur repeatedly in communication are regarded by the system as worth remembering due to their *redundancy*. As a result, the memory condenses them into *identities* and remembers them in future communication (2002, 25 ff.).

Through remembering and forgetting, memory enables both redundancy and variety in communication. The sum of identities formed based on redundancy and remembered in new communications constitutes the *structure* of the system. Structure here does not refer to a set of fixed elements and the relationships between them, because social systems are composed of communication units that are events with a temporal rather than spatial character. Communication units, as events that appear and disappear in a moment, are not fixed, and precisely because of this, fixed connections cannot be established among them and then observed. Therefore, as Corsi points out, the structures of social systems do not have a tangible nature; rather, they are structures of expectation (2021c). This means that the system anticipates certain topics and schemata in each new communication, based on the condensed identities that constitute its structure.

Two further important aspects of memory should be noted here. The first concerns the versatility of identities and structure. The communication system's memory is continually active in adjusting identities, forgetting those that are no longer redundant and adding new ones, thereby constantly renewing the system's structure. If structure were not this flexible and dynamic, social evolution would not be possible. The second point concerns the question of what happens to information that is forgotten by memory: Does it get lost? If not, and if memory does not function as an information reservoir, then where is this information stored?

Esposito (2002) has answered this question by identifying a parallel evolutionary trajectory for society's memory and dissemination media. She examines the evolution of memory alongside societal evolution and argues that societies with an oral culture had to rely on rituals to repeatedly remember identities that were crucial for communication and the maintenance of society. With the evolution of society on the one hand and the development of dissemination media capable of preserving information—followed by mass media and the internet—on the other, information can be more easily forgotten by communication because it can be stored through these media and thus preserved for future reference. In this way, forgotten information is not lost and it can still be referred to. Being forgotten simply means that certain information, topics, or schemata are no longer redundant and should not be remembered to ensure that current communication can connect with other recent communications. Instead, these can be stored in books, archives, or digital storages to be accessed whenever necessary.

Contradiction and Conflict

The expectations that form the structure of social systems and are constituted by their memory are not always fulfilled. This occurs when a communication that was expected to be accepted is instead rejected. According to Luhmann, these rejections of expectations can sometimes, though not always, produce *contradictions*. In logic, contradiction takes the form of tautology with an added negation: "A is (not) A" (Luhmann 1995, 361). Luhmann understands contradictions as unexpected forms of meaning that manifest in thoughts or communications—that is, in the operations of psychic or social systems. Therefore, contradiction, in social context, is not merely equivalent to the rejection of an expectation but rather arises when communication "incorporates the incompatible communication (and not just the rejected meaning!) within itself" (Luhmann 1995, 365).

For example, if the parliament invalidates the results of an election won by a certain candidate through the majority of votes, the expectations of the voters who elected him in a democratic political system remain unfulfilled. If these voters neither reflect upon nor communicate about the rejection of their unmet political expectation, then the event is simply forgotten without producing a contradiction. However, if this decision by the parliament, which represents the political system, becomes the subject of debate among individuals in the workplace, in mass media, or among political parties who did not anticipate it, then a contradiction can be said to have emerged. Following Luhmann's logical model, the contradiction takes the form of "the elected candidate is (not) president."

Society produces contradictions because they are necessary for its evolution. According to Luhmann, contradictions are alarm signals that strengthen society's immune system. Whenever a communication that was expected to be accepted is rejected, it temporarily places the system in a situation similar to one in which its autopoiesis would be at risk (Luhmann 1995, 373). By changing and adapting its structure in response to contradictions that resonate with it, the system ensures that its autopoiesis is maintained.

Contradictions do not block the system because they do not have operational consequences. In other words, the system continues to function in the face of contradictions, while simultaneously being alerted by them. This is because, in autopoietic systems, contradictions are treated differently at the levels of observation and autopoiesis. For an observer, contradiction means "undecidability" (Luhmann 1995, 360). System operations, however, continue even in the face of contradiction (Luhmann 1995, 360). Hence, "a contradiction is an indeterminacy of the system [at the level of observation], not an indeterminacy of individual operations [occurring autopoietically]" (Luhmann 1995, 361). In the example above, the government and the parliament continue to function through the medium of power and the code government/opposition, even when heated political debates surrounding the election results question the foundations of democracy in that specific national society.

The political system in the above example can, while maintaining its operations, respond in three different ways to the contradictions being thematized in political communication, in the mass media, or by citizens demonstrating in the streets. The first option is to ignore these communications and treat them as irrelevant. The second is to allow them to resonate with the current structure of the political system and to update this structure—for example, by passing new laws regarding who is eligible to run for the presidency or under what circumstances the parliament is permitted to annul election results in the future. The third option is for the political system to reject the critical communication about the contradiction directed at it—for example, through party leaders voicing their rejection of the critique coming from the opposition at a press conference, or by suppressing the demonstrations and arresting their leaders. In this case, when "expectations are communicated and the nonacceptance of the communication is communicated in return," a *conflict* arises (Luhmann 1995, 388). Hence, two communications are always initially involved in a conflict: one that expresses a contradicted expectation, and a subsequent one that rejects the expressed expectation (Luhmann 1995, 389).

In the above example, I am treating protest movements as the public's means of communicating the contradictions they have observed in the political system's decisions, demanding that politics address their unmet expectations. Luhmann distinguishes protest movements from political opposition within a constitutional democracy by emphasizing their different systemic roles. According to him, political opposition is integrated into the political system and must be prepared to govern or cooperate, which disciplines both its actions and rhetoric. In contrast, protest operates outside the political system, driven by ethical principles rather than political strategy, and positions itself as representing society in opposition to the political system. Luhmann argues that modern protest movements emerge due to the political system's increasing autonomy and lack of responsiveness. The constitution, by restricting the political system to its own operations, isolates it from broader societal concerns and thereby provokes protest as a reaction to this exclusion (Luhmann 2012b, 159).

In his observation, Luhmann does not deliberately acknowledge protest movements—including demonstrations, strikes, and other forms of civil disobedience—that lead to revolutions and the overthrow of the political system, replacing it with a new one. To fill this gap, I argue that the dynamics of a revolution unfold as follows: when protesters' expressions of their expectations are met with indifference or with violent or non-violent rejection, thereby creating a conflict, the protesters experience a second set of unmet expectations—namely, the expectation that their original expectations be addressed after having been voiced through protest. This accumulation of unmet expectations escalates and intensifies the protesters' actions, and can ultimately lead to a revolution that overthrows the existing political system. From this point of view, a revolution is the consequence of the political system's failure either to resonate with the demands of the protesters or, if such resonance is not intended, to fully suppress the protest movements.[7]

Evolution

The discussions of this entire chapter can be condensed into the concept of *evolution*. Each time irritations from the environment are experienced as a negation of the system's expectations, they can trigger an evolutionary step by introducing a *variation* into the system's structure (Luhmann 2012a, 278). For example, when Rosa Parks refused to comply with the legal directive of racial segregation in 1955 by not giving up her seat on the bus to a White passenger, she addressed a contradiction between the existing discriminatory laws, forming the expectations of the political and legal systems, and her own expectation, as a Black citizen, to be treated equally to white citizens. Her act of rejecting the racist legal program of the political system gained support from more individuals during the Civil Rights Movement, who, through the repeated articulation of their demand to end racial segregation, introduced a variation to the law and irritated the legal and political systems into accepting this variation.

Variations can either be treated as one-time occurrences and thus ignored by the system or they can be perceived as emergences that recur or are deemed worth repeating in future communication. In the latter case, the system is more likely to select them as identities and integrate them into its structure (Luhmann 2000a, 225). This is what happened during the Civil Rights Movement, when the legal system selected the newly introduced variety—due to its redundant repetition by an increasing number of citizens beyond Rosa Parks's singular act—as a new identity. This new identity was the Civil Rights Act (1964), which outlawed discrimination in public accommodations and employment based on race, color, religion, sex, and national origin.

After selecting the variation as a new identity and adjusting its structure accordingly, the system restabilizes and maintains its self-reproduction. Similar to the concept of autopoiesis, which originates in biology, Luhmann also borrowed the triad of *variation*, *selection*, and *restabilization* from Darwin's theory of evolution to explain the evolution of society (Luhmann 2012a, 258). As Corsi explains Luhmann's evolution theory, these steps exist in a circular relationship: contradictions that serve as variations only emerge when the system already has a stable structure and can observe such variations as contradictory to it. At the same time, the system can select these variations to destabilize, reconfigure, and subsequently restabilize its structure (2021a, 91). In other words, stabilization is only a temporary stage, as social systems continuously select new variations and create new stabilized states in their place, allowing the course of evolution to persist in this manner.

Memory plays a key role in the process of evolution by examining the compatibility of variations with the system's structure and by continually selecting between remembering and forgetting—retaining certain variations as new identities to be remembered for future communication, and forgetting both old identities that are no longer compatible with the structure or variations deemed unworthy of integration into the system's structure.

Evolution only seldom takes the form of radical developments, such as those following the Civil Rights Movement (Luhmann 2012a, 278). Rather, it is an ongoing process that continually changes and adapts the system's structure through repeated cycles of variation, selection, and restabilization. Furthermore, for Luhmann, evolution occurs not only at the level of the overarching societal system—as seen in the transition from societies with segmentary differentiation to center/periphery, stratified, and functionally differentiated societies—but also at the level of functional systems. For example, he examines the evolution of art as a functional system of modern society in his book *Art as a Social System* (2000a). Art is the functional system, the evolution of which, particularly through new waves of cinema, lies at the heart of this book.

1.2

Film as a Subsystem of Art

I argued in the introduction that Luhmann's systems theory of society can form a highly abstract theoretical continuum capable of encompassing a wide range of observations—from micro-level analyses of filmic form and communication to major transformations occurring at the scale of the societal system, including significant shifts in the political system or protest movements. To lay the groundwork for this, I briefly outlined Luhmann's systems theory and some of its key concepts in the previous chapter. In this chapter, I will sketch a theory of filmic communication grounded in Luhmann's systems theory.

In the previous chapter, I discussed that Luhmann regards art as a functional system of modern society. The discussions in this chapter will be based on the axiom that film is a subsystem of art. By grounding my discussions in this axiom, I align myself with a tradition of thought that originates with Canudo (1993) and Arnheim (1957), and remains present and valid today—for example, in the writings of David Bordwell and Kristin Thompson. While Canudo, in his manifesto, and Arnheim, in his book, sought to justify film's inclusion in the realm of art, Bordwell and Thompson treat this as a given, as evidenced by the title of their book *Film Art: An Introduction* (2013).

Considering film as art within the framework of Luhmann's systems theory has several implications. First, it suggests that individual films, like other artworks, are artistic utterances, and that filmic communication is understood when the viewers differentiate information from the utterance. Furthermore, filmic communication relies on various media for its operation—from its specific communication medium to the medium of meaning and the symbolically generalized communication medium of art. Moreover, as an artistic communication, film possesses a memory and undergoes evolution, just like the overarching systems of art and society. Finally, filmic communication is structurally coupled with other functional systems of society—couplings that can be observed and analyzed.

The film-theoretical framework I will outline below, rooted in Luhmann's systems theory of society, addresses all the aspects mentioned above—except for the precise mechanism of the structural coupling between film as art and the economic and political systems. This mechanism will be explored in detail during the case studies presented in Part Two. In that part, I will apply the theoretical framework developed here to analyze three distinct new waves of cinema and their correlation with their contemporary social crises.

Media and Forms of Filmic Communication

As mentioned in the previous chapter, identifying media as sums of loosely coupled elements and forms as the result of the strict coupling of those elements is not an objective process. Rather, it depends on the observer's perspective and the distinction he draws between form and medium. I find the distinctions I have made between forms and media of filmic communication in this chapter particularly helpful for understanding the evolution of film in the context of a new wave, as will be demonstrated in the second part of the book.

Like other types of communication, filmic communication relies on a multitude of media. From a historical perspective, the dissemination medium of film has been the most significant among these. Initially, this was the film strip, on which images—and later sound—were recorded optically. Thanks to the film strip's capacity for optical reproduction, it became possible to disseminate filmic communication across time and space. Today, digital technologies for storing and reproducing films have been added to the formerly analog dissemination medium of film. This medium belongs to the environment of filmic communication and is therefore not thematized in this chapter's discussions.

In the previous chapter, I argued with Luhmann that the medium of artistic communication is a second-order medium. By this, Luhmann means that art has the capacity to convert virtually any material medium into a communication medium by creating forms from that medium and attaching meaning to them. For example, you might come across a piece of wood in the forest with an interesting shape that captures your attention. However, it does not carry a meaning for you because you do not perceive it as a work of art shaped intentionally by a human and placed there to communicate something. If, however, the same piece of wood is displayed in a gallery, you perceive it as an artistic utterance, because this time you are aware that an artist has either found or shaped the wood in that way and exhibited it to "express something" through it. In this example, wood as a material medium has acquired a form through the artist's observation—in Spencer-Brown's sense—which differentiates the form from the material itself. It is not the wood alone, but rather the artist's act of observation (differentiating a form from the medium of wood) and the expression of that observation (through exhibiting the form in a gallery) that enables the exhibited wooden form to function as a communication medium. It is in this sense that the medium of artistic communication is a second-order medium.

In the same way, the material medium of film comprises the sum of all possible images and sounds, arranged in every conceivable sequence, that can be technically produced and subsequently projected, displayed, or played as a unified utterance—namely, as a film. These may include recordings of objects, humans, actions, places, and sounds, as well as images and sounds generated using computer software or even artificial intelligence. From this material medium, concrete forms can emerge by selecting specific images and sounds, recorded or generated using specific technical means, and arranging them in a particular order and relation to one another. Such forms are the result of a creative person's or team's observations, who have distinguished the form from the material medium of film through making concrete technical choices and have thereby indicated it. This form, in turn, serves as the second-order medium of filmic communication, allowing viewers to attach meaning to it and extract information from it.

One might argue that it is not only the technical aspect of recorded and projected images and played sounds but also their "content" that communicates with film viewers. For instance, recorded sounds might include spoken words, which are elements of the medium of language, or they may be music, an artistic medium in its own right that is also capable of communicating beyond the context of film. As for the recorded images, they are primarily understood as icons in Peirce's terms, which manifest "a similarity or analogy to the subject" they refer to (Peirce 1960, 195). This means that we recognize the image of a tree or a dog in film as a tree or a dog. Marshall McLuhan addresses this issue with his thesis that "the 'content' of any medium is always another medium" (1994, 8). Hence, filmic communication implements visual and auditory communication media that were already available to society and art prior to its emergence, while adding its own specific material and communication media on top of them, namely the technical aspects involved in the production of images and sounds.

McLuhan's concept of medium as an extension of the human body does not align with Luhmann's concept of medium. I also deliberately avoid delving into the labyrinth of which other media films contain, and which further media those, in turn, encompass. However, for the purposes of this book, I draw the Luhmannian inspiration from McLuhan's thesis that the medium of filmic communication can be coupled with the communication media of other arts, as well as with non-artistic communication media, such as language. Hence, in making concrete decisions about film form, the production team can determine which actors to cast, how to design their costumes, how they should perform in front of the camera, as well as where to film—choices that are regarded as elements of *mise-en-scène* and are shared between film and theater. Furthermore, film creators can decide how to design the lighting, which camera and lenses to use, and how to frame the action—choices that film shares with photography. Finally, as decisions specific to film alone, film creators can choose how to move the camera, how and where to record the sound, which visual and auditory effects to include in postproduction, and how to edit the film.

If, as assumed above, the material medium specific to film consists of all possible "sequences" of "technically recorded images and sounds" that can be presented through projection and playback before an audience, and if the selections made from this material medium—selections that constitute the form of the film—serve as the communication medium of film and are capable of engaging in communication with the audience, then what are the loosely coupled elements of the medium of filmic communication? I argue that this medium is a synthesis of *camera work*, corresponding to technically recorded images; *sound design*, corresponding to technically recorded sounds; and *editing*, corresponding to the arrangement of these images and sounds into a sequence. Since camera work is meaningful only in relation to what is being recorded by the camera—namely, the *mise-en-scène*—film theorists and historians have developed the term *cinematography* to refer to their combination.

By camera work, I specifically mean the camera angle, the choice of lens (normal, zoom, wide-angle, or telephoto), depth of field, focusing, camera movements, and framing.[1] Even in animations or films produced by a computer, there is always an implied camera that provides the perspective from which images are recorded. The medium of sound design, in turn, is composed of decisions regarding music, dialogue, ambient sound, and sound effects, as well as their volume, direction, and recording techniques.[2] Finally, editing determines the order in which technically recorded or produced images and sounds are placed within the film, as well as their relationship to each other. Editing here is not simply understood as cutting the film but rather as *montage* in its literal meaning, which refers to the assembly of image and sound within individual shots, as well as arranging unified image-sound compositions into scenes and sequences. Hence, editing not only regulates the relationship between successive shots and successive sounds but, more importantly, the interplay between "the image track, taken in its entirety, and the sound track" (Aumont, et al. 1994, 43).

The Process of Filmic Communication

Treating the sum of all possible elements that can be created through camera work/cinematography, sound design, and editing as a communication medium means that viewers can attach meaning to the difference between each concrete form selected from this medium and all other possible forms that were not selected. As a result, they perceive that form as an utterance and derive information from it. Hence, viewers not only attach meaning to the difference between what is made visible and audible through film and what is not—media not exclusive to film and also employed by music, painting, photography or theater—but also to the difference between the actual and the potential technical means of making those things visible and audible, which marks the realm of film-specific meaning-making.

The meaning-making process of choices from the medium of filmic communication can be clarified with an example. If a dialogue between two women is shown in a full shot, with a dog standing across the street in the background, the dog's significance in the scene depends on how it is framed and how sharply it is in focus (camera work), or how prominently its barking is heard by the audience (sound + image-sound editing). If the camera zooms in on the dog during the dialogue between the women (camera work), or if the full shot of the women is cut to a close-up of the dog (camera work + editing), it becomes clear that the dog is an important part of the scene. Following these choices, an eyeline match in a shot/reverse shot sequence between the women and the dog indicates that they have noticed each other. In contrast, parallel editing between the approaching dog and the unaware women creates tension, suggesting that maybe the dog is about to jump on one of the women. These technical choices can make sense and reveal the information described above only because the viewers know that they have deliberately been chosen instead of all other possible technical options to make the dog visible and audible, in order to make a specific statement. The difference between the actualized choices and the potential ones lends meaning to these choices.

The result of all concrete selections from the medium of filmic communication is the form of a single film that is capable of communicating because, in Luhmann's terms, it functions as an artistic utterance. Filmic communication occurs when viewers understand the film as a complete whole by making distinctions between each formal choice of the film and the information unit they ascribe to it, and by relating these pieces of information to one another in order to grasp the film's overall information. The extent to which viewers comprehend a particular film, how they understand it, and how many of its formal selections hold meaning for them—or are even noticed—varies from individual to individual. Regardless of this, filmic utterance is always understood by viewers as soon as they distinguish any information from the forms that the film offers.

As discussed in the previous chapter, individual or collective understandings of a film only become observable when they constitute the topic of further communication about that film. For example, critics might thematize and reflect on their understanding of a film in a newspaper or magazine. Groups of viewers might discuss their interpretations at a bar after the screening, or they might even protest against the screening of certain films if they have distinguished information from the filmic utterance that they consider immoral or harmful. Furthermore, viewers can demonstrate their understanding and acceptance of a certain filmic communication through their economic behavior, buying tickets for the next film by the same director or within the same genre. In the same way, they can also reject certain filmic communications by choosing not to buy tickets, which indicates that they have understood films from a particular genre or by a certain director and do not favor the kind of information those films convey to them.

Here, an important question arises concerning the information conveyed by the entire film as a single utterance. I argue that, at least in the case of fiction films, the overarching information of filmic communication is a *narrative*. Narrative is a form of literary communication whose communication medium extends beyond language. Like the communication medium specific to film, the narrative communication medium is a hybrid composition of diegesis, plot, characterization, voice, and other sub-media.[3] Thus, for each individual viewer, discrete units of information revealed by the fiction film can be coupled with components from the medium of narrative to construct the grand information of filmic communication.[4]

Memory and Structure of Filmic Communication

While numerous theories regard films as communicative entities, films have not always been capable of communicating throughout their history.[5] A brief exploration of early film history illustrates this. A well-known anecdote recounts how the audience at a screening of *L'Arrivée d'un train en gare de La Ciotat* (Arrival of a Train at La Ciotat; 1896) by the Lumière brothers supposedly fled from the screen as the train entered the station in the projected film. Whether or not this story is accurate, it underscores an important point about the observation and meaning-making processes involved in filmic communication. As we have learned from Luhmann, communication is facilitated through the medium of meaning. Meaning, in turn, arises from the difference between the actualized form and all other potential forms that could have been realized based on the possibilities provided by the communication medium. The earliest films in history did not have access to a reservoir of all possible filmic forms, against which a specific film could become meaningful and thereby communicate. This was because film had not yet established its specific medium of communication or explored its full range of possibilities. The medium of filmic communication that we know today encompasses identities that have been recognized and condensed as such through their redundancy by the memory of filmic communication. Without this redundancy, early film lacked both a memory and a communication medium. In the absence of these two, audiences watching the first films were unable to perceive them as utterances and assign meaning to them.

Using Spencer-Brown's cross sign, which designates the differentiation of forms, the distinctions drawn by audiences familiar with the medium of filmic communication would appear as follows:

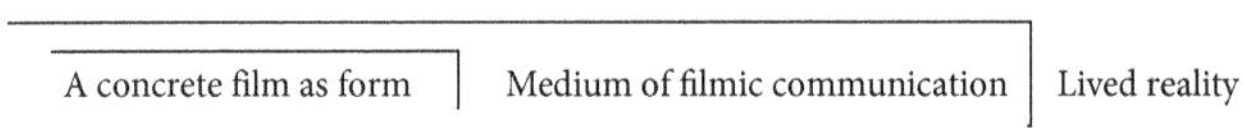

Early film audiences did not yet have access to the medium of filmic communication. As a result, the unmarked state of the film constituted their immediate lived reality, as illustrated below:

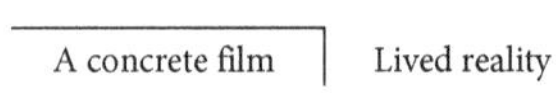

These two schemata highlight a key point regarding the observation of filmic utterance. In both cases—whether viewers are already familiar with the medium of filmic communication or not—they perceive the film as their lived reality if they are observing it as first-order observers. This is because the first-order observer can only perceive the marked state of the form, not its difference from the unmarked state. As Luhmann explains, in first-order observation, we only observe *what* we observe, but we cannot observe *how* we observe it. For instance, we see that "the sun 'comes up' and cannot see it otherwise" (Luhmann 2012a, 50). Therefore, the audience at the screening of the Lumière film could not help but believe that a real train is entering the projection room, just as a contemporary first-order observer of a horror film screams in fear when a vampire suddenly appears on the screen.[6]

The first-order observer can always adopt the position of a second-order observer and observe his own observation. This shift allows the observer to perceive the distinction between the marked and unmarked states. If the observer is already familiar with the medium of filmic communication, he recognizes that the unmarked state of what he initially perceived as reality is, in fact, the medium of filmic communication. Thus, his initial observation is merely a form emerging from this medium, not an experience of immediate reality. In other words, "it's only a film!" For the early film viewers assuming the role of second-order observers, however, the unmarked state of what they perceived as lived reality remained their lived reality. Consequently, they had difficulty drawing a distinction between the marked and unmarked states of their observation.

As contemporary film viewers who are well acquainted with the medium of filmic communication, we are able to watch films simultaneously as both first- and second-order observers. We can consciously adopt the role of first-order observers and allow ourselves to experience the film as reality.[7] At this observation level, "no distinction can be drawn between reality and the illusion of reality" (Luhmann 2012a, 50).

The film's impression of reality has been explored by film theories employing various theoretical approaches. Theories grounded in psychoanalysis—such as those developed by Mitry (1997, 82–3), Kracauer (1960, 157 ff.), and Baudry (1986)—argue that the perception of films in a darkened theater resembles a dream state, wherein the spectator experiences the film's diegesis as real, akin to the illusion of reality in dreams. Metz (1991, 3 ff.), by contrast, attributes the impression of reality in film to movement, as it renders all three dimensions of moving objects and humans visible. Sobchack (1992), in turn, approaches film's impression of reality from a phenomenological standpoint, highlighting the film's embodied "perception" and "expression" through the camera and the projector, which mirror the spectators' experience of lived reality. However, from the perspective of Luhmann's theory, it is unnecessary to delve into the specific psychoanalytic or phenomenological mechanisms through which the subconscious or conscious mind constructs the film's impression of reality. What matters instead is only the mode of observation—how individuals perceive a film as real during first-order observation.

The first-order observation of films involves simply observing what is presented visually and aurally, without considering what alternatives might have been possible—in other words, without reflecting on the unmarked state of the film form. First-order observation can thus be focused on perceiving, for example, the beauty of a little child's gaze as the camera lingers on their face, or the calmness of a vast meadow with a whistling train passing by in the distance. With Luhmann's systems theory, it is not possible to examine how the viewers feel while attending to the first-order observation of the scenes described, nor can one explore the filmmaker's intention in lingering on a particular shot. However, as we will see later, it is possible to discuss the *difference* between these formal choices and others that could potentially replace them, which renders these choices meaningful for the second-order observer. Sometimes, the second-order observer can ascribe a certain narrative or non-narrative information to such formal choices by comparing them with the non-selected, potential forms. At other times, the viewer might conclude that such forms were simply there for first-order observation, as they do not reveal any information.

The second-order observer considers the fact that the artists who made the film have thereby made a distinction between the actual formal choices made in the film and the potential ones that could have been made instead, thereby observing the film's form. With this knowledge, the second-order observer perceives the film as an utterance: the creative individuals who made the film have observed something and they are now uttering it through the screening.[8] The viewers can always switch from their role as first-order observers of the film to second-order observers and search for meaning behind every formal choice the film makes: "What did this dissolve mean? Was it meant as a flash back or was it meant to convey the character's dream?" or "Why was the protagonist's dialogue about her sorrow cut to the long shot of a foggy seashore? Is this choice of editing and cinematography a case of dialectical editing, trying to reveal her melancholy mood? Or is the seashore a diegetic place where something is about to happen?" These are the kinds of questions that second-order observers of a film quickly answer for themselves to attach meaning to individual formal choices that emerge as the film unfolds, often without even consciously asking them.

That film initially lacked memory, was therefore not coupled with the medium of meaning, and ultimately could not communicate was only true at the very first historical moment of its emergence. Every subsequent film, by recalling certain cinematic techniques from earlier films, contributed to the expansion and stabilization of the identities and structure of filmic communication. Engell discusses that Méliès's films, which appeared later than those of the Lumière brothers, no longer relied on the difference between film and the reality of everyday life, but rather on the difference between the actualized film and the potentials drawn from earlier films. In Engell's view, audiences who reportedly searched for water behind the screen after watching the Lumière film *Barque sortant du port* (Boat Leaving the Port; 1895) would have either misunderstood an early Méliès film or found it deeply confusing

(1995, 122). This would be because these viewers did not yet have access to the identities and structure of filmic communication that developed later in film history and could shape expectations when viewing a new film, thereby making the second-order observation of the new film as utterance possible.

Techniques such as different shot sizes, camera movements, and editing methods gradually stabilized as identities that could be expected with each new film experience. The maturation of editing—not merely as a simple cut but as an interplay between shots and later between visual and auditory levels—was achieved through the films of D. W. Griffith, on the one hand, and Sergei Eisenstein, on the other. Thanks to avant-garde films of the interwar period, Dadaist and Surrealist visual innovations were further integrated into the identities of filmic communication through their repeated appearances on the level of cinematography—for instance, abstract, geometric shapes moving on the screen (as in *Rhythmus 21* (Rhythm 21; 1921) and *Rhythmus 23* (Rhythm 23; 1923)), surrealist phenomena such as ants crawling out of a palm (in *Un Chien Andalou* (An Andalusian Dog; 1929)), or speaking statues and people diving into mirrors (in *Le Sang d'un Poète* (The Blood of a Poet; 1932)).

This compact overview illustrates how film history can be understood as the history of the structural development of filmic utterance. Through the redundantly repeated schemata in the media of camera work/cinematography, sound design, and editing, these schemata have condensed into identities of filmic utterance that can be expected in every film experience. Each of these schemata is coupled with a meaning. Parallel editing is one such schema, signifying that two events are occurring simultaneously in different locations. Another example is the shot/reverse shot technique, which conveys an exchange between two instances. Even when a shot of a person is followed by a shot of an object within a shot/reverse shot sequence, viewers assume that the person and the object are engaged in some kind of exchange—whether of states, emotions, or forces—despite the object's inability to interact. Similarly, a POV shot, a close-up, zoom-in and zoom-out techniques, or analytical editing (the cut from a long shot to close-ups of its details) each function as schemata that form the identities of filmic communication and often create meaning in a certain way.

The concept of the identities of filmic communication that I have developed here based on Luhmann's communication theory is very close to what Bordwell implies with the concept of *norms*. According to him, every film provides the audience with cues or hints that lead to drawing meaningful distinctions and understanding the film. These cues, according to Bordwell, point to schemata and norms already familiar to the audience. Norms in this context are the by-product of repeatedly used forms in past (filmic) communications. In Bordwell's words, norms consist of "customary practices" at different levels of filmic communication, such as camera work, sound design, or editing (2008, 137 ff.).

For Bordwell, one of the norms established by Hollywood cinema in the 1910s is the continuity system (2008, 137). Taken as a complex structure of filmic communication composed of certain identities, the continuity system primarily aims to make the story told by the film easily comprehensible (Bordwell, Staiger and Thompson 2005, 288). This involves: "the story as the basis of the film, the technique as an 'indiscernible thread,' the audience as controlled and comprehending, and complete closure as the end of all" (Bordwell, Staiger and Thompson 2005, 288). Classical Hollywood cinema achieved these ends by introducing specific technical selections at every level of its communication medium, which, through redundant repetition, became condensed into the structure known as the continuity system—a structure applied not only by Hollywood films but also internationally by the majority of fiction films.

One of the identities that constitute the continuity system is an establishing shot at the beginning of each scene in the medium of cinematography, which introduces the location, time, and main characters. Additionally, continuity in the direction of movement and gaze must be maintained during editing. Continuity is also ensured through the eyeline match and develops into the shot/reverse shot technique when there is an exchange of gazes, words, or gestures. The 180-degree rule (which involves camera work and editing) ensures that directions of movement remain comprehensible to viewers despite the cuts. Furthermore, the continuity system favors the synchronicity of sound and image and relations between them that are motivated by the narrative. Extradiegetic sounds (belonging to the medium of sound design) are often either narrator voices that advance the plot and provide additional information, the inner voices of film characters, or music that serves the plot and underscores certain emotional aspects of it.

Furthermore, the information conveyed through filmic utterance based on the continuity system is always narrative in nature and never extends beyond the narrative itself. Based on this principle, films that adhere to the continuity system avoid reflection—that is, they refrain from indicating the distinction between themselves as filmic communication and their environment—since such information does not support the story that forms the foundation of the film, which, as Bordwell, Staiger, and Thompson observe, is a key property of the continuity system.

Part Two

The Wave-Like Evolution of Film Art

This part encompasses the concrete analysis of three new-wave cinemas from three different continents—namely New German Cinema, New Hollywood, and New Iranian Cinema—using the Luhmannian theory of filmic communication outlined in Part One. In the introduction, I noted that new waves of cinema emerge in parallel with major social developments within their respective national contexts. In the following chapters, I will first demonstrate that the significant social changes occurring alongside the emergence of the West German, American, and Iranian new waves between the 1950s and 1970s were contradictions and conflicts in Luhmann's sense. I will briefly introduce these contradictions and conflicts at the beginning of each chapter, before proceeding with the analysis of the new waves of cinema.

New German Cinema takes precedence in the analyses of the new waves introduced in this section, and the chapter dedicated to it is almost twice as long as the other two. There is a film-specific reason and a sociological reason for this. The film-specific reason lies in the fact that, as you will see, this new wave has had a more complex course of evolution compared to the other two. It also included a prominent Feminist New Wave besides the nonfeminist one and was furthermore supported by two major film magazines—*Filmkritik* and *Frauen und Film*—and multiple manifestos and critical pamphlets. I therefore assume that the new wave of cinema in West Germany, due to its richness, can provide insight into the systems-theoretical analysis of the other new waves that did not demonstrate the same degree of complexity.

The sociological reason behind my choice is that, as will be shown in the next chapter, West German society in the 1960s and 1970s was confronted with the conflict arising from the political system's contradictory treatment of the immediate German past and the changing social norms and public expectations. In addition to this, the Iranian anti-Shah protests as well as the American anti-Vietnam War protests also found resonance within West

German society during this period and were intertwined with the protests of the German youth against the state of national politics. Hence, West German society had to deal with a more complex set of conflicts in this timespan as compared to the other two national societies that are introduced in this book. Therefore, it deserves a more thorough examination.

In introducing the contradictions and conflicts in West German, American, and Iranian societies in this part, I do not claim to offer a comprehensive historical account of all the dynamics within these national contexts during the selected time frame. Rather, in my brief introductions to these social settings, I will highlight only the most significant contradictions and conflicts that are observable alongside the development of each new wave. It is up to the reader to explore the histories of these contradictions and conflicts further, should they wish to gain a deeper sociohistorical understanding of them.

2.1

New German Cinema

Contradiction and Conflict in West German Society, 1960s and 1970s

The contradictions and conflicts that emerged in the 1960s and 1970s in West Germany had their roots in the period following the end of the Second World War in May 1945. These tensions reached a climax with the hijacking of the Landshut aircraft and the kidnapping of Martin Schleyer by the *RAF*, culminating in the deaths of the *RAF*'s leading figures—namely Ulrike Meinhof, Andreas Baader, Gudrun Ensslin, and Jan-Carl Raspe—in their prison cells in 1977.

Barely five months after the end of the Second World War and the occupation of Germany by the Allied forces—the United States, France, England, and the Soviet Union—these powers initiated a series of proceedings in the city of Nuremberg, which became known as the Nuremberg Trials. During these trials, which took place between 1945 and 1949, the central figures of National Socialism were convicted. Apparently, as Wehler points out, the news coverage of these trials opened the German public's eyes for the first time to the extent and severity of the atrocities National Socialists had committed (2008, 19). Regardless of the extent to which single German citizens continued to sympathize with Nazi ideology even after the lost war, the dominant discourse of mass media in West German society immediately after the war was a sharp break from National Socialism, owing to the Nuremberg Trials (2008, 20).

Beginning in 1949, the prosecution of Nazi perpetrators responsible for the genocide of Jews and Sinti and Roma, as well as the killing of queer individuals and members of resistance groups, was continued by both the first postwar government of West Germany under Chancellor Konrad Adenauer and the newly established state of Israel. According to Wehler, although the West German judiciary appeared to show a declining commitment to prosecuting Nazi perpetrators from the mid-1950s onward,

> this lull was disrupted by the Ulm *Einsatzgruppen* [Task Forces] trial of 1958. Even more significantly, the Auschwitz trial from 1963 to 1965 marked a turning point in public awareness, as the proceedings began to address the core aspects of the murder of Jews and the war of extermination in the East. These events—later further reinforced by the Majdanek trial from 1975 to 1980—entered public consciousness with far greater urgency than before.
>
> (2008, 21; my translation; emphasis added)

On the surface, based on the actions of the judicial system and the reports in mass media, it appeared that the judicial and political systems of the newly founded Federal Republic of Germany were committed to addressing the crimes of the Nazi regime and delivering justice to the surviving victims through these trials, thereby breaking with Germany's sinister past and attempting to start anew with a clean moral slate. However, critical German citizens came to see these trials as a façade for other political and economic agendas pursued by the West German government.

In the 1950s, West Germany began to experience a period of rapid economic growth, known as the *Wirtschaftswunder* (Economic Miracle), made possible by US support through the European Recovery Program (commonly known as the Marshall Plan). Named after US Secretary of State George Marshall, the plan aimed to rebuild war-torn European economies through extensive financial assistance, with the goal of preventing the spread of communism.[1] West Germany had become the easternmost country in noncommunist Europe, bordering the so-called Iron Curtain that separated it from the communist East. Consequently, it was deemed essential for anti-communist states to support the devastated West Germany post-Second World War and help reconstruct its economy and social structure at all costs in order to counter communism along its eastern frontier. This, in turn, meant that individuals with the potential to contribute to this anti-communist effort were welcomed into the new political and economic system—even if they had a history of active collaboration with the Nazi regime.

Besides economic support from the United States, West Germany's Economic Miracle also owed its prosperity to individuals and families who had made fortunes during the Nazi era and later became influential figures in rebuilding the country's economy. These were industrialists, bankers, or entrepreneurs who either collaborated with or directly benefited from Nazi policies, including "Aryanization" (the forced transfer of Jewish-owned businesses), the use of forced labor, and state contracts. These individuals were either not convicted or served only very short prison terms in the postwar period. Many were able to rehabilitate their reputations and continue or even expand their business empires.[2]

In 1955, West Germany joined the North Atlantic Treaty Organization (NATO). The rearmament of the German army and its accession to NATO had been an early aspiration of Adenauer. Since 1949, he had cited "protection against the Bolshevik threat" as the primary justification (Wehler 2008, 17; my translation). Citizens and veterans in West Germany who were critical of these developments opposed them through the pacifist *Ohne-mich* (Without Me) movement. The central message of this movement was that "the frontline generation, returned from the war and terribly decimated, never wanted to be soldiers again, never again to wear uniforms, never again to be forced to kill" (Holl 1988, 223; my translation).

In contrast to the pacifists, the spokespersons of the veterans' associations—aligned with the Catholic and Evangelical churches—launched campaigns advocating for the release of Nazi officers convicted in the trials, "all the more so in light of the rebuilding of German troops, since the imprisonment of numerous officers was deemed incompatible with this aim" (Wehler 2008, 19; my translation). As a result of these campaigns, "the vast majority of those convicted were released from prison after only a few years under the early amnesty laws of the Federal Republic [of Germany]" (Wehler 2008, 19; my translation).

The fact that former officers were released and permitted to serve in the army again after 1955 was, in turn, not a new development in West Germany. Since the founding of the federal state in 1949, there had already been a marked societal rehabilitation of those who had participated in National Socialist policy during the "Third Reich." Wehler severely criticizes the policies of the early Federal Republic of Germany for their lack of scrutiny in appointing former National Socialist personnel to key federal institutions. According to him, numerous former Nazis were placed in influential roles, particularly within the *Auswärtiges Amt* (Foreign Office), the *Bundeskriminalamt* (Federal Criminal Police Office), the *Bundesnachrichtendienst* (Federal Intelligence Service), and the *Verfassungsschutz* (Federal Office for the Protection of the Constitution). As Wehler emphasizes, this group of former officials, leveraging their well-established networks, not only influenced hiring decisions by citing their supposed expertise but also succeeded in blocking legal action or dismissal. Criticism was often met with temporary reassignment to less visible posts. As a consequence, many high-ranking officers from the *Reichssicherheitshauptamt* (Reich Security Main Office), *Einsatzgruppen* (Task Forces), *Gestapo* (*Geheime Staatspolizei*; Secret State Police), and other Nazi organizations who had been involved in wartime atrocities were reinstated into secure civil service positions. In their new roles, as Wehler notes, some even continued to work on the same issues as they had before 1945. Their anti-communist stance during the Cold War, which was genuine and required no fabrication, became the decisive factor in their reintegration. The long-term concealment of this dark legacy, which persisted for nearly sixty years, remains, in Wehler's view, a lasting stain on the internal political history of West Germany (Wehler 2008, 21–2).

By the mid-1950s, following these developments, "the elite in the civil service, judiciary, and academia had largely reverted to that of the Third Reich. Many young people growing up in West Germany felt they were 'surrounded by Nazis' [...]. By the mid-1960s, they had begun to see not just personal continuities but structural ones" (Kundnani 2024). In the eyes of the young, critical public, these continuities starkly contradicted the West German political system's claims of having moved beyond National Socialist policies.

Further contradictions in West Germany emerged in 1961, when *SPD* (*Sozialdemokratische Partei Deutschlands*; Social Democratic Party of Germany) declared simultaneous membership in the *SDS* (*Sozialistischer Deutscher Studentenbund*; Socialist German Student Union) and *SPD* to be incompatible (Langguth 1976, 39). Could the exclusion of *SDS* suggest that *SPD*, contrary to what its voters believed at the time, was not actually pursuing socialist politics as its program implied? This suspicion gained further credibility in 1967 with the formation of the grand coalition between *SPD* and *CDU* (*Christlich Demokratische Union Deutschlands*; Christian Democratic Union of Germany). According to Langguth, the formation of the grand coalition led many left-leaning students to believe that *SPD* was not a true alternative to the conservative *CDU* rule, causing them to lose faith in achieving change through parliamentary democracy. This disillusionment contributed to the radicalization of some protest leaders, with a few becoming openly hostile to the democratic system defined in the *Grundgesetz* (Basic Law) (Langguth 1976, 31–2).

Political repressions of the academics, beginning at *Freie Universität Berlin* (Free University of Berlin; FU Berlin), intensified the frustration of left-wing students even more. "On May 7, 1965, the rector of the Free University sought to prevent Erich Kuby's participation in a panel discussion at the university by issuing a ban from the premises. Approximately 500 students demonstrated on May 7 against the enforcement of this ban" (Langguth 1976, 42; my translation). On February 16, 1966, following the students' protests to censorship and to the Vietnam War, the university's academic senate imposed a ban on political activity within the university campus all together (Bergmann 1968, 20).

The actions of the political party *SPD*, as well as censorship and repression imposed on gatherings, talks, and sit-ins in FU Berlin, were perceived as contradictory to the expectations of left-wing voters, many of whom were students. These students had expected the political party *SPD* to hold on to the socialist program that it had declared and based on which it had gained their vote. Viewing *CDU* as the conservative party that was responsible for the reestablishment of former Nazis, these students expected to find a real opposition in *SPD*. Furthermore, students of FU Berlin expected their institution to adhere to its initial slogans of freedom of thought and speech. But their expectations were met with bans, censorship, and forced expulsions. Having experienced a contradiction due to the rejection of their expectations by the political system, the dissatisfied students communicated their disappointment back to the political system in the form of a series of protests that became known as the Student Movement.

The angry students, whose political activity was banned on campus, took their protests to the streets. Those who took part in the protests demanded freedom of thought and speech in the academic atmosphere as well as justice at national and international levels. In pursuit of these goals, "2000 people took part in a demonstration against the US Vietnam policy" on February 5, 1966 (Langguth 1976, 42; my translation). In June 1967, another demonstration with a foreign-related cause took place in Berlin. It was a protest against the visit of the Shah of Iran. During this demonstration, a student named Benno Ohnesorg was shot and killed by the police, and the officer responsible, Karl-Heinz Kurras, was acquitted in the subsequent trial. "After Ohnesorg's death, mourning rallies were held at almost all German universities, with 15,000 people accompanying the funeral procession in Berlin" (Langguth 1976, 44; my translation). In April of the following year, the attempted assassination of Rudi Dutschke took place—a Marxist sociologist and one of the charismatic members of *SDS*.

Shortly after the assassination attempt on Dutschke, the *Notstandsgesetze* (Emergency Acts) were passed in June 1968. This involved a constitutional amendment by the grand coalition between *CDU* and *SPD* that authorized the government to restrict citizens' fundamental rights in the event of a state of emergency. The legislators understood "state of emergency" to include natural disasters, wars, and uprisings[3] (*Siebzehntes Gesetz zur Ergänzung des Grundgesetzes vom 24. Juni 1968* 1969). The *Notstandsgesetze* were heavily criticized primarily because they evoked Article 48 of the Weimar Constitution (also known as *Notverordnung* (Emergency Decree)). The *Notverordnung* permitted the suspension of the democratic constitutional order in the event of an emergency, which subsequently facilitated the rise of National Socialism. It stated:

> If a federal state fails to fulfill the duties incumbent upon it under the Imperial Constitution or the laws of the Reich, the Reich President may compel it to do so with the aid of armed force. // The Reich President may, if public safety and order are seriously disturbed or endangered within the German Reich, take the necessary measures to restore public security and order, including, if necessary, the use of armed force.
>
> (*Die Verfassung des Deutschen Reichs vom 11. August 1919 (Weimarer Verfassung)*; my translation)

This legislation introduced by the political system constituted a new program that classified protests and uprisings as states of emergency. It thus enabled the political system to expand the domains it could control using its medium of power in the face of protests, clearly contradicting Article 5 of the *Grundgesetz* in West Germany, which states: "Everyone has the right to freely express and disseminate their opinions in speech, writing, and images, and to freely obtain information from generally accessible sources. Freedom of the press and freedom of reporting through broadcasting and film are guaranteed. Censorship does not take place" (*Grundgesetz für die Bundesrepublik Deutschland* 2025; my translation).

Furthermore, the methods by which the state suppressed the originally peaceful demonstrations—which were expressions of contradiction by the protestors—were in the protestors' eyes reminiscent of the forms of violence once employed against dissenting opinions during National Socialism. The radical responses of West German state to left-oriented student protests and organizations, as well as the legislators' surprising departure from the fundamental rights that had constituted the core of West German *Grundgesetz* after the end of National Socialism, were seen by opposition-minded students as evidence that the fascist mentality and methods persisted even after the war. As eyewitnesses reported, Gudrun Ensslin, one of the founders of the *RAF*, spoke the following words in the office of *SDS*, just hours after the shooting of Benno Ohnesorg during the anti-Shah demonstration: "This fascist state is out to kill us all. We have to organize resistance. Violence can only be met with violence. This is the Auschwitz generation—you can't argue with them" (cited in (Kellerhoff 2020, 19); my translation).

The political system's forceful suppression of protests expressing leftist groups' dissatisfaction with the contradictions they had perceived marked the beginning of an armed conflict between a fraction of protesters and the political system in West Germany. These protesters, who had shifted further to the left following the exclusion of the *SDS* from the *SPD*, founded the *RAF*. Through targeted assassinations, bombings, and kidnappings, the *RAF* sought to disrupt what it viewed as ongoing structural violence and authoritarian remnants within the West German state. Although the terrorist activities of the *RAF*'s first generation ended with the deaths of Ulrike Meinhof, Andreas Baader, Gudrun Ensslin, and Jan-Carl Raspe in their cells at Stammheim prison, the group endured through two subsequent generations.[4]

The Young German Cinema—later referred to as New German Cinema—emerged while West German society was dealing with these contradictions and conflicts.

Evolution of Film Art in West German Society, between the 1960s and 1980s

Film historical scholarship on New German Cinema often situates this new wave somewhere between an epoch and a category, both of which entail the construction of a specific filmic canon. As outlined in the introduction, I find these approaches problematic and instead advocate studying cinematic new waves as distinct, organic evolutional forms, which I consider more insightful. This evolution-based perspective, drawing on a conception of film as communication within the art system and grounded in Niklas Luhmann's theory, aims to trace how the utterance and information of filmic communication have evolved alongside the contradictions and conflicts discussed in the previous section. It also seeks to explore how these two concurrent developments might be interconnected. In this endeavor, I will not begin with the Oberhausen Manifesto, as do studies that frame New German Cinema as an epoch. Nor will I limit my analysis to the films typically identified as part of the New German Cinema canon. Instead, I will start by examining the structure and information of the *Heimatfilm*, which was most popular in West Germany during the 1950s and 1960s, before New German Cinema emerged.

Heimatfilm: The Calm before the Storm

Immediately after the Second World War, films produced in Germany under Allied supervision were required to depict the atrocities of National Socialism and the dire contemporary conditions of German life, which were direct consequences of the Nazi regime and the war. These films, intended to educate the German public about the mistakes they had made in supporting the Nazis, formed a genre known as *Trümmerfilm* (Rubble Film). From a Luhmannian perspective, a genre can be understood as a collection of specific topics and forms of filmic utterance that, through their redundant co-occurrence, establish a recognizable set of identities and filmic structure.

This structure, once consolidated through repetition and recognition, is subsequently labeled by film critics and scholars as a distinct genre. In the case of *Trümmerfilm*, it was the shared topic of the Germans' war traumata and the miseries they had to endure in the cities reduced to rubble—as materialized in the narrative and *mise-en-scène*—that defined the genre, while the film structure aligned with the continuity system.

Unsurprisingly, *Trümmerfilm* did not enjoy widespread popularity among German audiences. As Moeller notes, citing a film reviewer from the late 1940s, it was "time for spiritual restoration. We have had enough of violent emotions" (2003, 125). A subsequent film genre, *Heimatfilm* (Homeland Film), responded to this need for non-violent emotions by offering the West German public a sense of spiritual restoration. *Heimatfilm* was, unlike *Trümmerfilm*, the most popular film genre in West German society during the 1950s and early 1960s, demonstrating mass production and a "surprising" continuity (Ludewig 2011, 59). The *Heimatfilm* genre is defined by clear narrative conventions. As Tauber points out, authority figures like doctors, foresters, and priests play central roles in this genre. Good and evil are clearly distinguished. Typical conflicts include inheritance disputes, poaching, smuggling, and jealousy. Love between young men and women is central, with obstacles such as class differences, family feuds, intrigue, envy, and misunderstandings leading to a happy ending (Tauber 2016, 104). The conflicts addressed in *Heimatfilm* are often not matters of life and death, and they are peacefully resolved in the end.

The characters within the *Heimatfilm* narrative—which marks the information of this genre's communication—are often typified. Among them, the male main and supporting characters are physically strong men who, due to fate, become entangled in a misunderstanding with the women. The female main and supporting characters, on the other hand, are women who manage daily life independently, yet once they meet the protagonist, it becomes clear to both them and the audience that they absolutely need him for their life to become "complete." These patterns are evident, for example, in *Grün ist die Heide* (The Heath Is Green; 1951), in which Helga, the daughter of a secret poacher, meets the new forester, Walter Rainer, who embodies the morally upright position of law and order. The two are immediately drawn to each other. But Helga soon realizes that her father is the illegal poacher being pursued by the forester. His motivation for his outlawed actions, as he confesses to Helga, lies solely in the trauma he experienced after being forced to flee from the East after the war, a place to which he once belonged. The film does not delve further into the details of this trauma or how it might drive a man to illegally shoot animals.

In order to protect her father from punishment, Helga decides to leave the village where she and her father have resettled and take him with her. Here, she demonstrates a strong character by giving precedence to her father, who represents blood ties and family, over her love. When her father, having discovered a second poacher, is shot by him and lies in bed, Helga runs hysterically up the stairs to his room. It is only in Walter's arms, who is also waiting upstairs and who knows better that "everything will be alright" in the near future, that she regains her composure. The formerly strong-minded, independent Helga, who also acted as a mother to her father, appears helpless in strong Walter's arms, who is expected to provide her with security and support in the future.

In the previous chapter, I identified the continuity system as one of the most prominent and widely adopted structures of filmic communication. This structure was also extensively employed by *Heimatfilm*s, which placed uninterrupted storytelling at the core of their utterance. At the level of camera work, these films—much like classical Hollywood productions—typically open each scene with a long establishing shot that introduces the setting and characters. In terms of editing, they adhere strictly to synchronized diegetic sound and image, which are cut simultaneously. The diegetic music often consists of cheerful or romantic German folk songs, while extradiegetic music is typically used to reinforce the emotional tone of specific scenes. Other elements of the medium of filmic communication that require a deeper familiarity with the medium to be fully understood or that contribute less directly to the narrative—such as acousmatic sounds, jump cuts, unconventional shot types like extreme close-ups or long shots, unbalanced frame compositions, or varied depths of field—are deliberately avoided.[5] In short, the film directs the audience's attention exclusively to the diegesis and the actions unfolding within it.

As mentioned earlier, the dominant mass media discourse in post-Second World War West German society emphasized a radical break from National Socialism, driven by the trials of former Nazi functionaries, which received extensive mass media coverage. However, critics saw the themes of the popular *Heimatfilm* as a continuation of Nazi ideology, as they had already been explored in Nazi propaganda films. According to Trimborn,

> With regard to the ideals and values presented in West German *Heimatfilm* of the 1950s, as well as the preferred image of humanity portrayed therein, several parallels can be observed with the *Blut und Boden* [blood and land] ideology of the National Socialist worldview [...], such as the embellished, idealized depiction of the native German

> landscape—a conscious and demonstrative (and ultimately ideologically underpinned) demarcation from all that is considered "foreign"—or the portrayal of the "simplicity," "authenticity," "closeness to nature," and "contentment" of the rural population.
>
> (1998, 140; my translation; emphasis added)

Besides demonstrating these narrative characteristics from Nazi cinema, the romance-like narrative structure of the *Heimatfilm*—with a diegesis consisting of an idealized rural place, its typified character constructs lacking psychological depth, the decisive role of luck in the characters' fate rather than their conscious decisions, the complexity-reducing division between good and evil, and a happy ending in which conflicts are resolved, the good prevails and lovers get married—did not resonate with the complex contradictions shaping communications in West German society in the late 1950s and throughout the 1960s regarding politics, morality, and gender roles.[6]

The Wave Ventures to Take Shape

Heimatfilm was criticized as an escapist genre because it neither addressed the immediate Nazi past and the war nor engaged with significant contemporary communication topics of the 1950s, such as the remilitarization of West Germany and the reinstatement of former Nazi functionaries in key bureaucratic, governmental, and military positions. However, several other genres emerged in West Germany alongside *Heimatfilm* that ventured to incorporate these issues into filmic communication—films which Dillmann refers to as "sophisticated films." She defines "sophisticated films" in the Adenauer era as those that sought to confront contemporary problems, rather than depicting an intact world with reduced complexity, as was typical of *Heimatfilm* (2016, 31). In film historical literature, these works are categorized as war films, doctor films, problem films, and so on, depending on their themes and protagonists (Heinzlmeier 1988, 17). In this chapter, I will focus on war films, as they took the most significant risk of moving away from the popular *Heimatfilm* genre—whose financial success was already assured—and thematized, albeit in a conservative manner, significant topics of communication within their contemporary social context.

Although the 1950s war films too attempted to clearly distinguish between good and evil in their narrative, as *Heimatfilm*s did, the good and the evil in these films did not manifest as poachers and foresters—as in *Grün ist die Heide*—or thieves and honest people—as in *Schwarzwaldmädel* (The Black Forest Girl; 1950). Neither did their diegesis resemble the idyllic and timeless one of the *Heimatfilm*. Instead, the good and the evil in these films were represented within the context of the Nazi army and intelligence service. Thus, the supporters of National Socialism (NS) and *Schutzstaffel* (*SS*; Protection Squadron) as well as some high-ranking officers were portrayed as antagonists, while the lower-ranking soldiers, who had been drafted into the war but had participated involuntarily, were depicted as decent people. According to Stiglegger, instead of portraying a demonized external enemy, such as Britain or the Soviet Union from the Nazi perspective, the enemy in the war film genre of the 1950s West Germany was depicted within the ranks. Films of this genre, as Stieglegger interprets them, suggested that the average soldier was an upright and humane representative of Germany, often portrayed as a victim of the fanatical leadership. These films reinforced the myth of a noble army led to destruction by Hitler and the *SS*. As Stieglegger observes, the Holocaust and the persecution of Jews and other victims were often marginally addressed or never explicitly shown in these war films, with responsibility for the crimes placed largely on Hitler, Himmler, Göring, and other Nazi leaders. The simple soldier, however, was portrayed as relatable to audiences who remembered the bombings and the loss of loved ones, as well as the Allied invasion (Stiglegger 2016, 270).

As noted above, the remilitarization of West Germany and its accession to NATO were among the most significant communication topics of the late 1950s. In light of the Nazi regime's questionable war crimes, a moral discourse was necessary to justify both the rearmament of West German army and the reintegration of certain officials from the Nazi military into the new armed forces. The war film genre fulfilled precisely this function: at the narrative level, it condemned specific military factions while portraying others not only as innocent, but even as heroic and patriotic. In this respect, films of this genre engaged in communication on a topic fundamentally different from that of the *Heimatfilm*, while simultaneously retaining the latter's adherence to the continuity principle and its narrative structure, characterized by reduced complexity and a clear division between good and evil. Since the *Heimatfilm* owed its popularity precisely to offering an escape from the dark Nazi past and the pressing political and moral questions of the present, war films risked losing their appeal to audiences by diverging from this thematic approach. At the same time, war films failed to address the contradictions that critical West German citizens were perceiving; instead, they presented a story that, due to its simplified treatment of the Nazi past and the contemporary political climate, offered a contradiction-free narrative of West Germany's post-war political developments.

One of the most famous examples of these war films is considered to be the trilogy *08/15*. Released in 1954 and 1955, this trilogy—unlike the popular *Heimatfilm* of the time—deals exclusively and intensively with the Second

World War, in the same years when the rearmament and NATO accession of West Germany took place. Each part of the trilogy is set in a different location, which determines the subtitle of the respective film: the first part takes place *In der Kaserne* (In the Barracks), the second *Im Krieg* (At War), and the third *In der Heimat* (Back Home). *08/15* centers on the fate of an artillery battery across the three aforementioned locations and timeframe.

The character design in the narrative of *08/15* is marked by a clear division between the good and the evil. The protagonists of the film—namely Gunner Vierbein, Private Asch, and Corporal Kowalski—are all soldiers. The antagonists, on the other hand, are the authorities positioned higher within the hierarchical military system. These include the *SS* officers as well as those in the army who made decisions and issued orders during the war, such as Sergeant Major Schulz or Captain Witterer in the film. These figures exploit the soldiers and send them on suicide missions, while emerging unscathed themselves. Among them is Sergeant Platzek, an opportunist who always thinks of his own gain and profits from every emergency: whether in the barracks, at war on the Russian front, or back home when the barracks are taken over by the American troops.

However, not everyone in the upper ranks of the military hierarchy is portrayed as a manipulative villain in *08/15*. Lieutenant Colonel Plönnies, for example, considers the war to be meaningless and views Hitler as a foolish military leader. According to him, the incompetence of the commander in chief results in his subordinates carrying out ill-conceived war plans, thereby endangering the lives of soldiers. In the third part, Plönnies appears as a courageous and determined military judge who sentences a war criminal to death.

At the end of the third film, it is the corrupt and foolish—namely the high-ranking officers and their wives, who care only about living a luxurious life at any expense—who eagerly welcome the American soldiers. They immediately begin learning English, flirt with the Americans, and attempt to strike deals with them. In contrast, Plönnies and the "good," patriotic soldiers proudly keep their distance from the occupiers. This presents a clear commentary on the Allied occupation of Germany after the war, suggesting that the brave and upright soldiers were victims of both groups: the Nazis and the Allies.

Another war film, *Des Teufels General* (The Devil's General; 1955), draws the dividing line between the military, on the one hand, and the *SS*, on the other, portraying the former as conscientious patriots and the latter as corrupt and fundamentally evil adherents of National Socialism. As a result, the critique of the *SS* becomes sharper and more direct in this film. In one of the scenes, for example, Air Force General Harras (H), who is the protagonist of the film, spells out the word *Vaterland* (fatherland) for *SS* Group Leader Schmidt-Lausitz, who is trying to persuade Harras to switch from the military to the *SS* for the sake of their fatherland:

> H—*Vaterland*? [...] What do you even understand by that? Go ahead, spell it out: *V* as in *Volksgerichtshof* [People's Court], *A* as in *Aufhängen* [hanging], *T* as in *Totsagen* [declaring dead], *E* as in *Erschießen* [shooting], *R* as in *Rassenverfolgung* [racial persecution], *L* as in *Lager* [concentration camp], Auschwitz, Neuengamme, Dachau. See? That's how you spell Germany today!
>
> (my translation)

Harras in *Des Teufels General* is portrayed as such a decent and moral individual that he even attempts to protect a Jewish couple from persecution—a marginal gesture that occupies barely five minutes of the entire film. A military, then, in which such just and upright individuals occupy leadership positions, is considered desirable despite the atrocities of the Second World War: this is how the communications of 1950s war films should have been understood.

Nachts, wenn der Teufel kam (The Devil Strikes at Night; 1957) adopts a similar critical stance toward war and National Socialism to the aforementioned films. However, it also references a well-known motif from the history of cinema during the Weimar Republic, specifically Fritz Lang's *M* (1931). In *M*, a mentally ill man kidnaps and murders children. *Nachts, wenn der Teufel kam* is similarly about a psychopath, Bruno Lüdke, but his victims are women, not children. Criminal Inspector Axel Kersten, a wounded war returnee, follows the trail of the perpetrator. He is finally able to convict Bruno as the murderer of several women, one of whom is accidentally a Jewish woman.[7]

Despite his success in identifying the murderer, Kersten receives a direct order from Adolf Hitler, conveyed through the *SS* Group Leader, to keep the case confidential. This directive is issued because Lüdke is neither Jewish nor a foreigner, and the numerous murders he committed could be exploited as anti-Nazi propaganda. To suppress the case, Lüdke is executed without trial. Kersten, who seeks to reveal the involvement of high-ranking *SS* members in concealing the crime, is punished and reassigned to the frontlines.

In Luhmann's terms, *Nachts, wenn der Teufel kam* is a reflexive filmic communication, as it clearly alludes to an earlier German film, namely *M*. Through its reflexivity, the film ventures to prompt viewers to think beyond a second-order observation that merely derives a narrative from filmic utterance. Instead, it encourages them to recall a similar film they may know or still remember from the interwar period in Germany. This is a process that can be described as third-order observation in the Luhmannian sense, since viewers are expected to observe the difference between the outcome of their second-order observation, namely the narrative, and the narrative of the earlier film. By motivating observation beyond second-order observation, the film introduces a level of communicative complexity that was not available in *Heimatfilms*.

Nachts, wenn der Teufel kam presents another case of narrative venture that marks a clear difference to the *Heimatfilm*. Whereas the popular *Heimatfilm* always ended happily, some war films, such as *Nachts, wenn der Teufel kam*, risked their success at the box office and chose tragic endings. Another such film with a tragic ending is *Die Brücke* (The Bridge; 1959), which addresses the tragedy of war and National Socialism directly and without embellishment. The film opens by depicting the quiet everyday life of adolescents from a small German town near the end of the war, who are conscripted into the military the following day. They are assigned the meaningless task of defending the small bridge in their town against the approaching American troops. They are killed without exception, due to their youthful inexperience and the lack of competent leadership.

Not all war films in the 1950s had a tragic ending, however. For example, *Wir Wunderkinder* (Aren't We Wonderful?; 1958) and *Rosen für den Staatsanwalt* (Roses for the Prosecutor; 1959) were produced in the comedy genre. In addition to criticizing the injustices of National Socialism and the tragedies it caused—with which the previously discussed films concluded—both films trace former Nazi officers and judges into the present day (the late 1950s), where they now occupy prominent economic and judicial positions. Within the narratives of both films, these former criminals are punished in a humorous fashion. In *Wir Wunderkinder*, Bruno, the former opportunistic Nazi and now managing director in the era of the Economic Miracle, accidentally falls into an elevator shaft and dies. The fate of the senior public prosecutor in *Rosen für den Staatsanwalt* is less dramatic: he is merely suspended, because under National Socialism he had sentenced Private Rudi Kleinschmidt to death for stealing a tin of chocolate.

Besides its thematic venture, *Wir Wunderkinder* also undertakes minimal but significant innovations in its narrative structure. It uses certain elements from the medium of filmic communication to implement a narrative strategy that was unconventional at the time of its release, given the dominant structure of filmic utterance defined by *Heimatfilm*. The film opens as a silent film accompanied by a narrator's voiceover, introducing the small town depicted on screen. Suddenly, a pointer stick appears on the screen, and the camera zooms out to reveal a film theater where the silent film has been playing, along with a narrator holding the stick and a musician accompanying the silent film. This *mise-en-scène* decision to reveal the stick and the zoom-out, which is a camera technique specific to the medium of filmic communication, momentarily disrupt the viewers' dual options of first- and second-order observations, leaving them with only the option of second-order observation. This occurs because the viewers can no longer remain immersed in the unfolding plot, and for a few seconds, they have no choice but to search for the meaning behind the film's formal choices. As a result, they become aware that they have been watching a film projected within the main film.

The film theater, which includes the narrator and the musician accompanying the film with singing, piano, and accordion, constitutes the meta-diegesis of the projected film. Throughout the narrative, there are transitions between the diegesis and the meta-diegesis, particularly when signaling the passage of time. For example, the initially projected silent film begins by introducing the protagonist and antagonist, Hans Boeckel and Bruno Tiches, as children during the interwar period in Germany. The narrator comments on a small adventure the two undertake in the projected film: breaking away from the crowd to climb into a balloon just as it is about to lift off. The narrator then announces the end of the first act, and the camera zooms out from the screen to the film theater within the meta-diegesis, where the piano player and the narrator, looking directly into the camera, begin to sing a melancholy song about how the "Third Reich" came to power. In the second act of the diegetic film, which is projected following the song, Hans and Bruno are depicted as young adults during the Nazi era. This time, the diegetic film is a sound film, hinting at the fact that films in the 1930s, unlike those of the interwar period, included sound.

The direct address to the audience by the narrator and the musician constitutes an instance of *attraction* in Gunning's sense. With his concept of the "cinema of attractions," Gunning characterizes early cinema (between 1895 and 1906) as a mode centered on visual spectacle and direct audience engagement, rather than immersive narrative storytelling. These early films were exhibitionist in nature, openly acknowledging the viewer and drawing attention to their own cinematic form. Rooted in popular entertainment such as vaudeville and stage magic, this mode of cinema aimed to provoke reaction and wonder (Gunning 2006). The metadiegetic attraction of *Wir Wunderkinder*, through the narrator and the musician addressing the viewers directly as "members of the audience," leaves the viewers, for a moment, with no choice but second-order observation of the filmic utterance, reminding them that "they have only been watching a film" and should not engage with it emotionally as mere first-order observers. Such disruptions of observation mode were unimaginable within the uninterrupted, linear narrative of the *Heimatfilm*.

Rather than criticizing or intending to undermine *Heimatfilm*'s dominant mode of perception, the two diegetic levels in *Wir Wunderkinder* and the formal filmic strategies used to transition between them appear to serve two different functions. On the one hand, since the film is an adaptation of a novel of the same title, the two diegeses function as a narrative device to bypass sections of the novel that are not included in the film's storyline. On the other hand, breaking away from the diegesis into the meta-diegesis provides viewers with relief from having to re-experience the traumata and hardships of the Nazi era and the war as first-order observers. The meta-diegesis, featuring the narrator and the musician, allows them to step back from their intense, immersive emotional engagement and resume watching the unfolding events of the plot after a brief musical interlude.

The war films introduced thus far share a common quality: although they formally adhere to the dominant structure of the *Heimatfilm*—namely, the continuity system—they raise moral questions about the German military in the Second World War and the ethical backgrounds of millionaires and judiciary personnel during the era of the Economic Miracle. These were contemporary topics of communication in 1950s West German society, although war films treated them in a conservative and superficial way. Therefore, the war films stood in stark narrative contrast to the timeless, fairy tale-like diegesis and narrative typically associated with the *Heimatfilm*.

Furthermore, some of these war films take the risk of disrupting the viewers' first-order observation through minor instances of reflexivity or attraction in their formal utterance strategies and information choices. *Nachts, wenn der Teufel kam* becomes reflexive through its narrative allusion to *M*, encouraging engagement with the film's communication on additional observational levels beyond simply following the narrative. The cinematographic transitions between diegesis and meta-diegesis as well as directly addressing the audience in *Wir Wunderkinder*, in turn, represent examples of attraction and disrupt the viewers' first-order observation, reminding them constantly that they are just watching a film. I consider these choices as risks, as they mark a significant difference to the narrative and structural conventions stabilized by the *Heimatfilm*, whose box office success was still highly probable and therefore expectable in the 1950s.

A collection of the above-mentioned risky decisions is evident in the war film trilogy *08/15*. It is therefore worth examining more closely how *08/15* makes certain formal decisions to open up new possibilities for meaning-making in a filmic communication that engages with a topic very different from the *Heimatfilm*.

Depth of Field and Mise-en-Scène in 08/15

One of the key identities of filmic utterance that is extensively employed in *08/15* is the depth of field, a technique specific to cinematography. This technique is frequently used to convey information about characters' personalities or power dynamics in certain situations—information that, in *Heimatfilm*, would typically be communicated through *mise-en-scène*, including acting and costume design, or dialogue. In such shots, the camera remains static long enough to ensure that the *mise-en-scène* designed for the depth of field is clearly perceived by the viewers. Figure 1, for example, shows Private Asch playing cards and smoking with a superior officer in the barracks' cloakroom, while a sign reading "*Rauchen verboten!*" (No Smoking!) is visible on the wall behind the officer to the left. This frame composition, along with the written message in the background, offers a pointed commentary on higher-ranking officers who consider themselves above the strict rules governing the barracks.

Another example of filmic communication through depth of field and framing is illustrated in Figure 2, where Vierbein is framed within a triangle created by Schulz's arm, resting on his hip after catching Vierbein playing the piano. The scene reveals Vierbein's soft, romantic nature, which starkly

Figure 1 Screenshot from *08/15*, Part 1. Communication through depth of field.

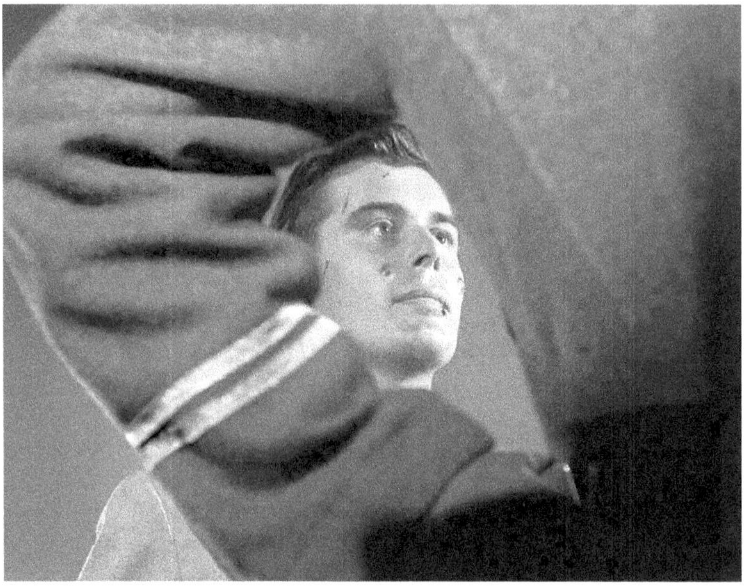

Figure 2 Screenshot from *08/15*, Part 1. Communication through depth of field.

contrasts with the harsh military dynamics prevailing in the barracks. The composition in this shot suggests Vierbein's submissiveness to Schulz, who embodies authority as a figure of higher military rank.

In the third part of *08/15*, the combination of *mise-en-scène* and sound through editing enables the retrieval of allegorical information from the filmic utterance—an approach not found in *Heimatfilm* with its limited formal and straightforward narrative strategies. Near the end of the trilogy's final installment, an elderly couple is introduced whose home has been occupied by American soldiers and repurposed as a military command base. The couple is escorted to the door by a German official, now working for the occupying Americans, as the camera follows them in a tracking full shot. This shot not only captures the couple being expelled from their home but also reveals the artworks on the walls and the refined *art nouveau* furniture and architecture of the house. The elderly man and his wife pause at the doorway, where the Americans have placed two Coca-Cola boxes on a commode. Having spoken with the German soldier about the artworks during the tracking shot, the man now rests his hand on the top Coca-Cola box and remarks that he has never had anything like that in his house (Figure 3). These cinematographic choices highlight the visual contrast between the "cultivated" German home, filled with fine art and elegant furniture, and the influx of "degraded" American goods, such as Cola bottles, now occupying the space. While the house can

Figure 3 Screenshot from *08/15*, Part 3. Allegorical communication through cinematography and diegetic sound.

be read as an allegorical representation of Germany as a land of high art and culture, the Coca-Cola boxes serve as an allegory for the American culture perceived as inferior.

Another degradation of the American occupiers' culture is conveyed later in the film through *mise-en-scène* and diegetic sound. In this shot, a Black American soldier is shown with an untidy uniform and an open collar, sitting on the floor with his legs spread, smoking a cigar, and listening to jazz music on his radio (Figure 4). Given the still pervasive racism in West German society during the mid-1950s, the contrast between this Black soldier's disheveled appearance and casual demeanor and the consistently tidy uniforms and upright postures of the white German soldiers depicted throughout the trilogy can be interpreted as another allegorical suggestion of the "seriousness" of the German soldiers versus the perceived "sloppiness" of their American counterparts. Additionally, the contrast between the jazz music playing on the untidy Black soldier's radio in the third part and the classical music performed by Vierbein—a white, tidy soldier—on the piano in the first part of the trilogy further reinforces the portrayal of German culture and music as more refined and superior to that of the American occupiers.

Figure 4 Screenshot from *08/15*, Part 3. Allegorical communication through cinematography and diegetic sound.

Allusion and Reflexivity in 08/15

As the next example of formal ventures in *08/15*, instances of reflexivity in filmic communication through *mise-en-scène* and depth of field come into focus. In a scene from the third part of the trilogy, the American occupiers are shown with their feet propped up on a desk in the office of the German barracks (Figure 5). In this scene, the audience is offered a textual commentary via a poster on the wall behind the American commander, which reads "*Feind hört mit*" (the enemy is listening). This directly references the domestic propaganda campaign of the "Third Reich" that used the same slogan to raise public awareness about espionage during the war and to discourage unnecessary conversation in public spaces. However, the poster simultaneously—and more significantly—alludes to the 1940 Nazi film *Achtung! Feind hört mit!* (Beware! The Enemy Is Listening!; 1940).

In the depth of field, this scene creates a satirical juxtaposition between the poster's warning and the actual "enemies" who now sit, victorious and relaxed, in the very space where the warning was once issued. This contrast not only carries ironic meaning but also produces a moment of reflexivity

Figure 5 Screenshot from *08/15*, Part 3. Reflexivity in cinematography.

in filmic communication, as the third part of *08/15* alludes to the legacy of Nazi film and its dissolution. The visual emphasis on this poster, along with another poster on the adjacent wall—which may also derive from a Nazi film—can be read as connoting the simultaneous end of Nazi cinema and the political system of National Socialism. Moreover, it suggests the conquest of the German film landscape by American cinema, mirrored by the physical occupation of the barracks by American forces.

A further example of reflexivity is offered by two shots from the first and third parts of the trilogy. Figure 6 shows a shot from Part 1 on the left, in which a pair of hanging boots is visible in the foreground inside the barracks' cloakroom, with three military men in the background. This composition serves as a prophecy of the future, where people wearing boots are executed, as depicted in a shot from Part 3 of the trilogy shown in Figure 6 on the right. This is less a prophecy of the audience's future—since the film was released in 1954, when the war was already part of history—and more a prediction of a future installment within the same trilogy. The two shots from Parts 1 and 3 of *08/15* can therefore be considered an instance of reflexivity in Luhmann's sense, as each filmic utterance references the other.

There are two further allusions to German and American films in Parts 1 and 2 of *08/15*. Figure 7 shows the scene from Part 1 in which Asch returns

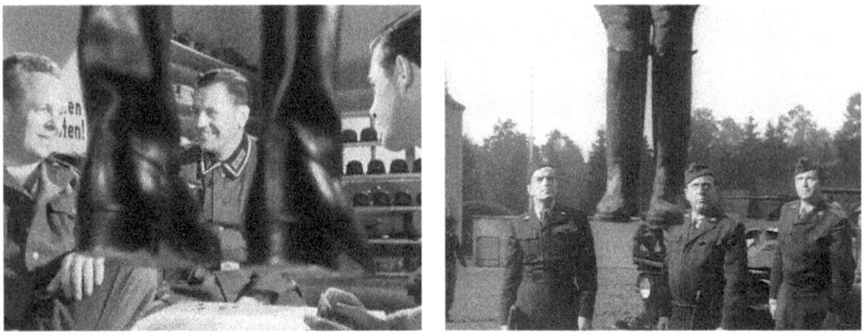

Figure 6 Screenshots from *08/15*, Part 1 (left) and Part 3 (right). Reflexivity in cinematography.

Figure 7 Screenshot from *08/15*, Part 1. Reflexivity in cinematography and diegetic sound.

half-naked to the barracks over the weekend, having left his clothes in his girlfriend's bedroom while fleeing from her father, who had unexpectedly come home. In the courtyard, he encounters the sergeant. However, the sergeant's body is not visible and only his enormous shadow cast on the façade of the barracks is seen, as he urinates around a corner, drunk from a celebration. The conversation between Asch and the acousmatic voice of the urinating shadow creates a grotesque moment, while the exaggerated shadow alludes to the expressionist cinema of the Weimar Republic, with its pronounced light-shadow contrasts and side lighting. The connection to expressionist film becomes even more apparent at the level of diegetic sound, when Asch explains to the sergeant's shadow that he is a sleepwalker, which is why he is in the courtyard without trousers and wearing only an undershirt. This directly references *Das Cabinet des Dr. Caligari* (The Cabinet of Dr. Caligari; 1920), an expressionist German film made during the Weimar Republic, in which Cesare, the sleepwalker, roams the city at night committing murders.

Even though the cultural offensive of the Americans is clearly mocked in *08/15*, as previously discussed, the trilogy itself, as a cultural product, is not exempt from the formal influence of Hollywood films and alludes to them in at least two scenes. While in *Heimatfilm*s common up to that point, kissing and sex scenes were typically avoided—either through cuts or by, for example, having the dancing lovers exit the frame of a static camera, as at the end of *Schwarzwaldmädel—08/15* employs a technique that was very likely inspired by classical Hollywood cinema. This method was used to tactfully censor scenes of violence, kissing, and sex following the introduction of religious-moral censorship by the Production Code Administration (PCA) in the 1930s.[8] This technique involves the indirect depiction of prohibited actions, for example, through the shadows of the acting figures or through specific framing and shot size choices that display only a portion of the action within a confined frame rather than revealing the entire event in a full shot. In the second part of *08/15*, there is a scene where Asch and a girl begin to kiss. To censor the kiss, the camera tilts downward to show their legs beneath the table. As they kiss, accompanied by a cheerful extradiegetic brass melody, their feet lift in a gesture known as a "foot pop"—a cinematic shorthand indicating that the kiss is thrilling and emotionally charged (Figure 8). Showing only the foot pop of a couple engaged in erotic interaction was a well-known censoring strategy in classical Hollywood cinema.

In a further allusion to post-Second World War Hollywood cinema, the third part's narrative temporarily adopts the form of a crime story, in which Asch suddenly assumes a role similar to that of a detective in a film noir. He is tasked with uncovering a murder and the theft of a platinum shipment committed by two members of the *SS*. In addition to the thematic parallels to film noir, Asch acquires a blonde female companion who assists him in solving the crimes, much like Humphrey Bogart is accompanied by a female counterpart in films such as *The Big Sleep* (1946). In their two-shot, the same extreme side lighting of faces can be observed, as is characteristic of film noir (Figure 9). Notably, in the shot from the third part of *08/15* shown in

Figure 8 Screenshot from *08/15*, Part 2. Reflexivity in cinematography.

Figure 9 Screenshots from *08/15*, Part 3 (left) and *The Big Sleep* (right). Allusion to film noir.

Figure 9, the camera awkwardly allows excessive headroom, revealing the large light spot cast by the upward-facing spotlight on the ceiling.

These instances of allusion in *08/15*, which exemplify reflexivity in the Luhmannian sense and were also present in other previously introduced war films, are significant because filmic reflexivity, by its nature, can only be perceived and understood by the third-order observer. This observer not only distinguishes narrative information from filmic utterance through second-order observation but also recognizes the difference between this filmic information and that found in other films. The allusions mentioned above playfully offer bonus information for those members of the audience who are more familiar with earlier films. In doing so, they extend beyond the *mise-en-scène*-based utterance and the linear narrative found in their contemporary *Heimatfilms*.

Attraction in 08/15

Besides its formal and narrative divergence from *Heimatfilm* conventions already discussed, *08/15* also exhibits attraction in Gunning's sense. This occurs when Asch and the girlfriend of an *SS* criminal, who is accompanying him, are speaking in the apartment of the criminal's victims. The woman urges them to leave quickly before anyone sees them. However, Asch replies, "well, anyone can see us here," and then casts a fleeting, sly glance into the camera (Figure 10). Thereby, he is referring to their visibility to the film's audience. This moment of engaging with the camera, which allows the diegesis to merge with the viewers' space, breaks the continuity system's convention, which traditionally forbids direct eye contact with the camera to avoid the interruption of the film's first-order observation.

Venture as Variation

The close analysis of the war films produced alongside the extremely popular *Heimatfilms* in 1950s West Germany reveals a distinct formal and narrative trend in the former. To ensure easy comprehension for viewers, the *Heimatfilm* avoided communication beyond the film's closed, linear narrative itself. As a result, *mise-en-scène* became its primary communication medium, while the film-specific medium of communication consisting of camera work, sound design and editing remained unobtrusive and served solely to convey the narrative through *mise-en-scène*—encompassing character actions, dialogue, and other visual elements. Consequently, the structure of *Heimatfilm* complied with the continuity system and its formal choices were limited to a small set of shot types, minimal camera movement (primarily tracking shots motivated by the action), rare use of zoom, and consistent synchronization of sound and image.

At their information level, *Heimatfilms* have often been criticized as escapist, portraying an idealized, unrealistic world rooted in idyllic rural German villages seemingly untouched by the war and subtly aligned with the *Blut und Boden* ideology of National Socialism, though without explicit reference. Within *Heimatfilm* narratives, characters were one-dimensional

Figure 10 Screenshot from *08/15*, Part 3. Attraction via direct address to the audience.

and polarized, conflicts minor and swiftly resolved to ensure a happy ending. This configuration, consisting of a predetermined repertoire of straightforward narrative forms and themes, defined the information of a filmic communication that was widely accepted by West German audiences in the 1950s, telling from its profitable sales at the box office.

In contrast, as demonstrated above, war films of the 1950s took risks at both narrative and formal levels by making choices that diverged from the *Heimatfilm* formula, even at the potential cost of box office success. The most significant of these choices lay in the topic of filmic communication itself, which resonated with some of the most pressing issues in West German society at the time: reflection on the war and the National Socialist past, the rearmament of the German military, and the reinstatement of former Nazis to their previous positions.

Alongside this shift in its other-reference, filmic communication also underwent a conservative but nonetheless daring formal reform within the war films. This reform took shape through an increase in both the number and complexity of selections from the medium of filmic communication—embedding more complex meaning within each shot and in the interplay of visual and auditory elements through allegory and allusion/reflexivity. These formal selections included, in part, more sophisticated uses of depth of field, framing, and the editing of sound and image than what *Heimatfilm* typically offered.

Thereby, war films in 1950s Germany demonstrate a specific tendency by risking to diverge from the *Heimatfilm* tradition—a genre that had already proven successful with audiences—by significantly updating their topic (information) and introducing greater variety in their form (utterance). In doing so, war films aligned the information of filmic communication with the ongoing communication in their environment. At the same time, they introduced limited modifications and extensions to their form by reactivating identities already familiar to filmic communication but abandoned by *Heimatfilm*—or, in Luhmann's terms, forgotten by *Heimatfilm*'s memory. I refer to this tendency as *venture*.

I argue that films manifesting the tendency of venture laid the groundwork for what would later emerge as new-wave cinema in West Germany. This is because the films subsequently associated with this movement display a radical expansion of the ventures these earlier films had cautiously initiated—namely, contemporizing the information of filmic communication and implementing identities of filmic utterance that enabled communication beyond the realm of a linear narrative derived mainly from the *mise-en-scène*. None of the existing studies on New German Cinema has acknowledged the contribution of venturing war films to this cinematic shift. However, when examined through the evolutionary lens provided by Luhmann's systems theory, their role in the development of New German Cinema becomes apparent.

It is important to emphasize that venture does not denote a film canon or a historical epoch. Rather, it refers to selections at the levels of information and filmic utterance that may or may not be present in specific films. Crucially, the term *venture* only acquires meaning within the context of film evolution when used relationally: a dominant film structure—characterized by its redundancy and popularity—must exist for venture to hold the significance attributed to it here, as a more or less conservative alternative to that structure. Moreover, venture itself must be sufficiently redundant to be recognizable as such and to constitute an evolutionary step in the development of filmic communication. Consequently, merely one or two "different" films exhibiting venture-like tendencies in their selections of information and form are insufficient to initiate a wave-like evolution.

West German cinema's venture, as the preparatory stage of New German Cinema, apparently emerged to resonate with the contradictory political and moral communications in its environment. However, films embodying this venture did not fully explore these contradictions in all their complexity.

Instead, they put issues such as military rearmament and the prosecution of former Nazis in uncomplicated, linear narratives, simplifying them by categorizing individuals as either "good" or "evil," and resolving the conflicts either through comedic closure—as in *Wir Wunderkinder* and *Rosen für den Staatsanwalt*—or through tragic endings in which soldiers perished as brave heroes or innocent victims, as in the rest of the war films analyzed. Hence, these war films avoided deep critical engagement with the dynamics of National Socialism and the complicity of ordinary citizens, soldiers, and high-ranking officers in its development.

The Wave Ruptures at the Shore

Film Industry's Crisis in 1960s West Germany

Whereas the *Heimatfilm* contributed to the growth and success of the film industry in 1950s West Germany, this industry entered a major crisis between 1957 and 1968. As Norbert Grob outlines, during this period the West German film industry lost more than 75 percent of its audience. The number of filmgoers declined sharply—from 800 million at the end of the 1950s to just 180 million by the late 1960s (Grob 2004, 217). This crisis was attributed in part to the increasing use and popularity of television. While many film studios, production companies, and distributors were forced to close, those that remained operational often shifted their capacity toward television productions (Grob 2004, 217).

This financial loss was noticed by the economic system, which is structurally coupled with the film system, forming the film industry. Having experienced this loss, the economic system irritated the film system and thereby indicated that the communication of *Heimatfilms* was being rejected by viewers, contrary to the expectations of success formed through a decade of repetitive experience. This loss demonstrated that neither the structure that had previously proven popular nor the narrative conveyed through this structure as information remained compelling to audiences. Additionally, venturing films, with their updated topics and slightly more diverse formal identities, also failed to attract viewers and thus could not rescue West German film from its financial crisis.

Compounding this financial failure was an artistic failure, which became evident at the 1961 Berlinale. According to Knörr:

> The official admission of their [that is, the films'] aesthetic failure came during the 1961 Berlinale, when the Ministry of the Interior demonstratively announced that not a single feature film would be

> awarded a Federal Film Prize that year. "It is bad. It is doing badly. It is being treated badly. It also wants to remain bad." These sentences from the much-quoted pamphlet *Der deutsche Film kann gar nicht besser sein* [The German Film Cannot be any Better] by Joe Hembus captured the tone of the young critics of the time.
>
> (2012, 170; my translation)

Following the aesthetic crisis of West German films, which was already noticed by multiple filmmakers and critics prior to the 1961 Berlinale, the period between 1957 and 1962 saw the publication of various letters, pamphlets, and manifestos that pointed to this and the financial crisis of film in West Germany, the most significant of which was the Oberhausen Manifesto, which will be examined later.

Simultaneously with these crises, a new group of films emerged. Despite the wide range of forms they explored from the medium of filmic communication, they shared a common tendency: they embraced filmic identities that, although previously established by earlier German and international films and already rooted in the medium of filmic communication, had long been forgotten by the memories of Nazi and postwar West German cinema. These earlier identities had been overshadowed by a limited set of identities characteristic of the *Heimatfilm* and the war film, which were continuously remembered by those traditions. The group of films I refer to here includes a segment of works commonly identified in film literature as Young German Cinema or New German Cinema.

The revolutionary formal choices of these films caused a *rupture* in the established structures of filmic communication. So stark was their contradiction to these structures and to audience expectations in West Germany that Elsaesser describes them as "cinephobic." Comparing these films to those of the French *Nouvelle Vague*, Elsaesser notes that the latter was already embedded within a tradition of artistic cinema with its own producers and its own audience (1989, 24). In contrast, what I call rupturing German films

> were made with a far less assured sense of an actual audience, and often bore little reference explicitly or implicitly to national or international film culture. The early films of Syberberg or Herzog, for instance, were to a remarkable degree objects *sui generis*, outside any recognisable tradition of film-making either commercial or avant-garde. Kluge's essays on celluloid, and even Jean-Marie Straub's or Vlado Kristl's films seemed, in contrast to the French directors' love of the cinema, inspired by what

one might almost call "cinephobia", a revulsion against the commercial film industry and its standard product, the fictional narrative film.

(1989, 24–5; emphasis in original)

If the films characterized by venture took the risk of shifting film's communication topic toward contemporary issues and modestly broadening the scope of filmic form, the films I address in this section—marked by rupture as their dominant formal tendency—pushed these boundaries to the extreme. These works not only integrated critical contemporary communication topics—such as the limited women's rights in West Germany, non-monogamous and homosexual relationship models, the uncritical thematization of the Nazi past by the political system, the suppression of leftist voices, and the division of Germany—into their information, but also came close to completely rupturing the established structure of filmic utterance established by *Heimatfilms*.

I will begin the analysis of rupturing films in this section with two works that have rarely been considered part of the West German New Wave in existing literature. This may be because both were produced before the declaration of the Oberhausen Manifesto, which many film scholars regard as the starting point of the German New Wave. Nevertheless, these two films exhibit nearly all the features of rupture that would later emerge in new-wave films produced in West Germany. Therefore, I will start with a comprehensive analysis of these films and then explore the features of rupture introduced by these two and demonstrated by other films in which rupture is the primary formal tendency. These films are *Jonas* (1957) and *Die Parallelstraße* (The Parallel Street; 1962).

Jonas

According to Prinzler, *Jonas* "paved the way for the Young German Film" (cited in (Vogt 2009, 434); my translation). As the *Frankfurter Allgemeine* newspaper noted on June 24, 1957, this film "transformed the German film situation in one stroke—regardless of how one may judge its meaning, its qualities, or its shortcomings" (cited in (Vogt 2009, 434); my translation). Although praised as an important film in its contemporary mass media, *Jonas* has not received the attention it deserves from film historians of New German Cinema. This is yet another reason to consider it more deliberately here.

Jonas's direct engagement with the unsettling contemporary communication topics of 1957 stands out as a key difference from the *Heimatfilm* and war film genres, which either avoided issues related to the war and the Nazi era entirely or reduced them to polarized character portrayals and simplistic storylines. During the opening credits of *Jonas*, set against the backdrop of a lighthouse in a nocturnal landscape, newspaper headlines from August 10, 1957, appear on screen: "More suicides than traffic fatalities" and "30 people voluntarily take their lives every day." Viewers also read that 47 percent of those surveyed experience *Angst* (anxiety), despite economic prosperity (Figure 11). Through these reports from a dated newspaper, the film clearly signals its intention to connect its communication to a current theme: the disturbed psychological condition of West German citizens. These intertitles, therefore, situate the film within the framework of contemporary mass media communication delivered by newspapers.

Jonas opens with tilted shots of the concrete façades of prefabricated buildings, street signs, and running printing presses in Stuttgart. The same voiceover that serves as narrator and commentator throughout the film—and also as the voice of Jonas and the other characters—explains that Jonas can be found behind a façade in this metropolis: a city full of signs, with its empty streets at dawn, where no people are yet visible and only the machines in the basements of the printing houses are operating. The tilted camera in the opening scene draws attention to its own presence by avoiding the perpendicular, eye-level framing typical of the continuity system.

Figure 11 Screenshot from *Jonas*. Addressing contemporary communication topics.

Here, the cinematography hints at the way the camera—as a technical equipment belonging to the environment of filmic communication—is being held. The film thereby engages in reflection in the Luhmannian sense, namely the thematization of the difference between filmic communication and its environment through the filmic communication itself.

A cut in this scene transitions from the flat cement façade of a building with small windows to the niches in the urn wall of a crematorium (Figure 12). This selection is an example of dialectical editing as conceptualized by Eisenstein, namely "the juxtaposition of two different images to create a sense which is beyond that of the two images which comprise it" (Robertson 2009, 37). In this case, the cut from the building façade to the crematorium wall suggests that the souls of those living behind these façades are already dead. The realization of meaning in filmic communication through complex editing strategies, such as dialectical editing, extends beyond the structure of the *Heimatfilm*, which conveyed its information primarily through the *mise-en-scène* and relied less on cinematic techniques that demanded greater interpretive effort from the viewers. While watching *Jonas*, viewers have no choice but to abandon their first-order observation for a few seconds and rely solely on second-order observation to discern the meaning of the difference between the two successive shots presented to them through dialectical editing.

Jonas, the film's main character, works for a newspaper. One day after work, he buys himself a hat, because, as the extradiegetic narrator's voice comments: "*Man geht heutzutage nicht mehr ohne Hut. Man geht nicht mehr unbehütet*" (Nowadays, one doesn't go out without a hat. One no longer goes out unprotected). This is one of the ambiguous statements repeatedly expressed by the voiceover in the film. It probably refers to the sense of insecurity that prevailed among West German citizens toward the end of the 1950s, having truly grasped the extent of the Nazi crimes through the trials and made aware of their own complicity as bystanders. Another example of such ironic and ambiguous remarks occurs when Jonas and Nanni, the main female character, are at a lighthouse. When Nanni, seemingly out of context, states that there are no more camps, Jonas replies that there are still "*Gefangene, Angeklagte, Verfolgte*" (prisoners, the accused, the persecuted), and that the spotlights continue to expose the guilty among the people. These remarks are made by one diegetic figure addressing another. However, the lack of sufficient narrative justification creates the impression that, although Jonas appears to be speaking to Nanni, he is in fact addressing the viewers. In doing so, the film seeks to prompt the viewers to reflect on their contemporary condition: how they remain silent about the past horrors of National Socialism—atrocities in which they themselves were complicit—

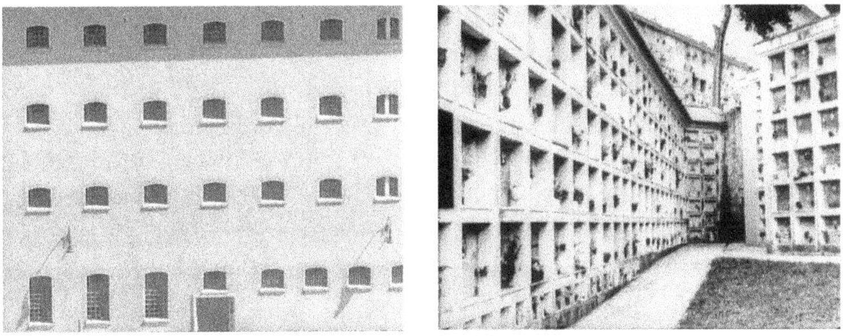

Figure 12 Screenshots from *Jonas*. Dialectical editing.

while continuing their daily lives. This direct address disrupts the audience's first-order observation of the film, which, in *Jonas*'s case, is almost impossible anyways!

After purchasing the hat from Nanni, the charming saleswoman at the hat shop, Jonas goes to a restaurant for a meal. Upon leaving, he notices that his new hat has vanished from the coat rack. Unwilling to leave without one, he quickly takes another hat hanging nearby and slips out. He soon discovers, however, that the hat is monogrammed with the initials "M. S."—those of a friend he once abandoned. A flashback reveals what happened: Jonas and M. S. escaped together from a "camp," but during their flight, M. S. was shot. As he lay on the ground, pleading with Jonas to take him along, Jonas fled to save his own life. Throughout the film, Jonas's voiceover repeatedly comments that he must wear this monogram on his forehead as a reminder of his past guilt, just as many others must do—another indirect remark intended to address the viewers.

Jonas wants to rid himself of both the hat and the unsettling sense of guilt that accompanies it. Yet the hat keeps finding its way back to him. "*Die Vergangenheit ist ein Boomerang aus Filz*" (the past is a boomerang made of felt), the voiceover emphasizes. Near the end of the film, Jonas believes he has found M. S. again, but he lacks the courage to confront him. In the final scene, Jonas—psychologically drained by his encounter with the past—wanders alone and aimlessly through the city, disappearing into the dark streets, as the voiceover notes: "*Jonas ist einer von uns: ein Mann mit vielen Schatten, ein Mann ohne Antwort*" (Jonas is one of us: a man with many shadows, a man without an answer).

Jonas gives the impression of being a silent film, despite having a soundtrack. This is due to the fact that most of the audio was recorded in the studio and later synchronized with the moving images. As a result, the soundtrack becomes autonomous. It opens up a space of its own, independent of the film's visuals, and contributes to a claustrophobic atmosphere. It is as if the reflections, dialogues, and the jarring, distorted city sounds—such as the police motorbike sirens and the officers' command: "*Weitergehen! Nicht stehen bleiben!*" (Keep moving! Don't stand still!)—are all unfolding within Jonas's paranoid mind. The blurring of boundaries between on-screen and off-screen sounds—which I consider a product of editing, that is, the assembling of sound and image—stands out as one of the film's most significant formal features.

Within the continuity system as an established filmic structure—with which both *Heimatfilm*s and war films complied—it is customary to use on-sound, so that the source of diegetic sound is also visually represented. In this framework, the role of extradiegetic music or voiceover narration is always to advance the plot or underscore it emotionally. Through this sound-image relationship, the continuity system fulfills its objective of mobilizing and coordinating all elements from the filmic communication medium, which it chooses for strict coupling, in the service of conveying a coherent narrative. The sound-image editing principles of the continuity system are subverted in *Jonas*, where the relationships between the images and voices, music, and city noise are not straightforward. These sounds shift between Jonas's paranoid and schizoid monologues, the narrator's voice, the distorted sounds of machines and vehicles within the diegesis, and the music, which alternates between Duke Ellington's jazz and the score composed by Winfried Zillig. These sounds have rarely a visible diegetic origin. The only scenes in which the diegetic voices of the characters are heard are the conversations between Jonas and Nanni, as well as between Nanni and M. S.—as if Nanni were the only anchor to reality in this chaotic, paranoid world. One could conclude that all other voices, sounds, and pieces of music unfold within Jonas's nightmarish thoughts.[9]

As the above analyses demonstrate, *Jonas* enacted a rupture in the structure of both *Heimatfilm*s and war films through two primary strategies. The first involved fully liberating the film's sound from its images, thereby granting sound an autonomy previously unknown in German cinema. Through this autonomy, the voiceover could comment on the film's visuals, reflect the protagonist's inner thoughts, and directly address the audience. By producing the sounds of vehicles and machines in the studio, applying distorting effects, and finally editing these extradiegetic sounds together with diegetic images of machines and vehicles, *Jonas* continually disrupts the viewers' first-order observation and their immersion in the illusion of reality. On the level of second-order observation, the film compels viewers not simply to settle for the narrative presented as information but to search for the meaning of the image-sound combinations offered to them by observing the difference between these combinations and the synchronized sound-image pairings familiar from conventional films.

Jonas's formal ruptures align with its subject matter. Instead of linking its communication to the dominant cinematic conventions of the time—which either centered on trivial romantic themes set in idyllic rural landscapes or presented war stories with drastically reduced complexity—the film chooses to address the troubled mental state of contemporary German citizens, rooted in their trauma from war and NS complicity. It does so not merely by telling the story of a paranoid man but by becoming a formally paranoid film itself through its formal disobedience to the established structure of filmic utterance.

No further rupturing filmic communications were immediately aligned with *Jonas*'s unique topic and utterance. It took another four years before the next film appeared that succeeded in rupturing the conventional film structure—*Die Parallelstraße*.

Die Parallelstraße

Despite the radical ruptures *Jonas* imposes on the continuity system, it still tells a story—the story of a man who buys a hat, loses it, takes another hat marked with certain initials, and finds that these initials evoke a past trauma he is unable to confront or resolve, leaving him baffled and depressed. This is not the case with *Die Parallelstraße*, which is too fragmented to be coupled with any cohesive narrative.

Die Parallelstraße begins with the ending of another film, in which a meeting of six men concludes and the credits roll against the backdrop of a departing airplane. Over this scene, a seductive female voice is layered, saying the phrase "*je t'aime!*" (I love you!). This marks the end of "the second part of the film, *Die Parallelstraße*," as the credits imply. Thus, the actual film *Die Parallelstraße* appears to be the third part of a series of the same name. This is a highly unusual way for a film to reference itself. The film is not only itself but also the third part of itself—without the audience having seen or even known about the two previous parts.

This formal choice recalls Raymond Williams's concept of *flow* as it relates to television, in the sense of one television program blending into another (Williams 2004, 77 ff.). It creates the impression that one has turned on the television too late, having already missed the first two parts of the film. One only catches the credits of the last episode before the third installment begins. This use of formal identities specific to television triggers reflection as it thematizes the difference between forms expected of film and those expected of television—a mass medium in the environment of film. Observing this difference, viewers have to ask themselves questions like: "Why is the film behaving like television? Why did it not start with an establishing shot that introduces the action, just as all other films that I know do? What does the film want to say by making this television-specific formal choice?" This formal reference to other media is a significant aesthetic decision which, as will be discussed later, also appears in other New German Films with a dominant rupturing tendency.

The *actual* film begins with a male voiceover explaining that every day, five men enter the room—the same room shown in the final sequence of the previous film—and are given ninety minutes to discuss documents concerning a "*fragliche Persönlichkeit*" (questionable personality), to classify them and establish a connection among them. If they fail to do so within those ninety minutes, "their existence comes to an end," which, according to the narrator, has always been the outcome so far. Although these individuals, as the narrator notes, do not find the connection, they continue to reflect. This makes the entire procedure intriguing for the narrator—who is the same person as the moderator present with the five men in the room, overseeing the ninety-minute session. Who these men and the moderator are, and what the entire procedure means, is left to the viewers' interpretation.

The documents mentioned are individual footage segments, recorded in various countries and covering a wide range of topics—from spirituality, cultural customs, and everyday life to industry, economic and industrial development, the oil crisis, and more. These are apparently projected in the same room where the group of five men and the moderator are located. As a result, the desk lamps on the tables must always be turned off before one of the documents is projected and turned back on when the men wish to discuss it. According to the narrator, the documents concern the men themselves, yet they fail to recognize themselves as the "questionable personality."

On the level of cinematography, everything in this film is unusual for its time or, to use Luhmann's terms, not expectable by the memory of filmic communication—whether it is the frequent use of overhead shots when the men and the moderator are shown in the room (Figure 13), or the stark contrast in color and image quality between the diegetic black-and-white frames and the "documents," some of which were recorded on color film and with a different camera than the one used to capture the studio scenes.

Many of the formal choices in the cinematography and editing of *Die Parallelstraße* can be traced back to television. It is not only the flow effect at the beginning—which originally characterizes television communication—that stands out in this respect. The diversity and lack of connection between the documentary film clips, presented as "documents" and interrupted

Figure 13 Screenshot from *Die Parallelstraße*. Unconventional camera angle.

by cuts back to the meta-diegesis of the room with the five men and the moderator, also evoke the identity of television reports that alternate between documentary footage and studio segments, where moderators and experts comment on the clips. The film footage in *Die Parallelstraße* comes from all over the world—Asia, Latin America, Europe, the United States—much like the material produced for television news and reports. Therefore, the most significant contribution of *Die Parallelstraße* to the rupture of established film structures in 1960s West Germany lies in its adoption of identities from a different mass medium: television. These identities transform the film into a collage of sounds and images, connected through editing but not guided by narrative logic.[10]

Both *Jonas* and *Die Parallelstraße* can be seen as contradictions—in the Luhmannian sense—to the dominant film structure of their time, due to their choices in cinematography, sound design, and editing. In this sense, their information can only be fully grasped when viewers not only engage with the narrative of these films—which is not present in *Die Parallelstraße*—but, more importantly, recognize the divergence of their formal choices from the prevailing film structure at the time of their release. This divergence represents a significant distinction between the actual and the potential, which constitutes meaning in Luhmann's systems theory. The forms actualized by these films were meaningful to their contemporary audience mainly through their contradictory difference from the potential film structure anticipated by film memory in late 1950s and early 1960s West Germany. This quality marks the most prominent feature of rupture in New German Cinema, which also explains why rupture is a short-lived occurrence: as soon as its formal choices become expectable, it ceases to function as rupture and, consequently, as an evolutionary stage of a new wave.

Although *Jonas* and *Die Parallelstraße* have not been regarded as canonical New German Films in the existing literature, the following analyses will demonstrate that many of the films considered canonical to this new wave reflect the selections from the medium of filmic communication originally made by these two works. These selections—which later, due to their redundancy, come to form identities specific to films characterized by rupture—include the autonomy of film sound from the image, the appropriation of identities from other arts and mass media, the insertion of spontaneous shots, rupturing camera work, rupturing forms of editing, and unexpected *mise-en-scène* features. Below are analytical examples of how these features are represented in other New German Films that also embrace rupture.

The Autonomy of Film Sound from the Image

As seen in the analysis of *Jonas*, the decoupling of image and sound in film grants sound higher degrees of autonomy and opens up new editing possibilities. This autonomy, as a new form of filmic communication unfamiliar to conventional *Heimatfilms* in West Germany, found revolutionary application in many rupturing New German Films, particularly during the 1960s and 1970s.

One remarkable example of the separation of sound and image—and therefore the closest to the case of *Jonas*—is *Fata Morgana* (1971). In this film, the soundtrack consists solely of extradiegetic music, accompanied by excerpts from a Guatemalan creation saga read by a female voice, which bears no direct relation to the images. The autonomy of the sound layer makes the film appear as two distinct artworks presented simultaneously to the audience: a soundtrack and a collage of moving images, with no evident connection or mutual reference.

The absolute dominance of silence is another variant of sound autonomy that marks an instance of rupture in New German Cinema. In the continuity system, sound perception approximates the viewers' experience of lived reality by ensuring that there is almost always something audible in the film—ambient sound, footsteps or breathing, dialogue, diegetic or extradiegetic music, and so on. Even when total silence occurs in such films, it is diegetically justified. Rupturing New German Films, however, do not hesitate to switch off the sound entirely for a few seconds without offering a diegetic explanation. Here, second-order observers not only differentiate a story from the forms they perceive as first-order observers but must also discern meaning between the choice to present a given scene with sound and the choice to present it without.

The absence of sound occurs, for example, in *Lebenszeichen* (Signs of Life; 1968), when Stroszek, a soldier wounded in the Second World War who is to spend the remainder of his service on the Greek island of Kos, is confronted with a wind farm. Stroszek, whose sanity has already begun to deteriorate, climbs a hill at the beginning of this scene, accompanied by nondiegetic Greek music. A few seconds of total silence follow as he takes his first look at the windmills. While the music resumes after this moment, Stroszek begins to scream and fire wildly at the windmills, yet neither his screams nor his gunshots are audible. This moment of silence, followed by extradiegetic music while the diegetic sound remains inaudible, limits the viewers' access to diegetic sound and, consequently, to an immersive understanding of the story and the character. It is as if the viewers were watching Stroszek through the glass of an aquarium—able to see him but not hear him. This implied barrier creates a sense of distance between the viewers and the protagonist's deteriorating mental state. As we will see later, a comparable barrier is also constructed through choices in cinematography at the end of the film.

Alexander Kluge's films employ total silence in their sound design as well. *Abschied von gestern* (Yesterday Girl; 1966), which won the Silver Lion at the Venice International Film Festival in 1966, follows the journey of an East German woman, Anita G., across West Germany. Anita wants to say goodbye to her past and start a new life. She tries to find love and friendship, secure employment, and attend university. In the end, however, she remains a lonely stranger in West Germany, and prison appears to be the only place where she is accepted and integrated, and where she finally finds a place to stay. In this black-and-white film, the soundtrack cuts out at several points, particularly when the displaced Anita wanders through the city or across fields. These interruptions are so disconnected from the film's images that they seem to serve no purpose other than just to disrupt the viewers' auditory perception.

In *Abschied von gestern*, another level of the decoupling of image and sound as an editing strategy becomes evident—namely, their asynchrony. This occurs in a scene toward the end of the film, in which Anita, after the stillbirth of her child, is sitting in a prison room with a counselor, answering her questions. During their conversation, there is a cut away to Anita in the clinic where she gave birth. In this brief medium shot, Anita is seen hugging the nurse, both laughing heartily, while the conversation between Anita and the counselor continues on the soundtrack. This shot could be interpreted as a flashback to Anita's miscarriage in the prison clinic. But if it is, why are Anita and the nurse laughing so gaily?! The scene then cuts back to the room where Anita and the counselor are seated, while their conversation continues. Such ruptures of diegetic temporal continuity and spatial integrity, together with undermining the image-sound synchronicity, which interrupt the viewers' immersive first-order observation of the film, are Alexander Kluge's aesthetic signature.

A similar image-sound asynchrony is present in *Mahlzeiten* (Lust for Love; 1967), where Elisabeth delivers a long monologue about the advantages of being married. In the middle of her speech, as she talks about the sad life of an unmarried friend, a close-up of the friend's smiling face is shown through a cutaway, even though she is not in the same location as Elisabeth. Meanwhile, Elisabeth's monologue continues to be heard by the viewers.

Another characteristic of rupture in New German Cinema, resulting from the autonomy of sound, is the dominance of the voiceover over the film images in delivering information. While voiceover narration was not a novelty in fiction films of 1960s West Germany, the voiceover in some films of the German New Wave assumes a non-narrative, rupturing role. Rather than advancing diegetic action, this voice offers free commentary on the film's images or on unrelated topics that bear no connection to humans, objects, actions, or scenes visible to the camera. In other words, the camera and the film sound convey entirely separate pieces of information on two different levels, rather than merging their information into a narrative unity.

Keitz, citing Reinhold Rauh, describes this decision regarding the editing of image and voiceover as follows: "Alexander Kluge, Edgar Reitz, and Wilfried Reinke emphasize the possibilities opened up by the traditionally considered 'unfilmable' image-independent narrative commentary for an aesthetics of alienation: 'In this regard, it does not matter whether the audible voice belongs to a character in the plot and is mentally connected to them, or whether it is an entirely foreign voice'" (1997, 240; my translation). For example, the voiceover sometimes reveals the thoughts and feelings of the film characters, significantly relieving the plot and the acting from the burden of emotional expression and realistic performance. At other times, certain topics are conveyed through this voice in a declarative manner, without any visual equivalent or narrative justification.

Such liberties with voiceover frequently appear in Alexander Kluge's films—such as in *Abschied von gestern*, *Die Artisten in der Zirkuskuppel: ratlos* (Artists Under the Big Top: Perplexed; 1968), *In Gefahr und größter Not bringt der Mittelweg den Tod* (In Danger and Deep Distress, the Middleway Spells Certain Death; 1974), and *Deutschland im Herbst* (Germany in Autumn; 1978)—but also in other rupturing films like Reitz's *Mahlzeiten*. Kluge often has his characters sit in front of the camera and look directly into the lens, while their life stories, goals, and thoughts are narrated by the voiceover. At times, this voice even belongs to the characters themselves but is presented as a voiceover or as an inner voice, while they remain motionless and silent in front of the camera. This occurs, for example, in the opening scene of *Die Artisten in der Zirkuskuppel: ratlos*, when the following conversation between Manfred Peickert—a circus artist—and the circus director is narrated by a voiceover. During this, Peickert is first shown frontally in a medium shot, like a portrait (Figure 14), and then performing everyday tasks in the next shot, while the voiceover narrates:

> Voiceover—Manfred Peickert works as an artist. He has plans.
> Manfred Peickert's voice—I say: "Mr. Director, could we hoist the elephants into the circus dome?" The director says: "Of course, but just consider whether the structure can support it." I say: "But you must admit, it would be something entirely new." Director: "Why new? I find it strange and very irrational." I say: "Something has to burst, and if the elephants are hoisted with a balloon."
>
> (my translation)

Even more rupturing than conveying information about diegetic film characters through a voiceover rather than through the plot or the characters themselves, is the use of voiceover in Kluge's subsequent television film, *Die unbezähmbare Leni Peickert* (The Indomitable Leni Peickert; 1969)—considered an epilogue to *Die Artisten in der Zirkuskuppel: ratlos*. In one scene, the voiceover reads aloud an excerpt from the chapter *Zur Genese der Dummheit* (On the Genesis of Stupidity) in Adorno and Horkheimer's book *Dialektik der Aufklärung* (Dialectic of Enlightenment). This voice initially belongs to Leni Peickert, the film's main character, who is shown reading *Dialektik der Aufklärung*. After the first sentence, the voice changes, and viewers then hear the voice of Evelin, another diegetic character and Leni's former circus colleague, continuing the reading, without herself appearing on the screen or being in the same room with Leni. This change of narrator implies that this scene is not merely about conveying the content of the book

Figure 14 Screenshot from *Die Artisten in der Zirkuskuppel: ratlos*. Voiceover autonomy relieves actors from the demands of realistic performance.

that a diegetic figure is reading to the viewers but rather about reading the book aloud to them. During this vocal quotation from the book, the screen briefly turns black before displaying the very page from the book being read aloud (Figure 15). What stands out here is not only the autonomy of sound but also the decision to place a page from Adorno and Horkheimer's book directly in front of the viewers and read it aloud to them. While this gesture may strike the audience as offensively elitist, it nonetheless remains—on the formal levels of sound design, cinematography, and editing—revolutionary and counter to the identities of filmic utterance remembered by the memory of film in 1969, when the film was released.

The Appropriation of Identities from Other Arts and Mass Media

As already seen in *Die Parallelstraße*, identities from the utterances of other art forms and mass media find their way into New German Cinema, marking a further rupture in the established film structure, which had previously relied solely on film-specific identities serving the continuous and coherent conveyance of a narrative. These identities manifest themselves across all levels of the filmic communication medium—namely, cinematography,

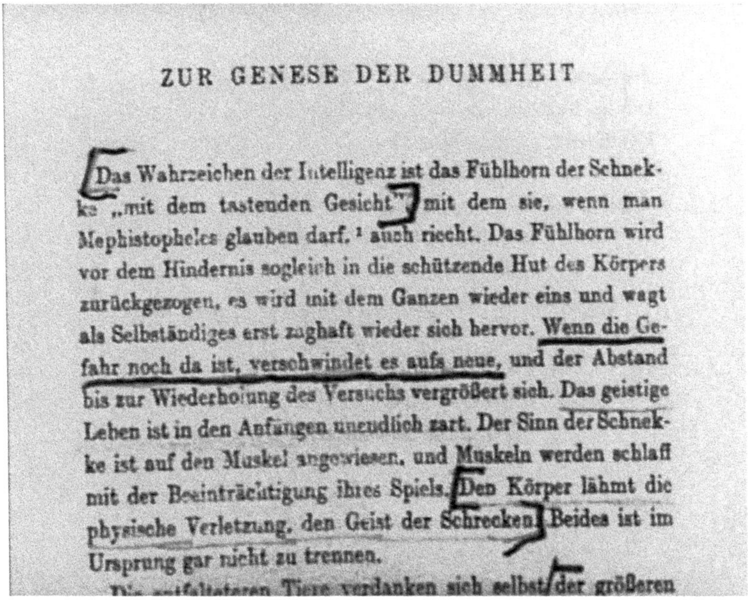

ZUR GENESE DER DUMMHEIT

Das Wahrzeichen der Intelligenz ist das Fühlhorn der Schnecke, „mit dem tastenden Gesicht", mit dem sie, wenn man Mephistopheles glauben darf, [1] auch riecht. Das Fühlhorn wird vor dem Hindernis sogleich in die schützende Hut des Körpers zurückgezogen, es wird mit dem Ganzen wieder eins und wagt als Selbständiges erst zaghaft wieder sich hervor. Wenn die Gefahr noch da ist, verschwindet es aufs neue, und der Abstand bis zur Wiederholung des Versuchs vergrößert sich. Das geistige Leben ist in den Anfängen unendlich zart. Der Sinn der Schnecke ist auf den Muskel angewiesen, und Muskeln werden schlaff mit der Beeinträchtigung ihres Spiels. Den Körper lähmt die physische Verletzung, den Geist der Schrecken. Beides ist im Ursprung gar nicht zu trennen.

Die entfalteteren Tiere verdanken sich selbst der größeren

Figure 15 Screenshot from *Die unbezähmbare Leni Peickert*. Autonomous voiceover reads a book page to the audience.

sound design, and editing. What is at stake here are the formal choices specific to television on one hand, and those of photography on the other.

From television, it is above all the forms of reports and interviews that are adopted—a practice originally initiated by *Die Parallelstraße*. In *Mahlzeiten*, for example, there is a scene in which the film's main character, Elisabeth, sits in front of the camera and speaks about her views on marriage—without any narrative justification introduced by the film's plot:

> [As a married woman,] I know I belong to someone. I belong to Rolf. He is there for me, I am there for him. I have my home. I know where I'm supposed to go. I know who I can talk to, who I can confide in. It's just that … you belong to someone. And I believe every woman should get married. You feel it in your heart and soul. You feel free, happy. You're simply happy. It has nothing to do with the physical.
>
> (my translation)

While delivering this monologue, Elisabeth does not look directly into the camera but appears to be looking at another person seated across from her, just beside the lens (Figure 16). This other person is neither heard nor seen,

Figure 16 Screenshot from *Mahlzeiten*. Adopting the form of television interviews.

but his presence is implied and motivates both Elisabeth's gaze and her speech. This creates the impression that Elisabeth is being interviewed at home by a host for a television program, such as a reality show.

In Alexander Kluge's films as well, characters sit in front of the camera to speak or introduce themselves. In *Abschied von gestern*, for instance, the director of a company looks directly into the camera and introduces the function of his enterprise—"the distribution of a compact audio program for learning foreign languages, composed of 36 cassettes" (my translation)—as well as the working conditions within the company (Figure 17). The transition to this frontal close-up from the shot preceding it—which shows Anita and the director in the same room—does not comply with the 180-degree rule. Furthermore, the tone and the manners of the director change to more formal ones as he begins to deliver his monologue. Hence, it is evident that the intended addressee of this presentation is not the diegetic Anita, who has applied for a position at the company, but rather the viewers of a simulated television program. The company director's direct gaze into the camera, along with his formal tone and the content of his introductory monologue, reinforces the impression of a mode of address specific to television interviews or advertisements.

Another identity of television communication used in New German Films is the insertion of historical footage or photographs between shots in which

Figure 17 Screenshot from *Abschied von gestern*. Adopting the form of television interviews.

the diegesis is interpreted as representing the film's contemporary society. These inserts—sometimes commented on or motivated by the diegesis and sometimes not—resemble those used in television commentaries and documentaries on past events. A prime example of this is the historical footage inserted into *Deutschland im Herbst*. In the film's third episode, directed by Alexander Kluge, a history teacher named Gabi Teichert begins researching the depths of German history, looking for material to teach at school. Following Gabi's inquiry, the film inserts low-quality black-and-white footage of Nazi marches and events between the episode's otherwise color images (Figure 18).

Fassbinder, in turn, uses the film camera as a photo camera in some of his films, as both the camera and the actors in the *mise-en-scène* remain static or the actors in their frozen postures make only minimal movements. This is the case in multiple shots in the opening sequence of *Liebe ist kälter als der Tod* (Love Is Colder Than Death; 1969), in which movements are kept extremely minimal without significantly changing the composition of actors within the frame—such as in the shot where Franz is being interrogated, and the interrogator tries to persuade him to cooperate with "the syndicate" (Figure 19). In this shot, the actors placed in the *mise-en-scène* barely move or change their posture while speaking.

Figure 18 Screenshot from *Deutschland im Herbst*. Adopting an identity from television.

Figure 19 Screenshot from *Liebe ist kälter als der Tod*. Adopting an identity from photography.

The cinematography's adaptation of photographic identities becomes even more explicit in *Händler der vier Jahreszeiten* (The Merchant of Four Seasons; 1971), in which the figures deliberately pose in front of the static film camera and remain motionless for several seconds, as if they were in front of a photographic camera. In one instance, Anna stretches out on the sofa and fixes her gaze on an indeterminate point in the distance, while being observed by her niece sitting next to her. This shot lasts for ten seconds,

Figure 20 Screenshot from *Händler der vier Jahreszeiten*. Adopting an identity from photography.

without any movement, dialogue, or change in the camera setup and without any sound (Figure 20). Here, both the camera and the elements of *mise-en-scène* are adapting a photographic identity.

The Insertion of Spontaneous Shots

Due to the dominance of fiction films that closely adhered to the continuity system, West German film audiences in the 1960s were accustomed to coherent and engaging narratives on the level of a film's information. These narratives revolved around questions such as: "Can Hans and Bärbele in *Schwarzwaldmädel* finally marry despite numerous obstacles and misunderstandings? Will Hans in *Grün ist die Heide* ultimately expose Helga's father as the poacher he is searching for, despite the love shared between him and Helga? If so, then how will their love story end?" Consequently, each unit of information that viewers distinguished from the filmic utterance brought the plot one step closer to answering these questions for them.

However, in rupturing films of New German Cinema, a tendency resurfaces that was already present in the works of the Lumière brothers but had been forgotten by the memory of filmic communication in West Germany due to the rise and widespread appeal of the fiction film. This concerns the act of showing things for their own sake, without the depicted elements contributing to the plot. In the systems-theoretical sense used in this book, this refers to selections within the medium of cinematography that invite viewers to engage in pure first-order observation.

This is precisely what Rancière calls *pure cinema* and what Epstein refers to as *photogénie*. Rancière understands pure cinema as films that have freed themselves from melodramatic fiction and instead turn toward the act of showing (2006). For Epstein, *photogénie* is a certain kind of beauty hidden within things, imperceptible to the naked eye. According to him, only the camera lens is capable of extracting this beauty and its sublimity and making them visible (Epstein 2008, 30 ff.). In rupturing New German Films, it is not uncommon for arbitrary events or people who happened to be present at the filming location to be captured by the camera in this way. For instance, Ula Stöckl and her cameraman in *Neun Leben hat die Katze* (The Cat Has Nine Lives; 1968) recorded "whatever happened to appear in front of their lens beyond the script [...]. Thus, Stöckl casually documents the takeoff and subsequent crash landing of a Starfighter, a demonstration against the Vietnam War [etc.]" (Sannwald 2012, 126; my translation). Figure 21 demonstrates the Starfighter landing mentioned by Sannwald. It is not necessary for viewers to be aware of the production circumstances, as Sannwald describes them, in order to distinguish these scenes. Rather, they stand out by occupying a considerable amount of screen time without contributing to the progression of the plot. Their long screening time and their lack of narrative value are likely the reasons why viewers come to realize that these scenes are intended primarily for first-order observation.

Figure 21 Screenshot from *Neun Leben hat die Katze*. Insert of spontaneous shots.

In a similar fashion, the camera in *Lebenszeichen* lingers on the inhabitants of the Greek island of Kos, who are sometimes aware of its presence and gaze directly into the lens. These include men gathered in the city center playing backgammon and children playing near the harbor. These individuals do not contribute to the progression of the plot. Instead, they lend the film a documentary-like impression and provide the audience with a brief respite from engaging with Stroszek's disturbing behavior caused by his traumata from the Second World War. Through the camera's lingering focus on the locals, the audience is given the chance to observe their expressions and postures, the tropical atmosphere of Kos in which they reside, and to explore the photogenic qualities of these static shots (Figure 22).

Observing the camera's autonomy from the plot, along with the independence of sound from the film images in the rupturing films of New German Cinema, reveals a pattern in this cinematic movement's formal choices. As the camerawork loosens its coupling with the plot and sound detaches from the images recorded by the camera, both cinematography and sound design—along with new forms of editing—become the topic of filmic communication. They draw the audience's attention to themselves rather than merely supporting the narrative. This is achieved by refusing to meet the audience's expectations of experiencing a fiction film structured within the continuity system. In doing so, these films reflect on the roles that the camera, sound, and editing—elements that constitute the medium of filmic communication and belong to its environment—should or could play within a filmic utterance, extending beyond merely conveying narrative information.

Rupturing Camera Work

Among the identities condensed by the memory of *Heimatfilm* were smooth, plot-motivated camera movements, meticulously balanced framing, and

Figure 22 Screenshots from *Lebenszeichen*. Insert of spontaneous shots.

shot sizes adapted to the unfolding action. In contrast, rupturing films of New German Cinema did not shy away from reminding the viewers of the camera's presence through apparent flaws in camera work. For instance, the use of portable cameras resulted in shaky frames. Thus, the camera's presence was overtly marked in a way that can be described, following Luhmann, as reflection. Through the shaky frame, the film draws attention to the difference between its utterance on the screen and the physical camera that belongs to the production circumstances of film and thereby to the environment of filmic communication. Shaking frames caused by handheld cameras can be seen, for example, in *Mahlzeiten*, *Lebenszeichen*, and *Neun Leben hat die Katze*.

A further example of rupturing camera work involves the use of disproportionate shot types in rupturing New German Films. At the end of *Lebenszeichen*, for instance, there is a scene featuring a long shot of the island's fortress. From within the fortress, the now-insane Stroszek is heard screaming and threatening to fire his rockets at the sun. His figure is so distant in the frame that it is barely recognizable (Figure 23). This choice at the level

Figure 23 Screenshot from *Lebenszeichen*. Disproportionate shot size relative to action (arrow added by me).

of camera work aims at not visually presenting the actions of a character who, although physically present before the camera, remains at a significant distance. This approach stands in contrast to the established structure of filmic utterance in the 1960s, which expected shot sizes to align with the action: if a character is acting and speaking, the camera should frame him in a way that allows his expressions and gestures to be seen.

Shot sizes defying the continuity system's principles can also be found in the extreme close-ups of characters' body parts in *Neun Leben hat die Katze*. In this film, for instance, Anne's eyes fill the entire frame after her attempt to smother a man with a pillow. The close-up is so extreme that it fails to convey Anne's complete facial gesture following the attempted murder. As a result, it cannot be regarded as contributing to the plot. Later, close-ups of Anne's mouth and chin are shown while she eats pralines. While the close-up of her mouth fetishizes and sexualizes it, the close-up of her chin serves no such function; instead, this shot appears in the film merely as an unusual, noninformative—in short: rupturing—selection regarding cinematography.

Other instances of rupturing camera work occur in scenes where the camera makes no attempt to maintain a centered composition around moving characters, failing to reframe them promptly and unobtrusively. In *Die unbezähmbare Leni Peickert*, for example, Leni Peickert and her colleague, Mr. Lüptow, march back and forth in front of the camera as Leni tries to convince him to work in television. In this sequence, the two are rarely seen frontally within a balanced frame. Instead, as the panning camera catches up to them, they reverse direction and move out of the frame. This results in awkward compositions (such as in Figure 24) where only the back of Mr. Lüptow's head and Leni's left shoulder from behind are visible.

Händler der vier Jahreszeiten features, in addition to the static, photography-like shots mentioned earlier, unsettling camera movements and zooms. Whenever the figures move, the camera tracks them using a rapid pan-plus-zoom technique. It pans to track their movements and zooms in to capture close-ups of their faces as they speak, even though their expressions remain cold and largely emotionless, hence questioning the reason for the zoom in. The camera then zooms back out and continues to follow the actors. Although this technique does not necessarily violate the continuity system, as it is motivated by the characters' actions and dialogue, the frequency of the pans, continuous reframing, and abrupt zoom-ins and zoom-outs are so exaggerated that viewers cannot help but notice the camera's presence and its "neurotic" behavior. Rather than simply conveying the narrative through framing, the camera appears to be deliberately unsettling the audience, producing an effect that borders on nausea when watching the film.

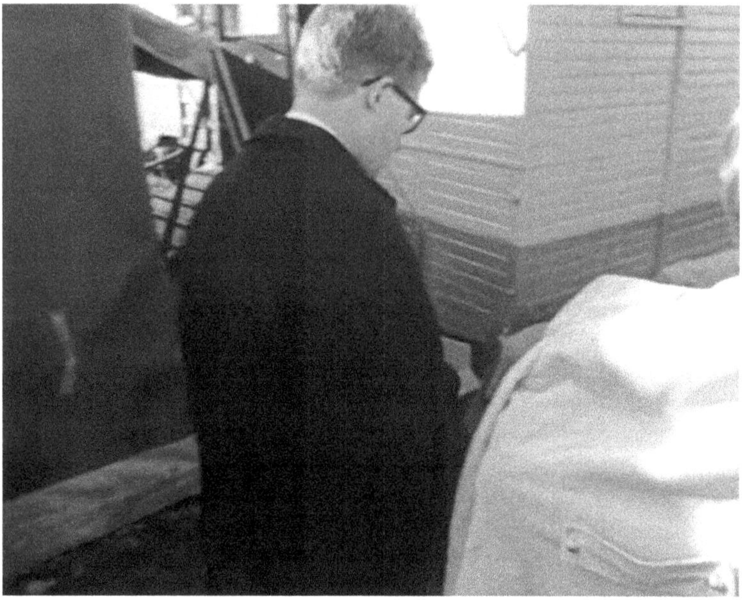

Figure 24 Screenshot from *Die unbezähmbare Leni Peickert*. Awkward framing of the action.

Finally, direct gazes into the camera lens are abundant in rupturing New German Films, with a prominent example being *Liebe ist kälter als der Tod*. In the film's opening sequence, for instance, Bruno is shown in a medium shot, staring into the camera without speaking or moving for a full minute (Figure 25). The shot is accompanied by suspenseful music played on string instruments.

Rupturing Forms of Editing

Like other submedia of filmic communication, editing in rupturing New German Cinema also contributes to the reflection of film by making itself perceptibly present. In doing so, it resists fulfilling the expectations of its contemporary audience, who anticipated seamless editing in service of the narrative. The most striking examples are the frequent jump cuts in films by Stöckl, Herzog, and Kluge. Kluge's use of jump cuts disrupts not only visual continuity but also the continuity of sound. In *Abschied von gestern*, for instance, extradiegetic music is abruptly cut to complete silence for several seconds, then replaced by music entirely different in style and mood, while there is no change of scene or sequence to justify this shift.

In addition to jump cuts, the insertion of non-diegetic shots also ruptures the editing style of the continuity system. Rauscher describes this in Kluge's

Figure 25 Screenshot from *Liebe ist kälter als der Tod.* The actor's prolonged gaze into the camera.

films, where he combines "seemingly random things that impress him" during shooting, thereby disrupting "the story's progression through inserts, outstanding text and sound collages, and documentary and spontaneously found material" (2012, 113–14; my translation). One example is the insertion of images of paintings and their details in the episode directed by Kluge in *Deutschland im Herbst.* These inserts are sometimes so disconnected from the diegesis that they solely occur to highlight the unexpected contrast between the inserted shot and the one preceding it, without any narrative function. Through contradicting audience expectation in this way, the film thematizing editing itself—as an element from the medium of filmic communication—which belongs to communication's environment. This observation of the distinction between the film system and its environment by the film itself counts as reflection in systems theory.

At other times, non-diegetic inserts in rupturing New German Films demonstrate the qualities that Sergei Eisenstein described as dialectical editing. The use of dialectical editing represents a rupture in 1960s West German cinema, as the film memory shaped by *Heimatfilm* was primarily accustomed to storytelling through cinematography, with editing merely arranging sequences and sound-image combinations in its service, remaining largely unnoticed by the viewers. In contrast, dialectical editing *à la* Eisenstein transitions from a diegetic scene to a non-diegetic one, thereby creating a semantic gap between the shots. The audience is expected to bridge this gap by attributing meaning to the difference between the two images. Viewers are thus led to ask themselves, either consciously or subconsciously:

"Why was this particular shot shown to me after the cut, and not another one referring to the film's diegesis? What does this difference between the actual and the potential mean?"

A strong example of dialectical editing in New German Cinema is *Gelegenheitsarbeit einer Sklavin* (Part-Time Work of a Domestic Slave; 1973). Roswitha, the film's protagonist, runs an illegal abortion practice while also managing the entire household for her family of five. Her husband Franz, a chemist, aspires to become an entrepreneur by studying business management in his free time. Despite Roswitha's considerable effort to work part-time alongside her other responsibilities in the family in order to support Franz's ambitions, he continually scolds her—for engaging in illegal work, for inviting friends over, and for not choosing the highest-quality groceries. In one shot, Roswitha stands in a room with Franz, who berates her for not having finished the books she borrowed from the library, thereby questioning her intellectual capabilities. This shot cuts to an intertitle—displayed in Figure 26, left—that reads: "*Gib mir einen Punkt außerhalb der Familie und ich werde die Welt bewegen*" (Give me a point outside the family, and I will move the world)—an allusion to Archimedes' saying, "Give me a place to stand and with a lever I will move the whole world" (*Archimedes* 2025). The intertitle then cuts to several drawings of mothers with many children, possibly from children's books, where the father is shown sitting leisurely by the mother's side smoking a pipe or going hunting, while the mother is burdened with caring for the home and the children (Figure 26, right). The dialectical editing here suggests that, if Roswitha were free of her family, or if she could think beyond the confines of the patriarchal power structures that have enslaved her in the name of family, she were capable of doing anything.

Another rupturing aspect of editing in New German Cinema, which exceeds the boundaries of what is expectable within the continuity system,

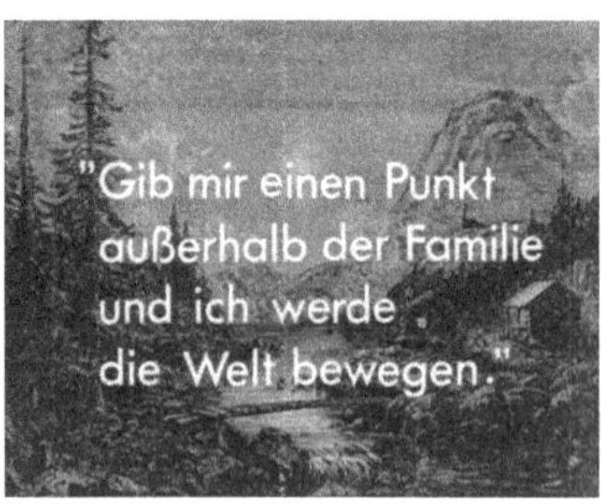

Figure 26 Screenshots from *Gelegenheitsarbeit einer Sklavin*. Dialectical editing.

can be observed in the repeated use of the same shot in sequence with minimal variation. This form of redundancy appears, for example, in *Die Artisten in der Zirkuskuppel: ratlos*, in a scene where the shot of Leni Peickert descending the ladder from the circus stage during her rehearsal is shown multiple times. In this sequence, the asynchronous voice of an English-speaking trainer can be heard, instructing Leni on how to position her body and move.

In the opening sequence of *Liebe ist kälter als der Tod*, similarly, three American shots follow one another against the backdrop of the same white wall. In each shot, Franz and Bruno enter from the right side of the frame, walk across at the same pace, and exit to the left, maintaining identical composition. Franz delivers a brief line in each shot, and Bruno responds with a short reply. This formal choice differs from other possible cinematographic and editing decisions in which Bruno and Franz might deliver the same lines—for example, in a two-shot of them standing or sitting, presented without any cuts. This difference can mean only one thing: the editing decision was made solely to rupture the established structure of filmic utterance through reflection.

Repeated shots in a sequence also appear in the opening scene of *Fata Morgana*, where the landings of several similar airplanes are shown consecutively in shots with identical compositions. This redundancy serves no other purpose than to draw attention to the editing choice causing the redundancy itself, thereby disrupting the viewers' expectation of a filmic form in which each shot is deemed legitimate only if it advances the plot, and in which editing functions merely to move the sequence of such shots forward.

Unexpected Mise-en-Scène Features

As should be clear by now, rupturing New German Films refuse to subordinate their formal choices at the level of utterance to uninterrupted narration at the level of information. Liberating filmic utterance from the obligation to tell a coherent story allows for new freedoms in camera work, sound design, and editing, as previously discussed. It also exempts actors from having to embody complex, realistic characters with understandable motivations and desires. As a consequence, the thoughts, emotions, and experiences of individual film characters either remain undisclosed or are conveyed through means other than realistic or dramatic acting. This is exemplified in Kluge's films such as *Die Artisten in der Zirkuskuppel: ratlos*, where the voiceover introduces the characters through verbal language, rather than allowing them to express their thoughts and motivations through diegetic action. Accordingly, the actors are not required to convey their inner states through performance and thus are not expected to act in a naturalistic style. Instead, they simply appear before the camera without attempting to embody their characters through facial expression, gesture, or vocal modulation.

This expressionless acting style also appears in *Nicht Versöhnt* (Not Reconciled; 1966), a film adaptation of Heinrich Böll's novel *Billard um halb zehn* (Billiards at Half-Past Nine). However, unlike in the above example, this acting style is not supported by voiceover narration that might otherwise fill the informational gap left by the lack of expressive acting. The film's characters appear lifeless and as if hypnotized—perhaps because they have undergone extreme traumata within the narrative, including two wars and the era of National Socialism. Further instances of this acting style can be found in Herzog's *Herz aus Glas* (Heart of Glass, 1976), in which some of the actors were reportedly actually hypnotized to enhance a detached, trancelike aura in their performances (Figure 27).

Many of Fassbinder's films employ this expressionless acting style as well. Characters in his films rarely demonstrate emotions through facial expressions or performance, and when they do, it takes the form of extreme outbursts—crying, laughter, furious screaming, or acts of violence. The stark contrast between the characters' rigidity and their occasional emotional eruptions makes Fassbinder's films profoundly unsettling. Consequently, it remains difficult for viewers to discern any information about the psychic properties of these characters based on their actions, other than the possibility that they are traumatized human beings. This approach to acting, which diverges from the

Figure 27 Screenshot from *Herz aus Glas*. Expressionless acting.

naturalistic style expected by the conventional film structure in 1960s West Germany, represents another instance of rupture at the level of *mise-en-scène*.

The depiction of sex and nudity marked one of New German Cinema's further unfamiliar *mise-en-scène*-related choices, contributing to the films' visual unpredictability. Figure 28 illustrates the contrast between the maximum permissible depictions of intimate relationships in *Heimatfilms* (top)—where even kisses were subject to censorship—and the freedoms that rupturing New German Films took in portraying sex and nudity (bottom). As an extreme example, Alexander Kluge's film *Gelegenheitsarbeit einer Sklavin* is notable for explicitly showing women's genitals as they visit the illegal abortion specialist, Roswita, to undergo an abortion. The film portrays in close-up the entire procedure, culminating in the removal of the dead fetus from the patient's vagina.

Figure 28 Screenshots from *Schwarzwaldmädel* (top) and *Neun Leben hat die Katze* (bottom). Displaying intimacy and nudity in *Heimatfilms* vs. New German Cinema.

Finally, homosexual relationships were visually brought to the forefront in rupturing films. In one of the scenes in *Neun Leben hat die Katze*, Katharina and Anne—who otherwise always share the same bed but are not deliberately introduced as lesbians in the plot—cuddle on a swing while Katharina talks to her boyfriend about work. The man comments on the women's behavior by saying to Anne: "I can't concentrate when I see you like this [. . .]. The world order could be restored if I were sitting there [next to Katharina]" (my translation). For him, the "world order" is "restored" by the assumption that such close and intimate physical contact should exist only within a heterosexual context, between a woman and a man. Thematizing a relationship of this kind—both physically and emotionally intimate between two women—would have been unimaginable in the 1950s film industry.

The extreme taboo break regarding the explicit portrayal of homosexual relationships at the level of *mise-en-scène* appears later in a scene in the first episode of *Deutschland im Herbst* directed by Fassbinder. This scene deliberately features Fassbinder—who also appears on camera as an actor in his own film—and his boyfriend, Armin, walking around the apartment naked and having sex.

The Role of Rupturing Films in the Evolution of New German Cinema

This overview of the formal selections made by rupturing films of New German Cinema clearly demonstrates how these films aim to disrupt nearly every identity in filmic utterance that had been shaped by the memory of filmic communication up to the early 1960s. These identities—arising from the medium of filmic communication as well as from elements of communication media belonging to other arts and coupled with film, such as *mise-en-scène* and narrative—had been established through their repetitive appearance in *Heimatfilm*s and venturing films of the 1950s. This repetition, in turn, resulted from the popularity of these genres. Their communication was accepted by the audience and therefore the memory of filmic communication kept remembering them.

The major selections introduced by rupturing New German Films in terms of camera work, sound design, editing, and *mise-en-scène* are centrifugal to the diegesis. Through constant disruptions in continuity, they prevent viewers from becoming immersed in a linear narrative. Rather, these selections foster the film's reflection, meaning that the film does not only present a narrative as its other-reference but more emphatically thematizes and thereby observes the difference between filmic communication—consisting of information, utterance, and understanding—and its environment, including filming equipment and the medium and identities of filmic communication. The analyses above have shown, for instance, how the presence of the camera is suggested through its apparent flaws resulting in a shaky or unbalanced frame; how the film sound is detached from the images and draws attention to itself through its autonomy; and how editing takes center stage in filmic utterance through jump cuts, inserts, repetition, and the integration of spontaneous shots.

All the rupturing characteristics introduced and analyzed in this section stand in clear contradiction to audience expectations in 1960s West Germany. As Elsaesser notes, these films were intended to be perceived by contemporary viewers as "an anti-cinema, anti-television and anti-press medium" (1989, 155). I argue that this contradiction has been the primary source of meaning in rupturing New German Films. Meaning, according to Luhmann, arises from observing the difference between the actual and the potential. In *Heimatfilms* and war films in 1950s West Germany, all potential and therefore expectable filmic identities that could have replaced the actual ones stemmed from the reservoir offered by the continuity system. In rupturing films, however, a considerable number of selections from the medium of filmic communication contradict viewers' expectations of what those selections could potentially be. Hence, the meaning in rupturing films functions as a second-order meaning. It is not merely generated by observing the difference between the actual forms and their potential alternatives. Instead, the viewers first recognize that the actual form rejects the expected alternatives by presenting a choice that does not align with them. Then, they must observe the difference between this actual rejection and the potential confirmation that was expected to emerge in the film's formal choices, thereby constructing second-order meaning. Viewed in this systems-theoretical light, rupturing films engage in reflection to generate second-order meaning. This is the communicative contribution that they make to the progression of the new wave through their contradictory formal choices.

The communication topics of rupturing New German Films address contemporary contradictions in West Germany between the protesting public's political expectations and the unprocessed Nazi past, the restriction of women's rights, and the suppression of socialist demands as well as demonstrations against the Vietnam War and the tyranny of the Iranian monarch. Furthermore, in a process of reflection, these films also turn the medium of filmic communication and the identities condensed out of it by film's memory into a communication topic. Through formal selections that contribute to their reflection, rupturing films express not only thematic opposition to the conventional, escapist, and simplistic narratives established by *Heimatfilms* but, even more radically, formal opposition to the structure of this cinematic tradition. These choices help rupturing films contradict both the information and the utterance of conventional films in West German society during the 1950s and 1960s.

Viewed in this way, rupturing films are meaningful as rupture only insofar as they can refer to—and thereby contradict—the film structures and narratives that they rupture. As time passes, and as viewers' memories become decoupled from the memory of *Heimatfilm*s and venturing war films, they inevitably lose access to the source of second-order meaning in rupturing films—which can only be generated by observing the difference between the form of rupturing films and the structures they oppose. This is why rupturing films, most of which are categorized as New German Cinema by film historians, gradually disappear.

Contradictions, as Luhmann points out, are negations of expectations that the system creates to sound the alarm and warn itself of a possible disruption to its autopoiesis. As discussed earlier in this chapter, filmic communication in West Germany was undergoing a crisis in the early 1960s, as the film industry suffered a massive loss of viewers and West German films were denied prestigious art film prizes. Rupturing films sounded the alarm on this crisis by contradicting the established structure of filmic utterance through reflection. To achieve this, they thematized the degraded structure by defying it, to warn that communications relying on this constantly rejected structure can block the film system's autopoiesis.

Thus, rupturing films, like venturing films, presented variations to the established structure of filmic utterance, although their variations were significantly more revolutionary and diverse than those of venturing films. While the variation introduced by rupturing films consisted of completely contradicting the established structure of filmic utterance while updating its topics, venturing films limited their variation to updates at the narrative level and isolated innovative formal choices.

As the above film analyses reveal, rupture signifies the sum of certain formal selections made redundantly by a group of films. It therefore does not constitute a genre or an epoch, as was also the case with venturing films. Moreover, it is important to note that there is no clear temporal or categorical division between venture and rupture. Alongside the emergence of the first rupturing films in the late 1950s and early 1960s—such as *Jonas* and *Die Parallelstraße*—venturing films were still being produced. These continued to reflect on Germany's sinister past and contradictory present through slightly modified forms of filmic utterance and simplistic, yet contemporary topics. *Schwarzer Kies* (Black Gravel; 1961) and *Herrenpartie* (Destination Death; 1964) are just two examples among many of such films. Additionally, a film like *Wir Wunderkinder* cannot be classified strictly as either venturing or rupturing, as it exhibits both tendencies: it leans more toward venture by adhering to the film's established, narrative-centered formal structure while attempting to align the story with contemporary communications. Yet, it also includes a few instances of attraction as rupturing formal selections regarding cinematography and editing, which, however, neither dominate the film nor appear redundantly in other films contemporary to *Wir Wunderkinder*.

In Luhmann's terms, a variation can only contribute to the evolution of an autopoietic system if it is selected and stabilized by that system. Stabilization in filmic communication means that other films adopt and repeat the variation, thereby transforming it into an identity that is henceforth remembered by the memory of filmic communication. Moreover, evolution is only possible if it is oriented toward the future. Future-orientation in this sense refers to the development of new structures that facilitate the continuation of further communications, thereby securing the system's autopoiesis.

Viewed in this light, the evolution of filmic communication cannot occur solely through films that primarily aim to rupture the structure of past films. West German filmgoers of the 1970s, who were more familiar with the structure of Hollywood films than with that of *Heimatfilms*, were more likely to accept filmic communication that conformed to the former rather than one that contradicted the latter. Therefore, in the context of New German Cinema, a final stage of filmic evolution with greater affinity to Hollywood cinema was still to emerge, in which the variations introduced by venture and rupture were selected and stabilized.

Rupturing films emerged almost simultaneously with the beginning of the peaceful Student Movement and the subsequent political conflicts in West Germany in the 1960s. They continued to evolve alongside the radical political upheavals caused by the *RAF* and came to an end almost parallel with the suppression of student and left-wing protests, the radicalization of the *RAF*, and the deaths of its leaders in their prison cells. These conflicts and their fatal conclusion constitute the main topic of *Deutschland im Herbst*. The film, released in 1978, begins with television footage from the funeral of Andreas Baader, Gudrun Ensslin, and Jan-Carl Raspe in October 1977. It ends by depicting the scattered crowds of despondent young people returning home from the funeral through heavily monitored streets.

Deutschland im Herbst may be considered the most mature New German Film with a dominant rupturing tendency, in which nearly all features of rupture introduced previously are realized. The participation of several of the most prominent directors of rupturing films from the 1960s and 1970s in the creation of this film symbolizes its role as a kind of declaration of completion for rupturing films. *Deutschland im Herbst* summarizes not only the formal characteristics of rupture but also the sociopolitical events in West

Germany during the 1960s and 1970s through the narratives of its individual episodes.

Toward the end of the 1970s, it was time for West German society to move forward and confront the future after the profound conflicts it had witnessed between protestors and the political system—just as new-wave cinema entered its final phase of evolution.

The Wave Departs into the Ocean

As mentioned, rupture can only be meaningful as such when the memory of filmgoers still has access to the structures being ruptured and can thus derive meaning from the difference. Otherwise, rupture loses its evolutional significance. Furthermore, as contradiction to film's established structure, rupture primarily functions as an alarm, alerting the film system that its autopoiesis is at risk. If the danger diminishes—that is, if filmic communication proves acceptable to audiences and films succeed at the box office or gain recognition from the critics and at film festivals again—the alarm signal can cease.

Both conditions were met in West Germany in the 1970s. During this period, film audiences returned to theaters despite the surge in popularity and widespread use of television. Furthermore, New German Cinema began to gain international recognition in this decade, thus reclaiming the artistic qualities of filmic communication that were at crisis in the 1960s. This recognition was in part indebted to the support of West Germany's political system and its cultural institutions. According to Elsaesser, "from the early 1970s onwards the Federal government, through its embassies, its cultural missions and Goethe Institutes, vigorously promoted the New German Cinema abroad. It gave interested audiences access to otherwise unavailable films, conducting seminars, inviting film-makers, supporting lecture tours, retrospectives and special events at colleges, festivals or arts centres" (1989, 301).

Around the same time, a third formal and narrative tendency emerged in West German cinema which, although not as revolutionary as rupturing films, is still regarded by film historians as part of the German New Wave. This new tendency draws on specific formal elements from the various innovations introduced by rupturing films, coupling them with information and topics different from the ones that rupturing films contradicted. In this sense, the new tendency corresponds to selection and restabilization as stages of evolution identified by Luhmann. It selects certain identities introduced by rupturing films and restabilizes the structure of filmic utterance by integrating these identities into the continuity system again, which had proven stable and successful due to the global popularity of Hollywood blockbusters during the 1970s. Because of its orientation toward the future—in contrast to the past-focused rupturing films—I refer to this third evolutionary step of New German Cinema as *departure*.

Restoring the continuity system in films tending toward departure required repositioning the diegesis and the narrative at the center of the film, with non-narrative references in filmic communication—including reflection—being minimized as much as possible. Consequently, although identities from rupturing films reappear in departure films, they are justified by the diegesis and the plot.

As the following analyses will demonstrate, two different tendencies can be distinguished in the reconciliation of departure films with the continuity system. These are chase films and road movies on the one hand and films made in documentary style on the other. Through their plots, these films create continuity without relying on drastic actions or dramatic stories to drive the narrative. Additionally, there are literary adaptations and historical films that film historians regard as part of the new wave of cinema in West Germany. I will briefly introduce these at the end of this section and explain, using this book's systems-theoretical approach, how they could have been seen as contributing to the new wave's departure.

Chase Films and Road Movies

A sign that the evolution of New German Cinema was to take place through the re-centering of the diegesis within the continuity system came with the great success of *Zur Sache Schätzchen* (Go for It, Baby; 1968), which was "the most successful German film of 1968" (Moltke 2012, 116). The film follows a day in the life of Martin, a young, intelligent man who disregards all social rules and norms. In the opening scene, Martin observes a burglary in the store opposite his apartment, but he shows no interest or curiosity toward it. After his friend Henry persuades him to report the incident to the police, he finds himself at the police station, indifferent and bored. His apathetic and reluctant responses make him suspicious to the officers. The rest of the film consists of a lighthearted comedic chase between Martin and the police, during which he meets Barbara, a free spirit like himself, still full of childish enthusiasm. Eventually, Martin is arrested in his apartment by the police and even shot at. What initially appears to be a tragic ending quickly turns into a happy ending as Martin, whose arm was lightly wounded by the bullet, stands up and leaves the apartment with the two policemen, still maintaining his sarcastic demeanor.

At the narrative level, characters in *Zur Sache Schätzchen* likely resonated with contemporary West German youth who, influenced by the hippie culture emerging from the United States, found Martin and Barbara's carefree way of being appealing. Formally, this film is nothing more than an eventless continuity, a mere linear causal connection.

Wim Wenders preserves continuity through uneventful rides and drives by making road movies. His road movie trilogy is composed of *Alice in den Städten* (Alice in the Cities; 1974), *Falsche Bewegung* (The Wrong Move; 1975), and *Im Lauf der Zeit* (Kings of the Road; 1976). These films follow their male protagonists on journeys across West Germany. The journey serves as the common thread that arranges the events in chronological order and gives them a narrative coherence. As long as the film characters—who meet by chance at the beginning of the film and part ways at the end—are on a shared journey, these films do not require a prominent or suspenseful plot to justify the encounter and interactions of the characters. It is the journey, rather than the characters' motives and actions, that propels time and the extremely nondrastic events forward. As Elsaesser describes the relation between time and narrative in Wim Wenders's films—including his road movies—"Wenders, whose stories emphasise *temps morts*, the passage of time when not consumed by action, has always been preoccupied with narrative. But the telling of stories matters only in so far as it is an occasion for creating a specifically filmic sense of time, and allows for characters not driven relentlessly forward by psychological motives and externally imposed causes" (1989, 134; emphasis in original).

The events in the road movies directed by Wenders serve no further function than to mark the stations of the journey and to punctuate the plot. Hence, these films' plots can be summarized in three stages: the film characters meet by chance and share a direction of travel; they inform the viewers about their feelings, thoughts, and complexes through their conversations and interactions with each other; and they part ways at the end of the film. The journey in this road movie trilogy is merely a schema, a diegetic pretext for revealing the film characters' state of mind. Occasionally, this schema is also used as a context for employing certain filmic identities condensed through rupturing films.

Among these identities is the element of film characters addressing the audience. In rupturing films, this occurred either through characters looking directly into the camera and speaking or through voice-over narration reciting philosophical texts or political messages—both methods lacking causal motivation within the plot. In Wenders's trilogy, the monologues addressed to the audience have a diegetic addressee. Nevertheless, their length and tone suggest that they are in fact directed at the audience, rather than the diegetic recipient. For example, in *Falsche Bewegung*, there is a scene in which the industrialist delivers a lengthy speech about loneliness on the night before he hangs himself. His addressees are the circle of weary travelers around Wilhelm, the film's main character, who are already established within the diegesis. However, the monologue continues for so long, without any meaningful reaction from the listeners, that the film audience inevitably feels it is being addressed directly (Sarkar Farshi 2021, 71).

Another example is the prologue of *Im Lauf der Zeit*, in which an elderly film theater owner recounts his working conditions during the Weimar Republic, under National Socialism, and in the postwar period to Bruno. In this monologue, he actually outlines the history of German film, as the viewers need this context to grasp the film's critical message about the catastrophic state of West German cinema in the 1970s. The film's epilogue is also seen as a critique in this regard. Here, another film theater owner concludes her conversation with Bruno with the following statement: "*So, wie es jetzt ist, ist es besser, es gibt kein Kino mehr, als dass es ein Kino gibt, so wie es jetzt ist*" (The way it is now, it is better that there is no cinema any more than that there is a cinema the way it is now). Although these statements are addressed to diegetic characters, they are not prompted by diegetic events or actions. They occur abruptly, without, for example, responding to a question or commenting on an action initiated by one of the film's characters. Their likely purpose, therefore, is to speak directly to the viewers.

The Documentary Style

A prominent advocate of narrative films with a documentary flair in New German Cinema has been Helke Sander. Her first feature film, *Die allseitig reduzierte Persönlichkeit—Redupers* (The Allround Reduced Personality—ReduPers; 1977), is a nonfiction work in which Sander portrays the everyday life of Edda Chiemnyjewski (played by Sander herself)—a photographer and single mother navigating a male-dominated West German society, where she encounters discrimination in both her personal and professional life. She also regularly gathers with her female friends and colleagues to engage in discussions on socialist and feminist topics. The film demonstrates the quality of a documentary at the level of information, as it directly addresses contemporary problems faced by the very individuals who appear before the camera. The film also incorporates formal elements characteristic of documentary cinema. These include depictions of the main character's work processes as a photographer, multiple tracking shots through West Berlin filmed from a moving car, the absence of professional acting due to the lack of a dramatic plot, and voiceover commentaries delivered by Sander herself.

Despite *Die allseitig reduzierte Persönlichkeit—Redupers*' overall adherence to documentary film conventions, there is one scene that ruptures these conventions. Here, Sander inserts the image of a newspaper page and creates

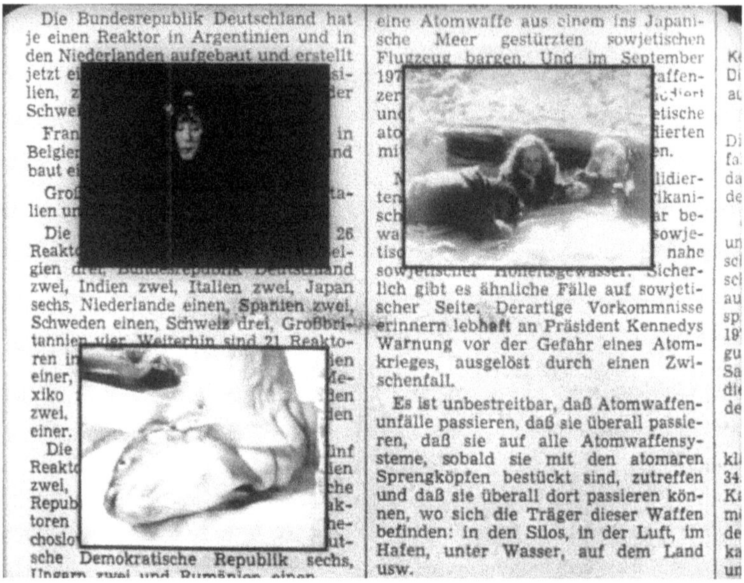

Figure 29 Screenshot from *Die allseitig reduzierte Persönlichkeit—Redupers.* Non-diegetic insert.

a split-screen effect on it by displaying three separate screens, each containing a different moving image. These images appear to depict women in various social roles: as an actor in a silent film, as a mother on holiday with her husband and child, and as a woman managing domestic responsibilities—preparing food in the kitchen and using a knife to first cut fruit and behead a fish, then to behead a mouse and slice a beetle in half (Figure 29). This shot is disconnected from the diegesis, as well as from Sander's voiceover that reads a friend's letter aloud.

Sander's later films, such as *Der subjektive Faktor* (The Subjective Factor; 1981) and *Der Beginn aller Schrecken ist Liebe* (Love Is the Beginning of All Terror; 1984), which place greater emphasis on narration than on documentation, interestingly present more of the identities introduced by the rupturing films of New German Cinema. In *Der subjektive Faktor*, for example, there is an abundance of shivering shots, rapid pans, and awry framings characteristic of the handheld camera, along with the autonomy of the sound level from the images—in which Sander's voiceover comments on people in the street captured by the camera in complete absence of diegetic sound.

In *Der Beginn aller Schrecken ist Liebe*, a stark contrast emerges between the documentary black-and-white footage from the Nazi and postwar periods or the student protest movements, and the colorful diegetic images—a combination that, as mentioned earlier, can be traced back to television communication. Furthermore, the difference of volume between the diegetic sound and the explosively loud extradiegetic pieces of music serves as filmic reflection, since the extradiegetic music does not merely underscore the plot, but rather draws attention to its unconventionally high volume.

Parallel to his prominent rupturing films introduced earlier, Werner Herzog also consistently produced documentary films—beginning in 1969 with his first, *Die Fliegenden Ärzte von Ostafrika* (The Flying Doctors of East Africa; 1970); followed by *Behinderte Zukunft* (Handicapped Future; 1971) and *Land des Schweigens und der Dunkelheit* (Land of Silence and Darkness; 1971), both focusing on handicapped individuals; *Die große Ekstase des Bildschnitzers Steiner* (The Great Ecstasy of Woodcarver Steiner; 1974), which portrays an athlete; *La Soufrière—Warten auf eine unausweichliche Katastrophe* (La Soufrière—Waiting for an Inevitable Disaster; 1977), filmed on the island of Guadeloupe, where a volcano was smoking and expected to erupt—an intriguing allusion to Jean Epstein's documentary *La Montagne Infidèle* (The Unfaithful Mountain; 1923), which captured the eruption of Mount Etna in Sicily in 1923; and many others.

However, Herzog's documentaries were never considered part of the German New Wave. The systems-theoretical framework established here can provide an explanation: these documentaries did not align their communication with rupture or departure, either by contradicting the structure of *Heimatfilm* or by adopting the new identities introduced by rupturing films and embedding them in the continuity system. Rather than integrating themselves into the wave's progression, these documentaries followed a trajectory of their own. This is most likely also the reason why Harun Farocki's essay films and documentaries are not generally recognized by film historians as part of New German Cinema: they did not align with the new wave's evolution and instead developed a completely different formal and narrative approach.

Literary Adaptations

Literary adaptations and film remakes were never regarded as new or innovative in West German cinema. The highly successful *Heimatfilm*, *Grün ist die Heide*, was a remake of a 1932 film of the same title. The venturing film *Wir Wunderkinder* was based on a novel with the same title by Hugo Hartung, published in 1957. None of these films was ever considered as new wave. However, the adaptation of multifaceted and critical literary works, combined with a complex and cohesive set of formal decisions, revitalized the faltering film industry in West Germany during the 1960s and 1970s and led to the production of films that film historians have designated as part of the canon of New German Cinema.

These literary adaptations were mainly directed by Volker Schlöndorff. Many of his films, such as *Der junge Törless* (Young Törless; 1966), *Baal* (1970), *Die verlorene Ehre der Katharina Blum* (The Lost Honor of Katharina Blum; 1975), and *Die Blechtrommel* (The Tin Drum; 1979), were adaptations of literary works or stage plays. Rather than critically rupturing the formal structure of *Heimatfilms*, Schlöndorff simply disregarded the *Heimatfilm* tradition, the form and narrative of which—compared to its contemporary Hollywood blockbusters—were already primitive and flawed. Instead, his films emphasized innovative and occasionally political subject matter, which unfolded through intricate plots and cinematic forms that were far more complex than those used in *Heimatfilms* and the venturing war films.

The significance of Schlöndorff's film narratives lies primarily in their nuanced character development. In Kolker and Beicken's words:

> Early in his career, Volker Schlöndorff readily adopted the classical Hollywood style, with its conventional cutting patterns, psychologically motivated characters, and linear chronology. From *Der junge Törless* [...] to *The Tin Drum* [...], he used the conventions of Hollywood to present character studies that allowed for identification and insight into the dark abodes of minds and souls confronted with the temptations of fascism.
> (1993, 32–3; emphasis in original)

Thus, Schlöndorff's films first followed the trajectory of 1950s and then 1970s Hollywood blockbusters, which were marked by more complex narratives and character designs, as well as an enriched medium of filmic communication capable of granting those narratives an appealing cinematic utterance. The introduction of a serious and sophisticated approach to film storytelling—one that was both popular and commercially successful, thereby achieving redundancy and promising to sustain the autopoiesis of West German cinema—may explain why these films are considered part of the new wave in film historical literature, although they did not select and stabilize any variations introduced by rupturing films. Given their future-oriented nature and support for the autopoiesis of film, one can regard them as contributions to the departure of New German Cinema.

Historical Films

This section on New German Cinema's departure can be closed by a brief overview of Fassbinder's project to explore contemporary German history with his films. Although rupturing formal selections were more dominant in Fassbinder's earlier films—like *Liebe ist kälter als der Tod* and *Händler der vier Jahreszeiten*—this trend changed with Fassbinder deciding to dedicate his films to exploring different phases of German history's development. According to Elsaesser, Fassbinder's historical chronology begins with the decline of Prussianism in *Fontane Effi Briest* (Effi Briest; 1974), followed by the turmoil of the Weimar Republic (*Berlin Alexanderplatz* (1980)), the rise of National Socialism (*Despair—Eine Reise ins Licht* (Despair; 1978)), the Second World War (*Lili Marleen* (1980)), the postwar rubble years (*Die Ehe der Maria Braun* (The Marriage of Maria Braun; 1979)), the Economic Miracle (*Lola* (1981)), the late 1950s (*Die Sehnsucht der Veronika Voss* (Veronika Voss; 1982)), the era of guest workers (*Angst essen Seele auf* (Ali: Fear Eats the Soul; 1974)), the "hot autumn" of left-wing terrorism (*Deutschland im Herbst*), and the end of the *RAF* (*Die dritte Generation* (The Third Generation; 1979)). As Elsaesser points out, these films focus on moments of crisis and turning points in German history, "portrayed through the often-failing lives of petty bourgeois, followers, anti-heroes, and social outsiders in a conflicted society" (2012, 13; my translation).

Fassbinder's historical films retained traces of the emotionless acting style and camera work he favored in his earlier rupturing films, although they became more narrative- and diegesis-driven in line with their aim to explore German history, rather than to rebel against the structure of the *Heimatfilm*, which had already been forgotten by the 1970s.

The Wave's Descent

The new-wave cinema in West Germany gradually faded in the 1980s, even though prominent figures of the movement—such as Sander, Kluge, Herzog, and Wenders, among others—continued to make films. During this period, other types of productions came to dominate West German film market, including the widely recognized works of the New German Comedy genre. Coury reviews the dawn of this new genre in 1990s West Germany as follows:

> While the future of the *Autorenfilm* [author film; that is, New German Film] is still being debated, there was a decided trend in Germany in the 1990s toward Hollywood-style comedies. These films, beginning with Doris Dörrie's 1986 box office success *Männer* [Men], have achieved a

> domestic popularity that the *Autorenfilm* never reached, primarily by utilizing the elements of the classic narrative cinema. Sönke Wortmann's 1995 hit comedy, *Der bewegte Mann* [The Most Desired Man] about a man who moves in with a shy gay man after being kicked out of his apartment by his girlfriend, for instance, grossed over $40 million dollars [*sic*] in its first ten months making it the third most successful German film since 1980. Moreover, Wortmann's follow-up films were equally successful and a general revitalization of the German film industry occurred in the 1990s, including the glamorization of the German film prize ceremonies. [...] This new genre of German-comedy [*sic*], "die neue deutsche Komödie," came as a bit of a surprise, for postwar German film had not garnered a reputation for its humor. What these new films had in common was their reliance on traditional elements of the classic cinema: causality, linear narrative, closure, and the most necessary element of all, a happy end.
>
> (2004, 110; emphasis in original)

As will also be demonstrated in the following chapters, new waves of film tend to disappear after fulfilling their evolutionary function. The fact that they are no longer recognizable as a wave from a certain point onward indicates that the new identities they introduced into filmic communication are now considered, by the memory of film, to be worth remembering. As a result, these identities have become part of the structure of filmic utterance, which has selected and restabilized them.

The analysis of New German Cinema does not end here. It remains essential to examine the correlation between the emergence of this evolutionary movement and the contemporary contradictions and conflicts within West German society, as mediated by communications in film's environment. Moreover, New German Cinema is the only new wave discussed in this book that was accompanied by an explicit Feminist New Wave, which warrants an introduction.

Irritation and Resonance: The Role of Magazines and Manifestos

In Part One of the book, I discussed with Luhmann that both the system of society and the functional systems differentiated within its internal environment—all of which consist of communication—are autopoietic and operationally closed. Hence, their operations cannot be directly determined by their environment. Rather, communication can make the environment its own topic, thereby addressing it through other-reference. Otherwise, any communication system operates based on self-reference, meaning that communication is always the synthesis of information, utterance, and understanding—regardless of its topic or any other environmental factors. I also discussed that, according to Luhmann, autopoietic systems have three different means of becoming aware of and interacting with their environment despite their operational closure, namely through irritation, resonance, and structural coupling.

With these concepts in mind, let us examine the system of filmic communication—as a subsystem of art—in the context of West Germany between the 1950s and the 1980s more closely. As an operationally closed system, film art can be irritated by the environment both as art and through its structural coupling with the economic system. This coupling is one of the reasons why film is referred to as an industry. Films as industrial products not only rely on technical means for their production but also create a product oriented toward generating profit. Therefore, any communication that contributes to acquiring the budget for film production and subsequently selling the film on the market qualifies as an economic communication coupled with film.

If a single film fails to secure production funding or performs poorly at the box office, the economic system coupled with film is likely to dismiss it as an isolated case. The same applies if a single film does not succeed in appealing to art film festivals or to the taste of film critics and other individuals and institutions representing the art system. However, an overview of West German cinema's economic and artistic crises have shown that when filmic communications are repeatedly rejected—whether by funders, viewers, or representatives of the art system—these rejections irritate the economic system structurally coupled with art in film, as well as the art system itself. In New German Cinema, the film system that was thus threatened by the potential termination of its autopoiesis, took measures to sound the alarm and alter its structure through rupture. This structural transformation enabled filmic communication in West Germany to resonate with the irritation it had received from the environment.

It was the irritation caused by the economic and artistic rejections of West German films that Joe Hembus referred to in his pamphlet *Der deutsche Film kann gar nicht besser sein* (The German Film Cannot Be Any Better)—which was quoted earlier, in the section on the film industry's crisis in 1960s West Germany. This pamphlet was not the first reference to the artistic crisis of film, which had already begun in the 1950s and reached its peak in the early 1960s. Rather, it was part of a broader series of manifesto-like pamphlets that had already been published in the 1950s to irritate the film system. These included, for example, "Wolfdietrich Schnurre's *Rettung des deutschen Films* [Rescuing German Film] (1951), [...] as well as Walther Schmieding's *Kunst oder Kasse—Der Ärger mit dem deutschen Film* [Art or Cash—The Trouble with German Film] (1961)" (Gass 2016, 47; my translation). In addition, attention must be drawn to the manifesto *filmform—das dritte Programm* (film form—The Third Program), which was published in 1957 as a letter sent to selected individuals and led in 1959 to the founding of the group DOC 59. Wedel describes this development as follows:

> DOC 59 was founded on April 9, 1959, in Munich at the initiative of Haro Senft and Ferdinand Khittl. According to its charter, its goal was "to contribute to the creation of culturally and artistically valuable films." [...] // In terms of content, the group's reform efforts aligned with ideas that Vesely, Senft, and Heiner Braun had articulated two years earlier in their manifesto *filmform—das dritte Programm*, written out of frustration over the artistic stagnation of German cinema. That manifesto already anticipated a number of the demands later expressed in the Oberhausen Manifesto. While the Oberhausen Manifesto primarily called for "new freedoms" for feature films [...], the demands of *das dritte Programm* were directed at both feature and documentary films, addressing cinema as well as television: "[...] There must be a form of production that restores binding force to film—which has become a medium of the culture industry, even of mass stupefaction—and allows it both artistic and social commitment."
>
> (2012, 161–2; my translation; emphasis in original)

The Oberhausen Manifesto is regarded as the most impactful utterance within West German film's environment to alert the film industry to the crisis it was facing. This is not only due to the manifesto's revolutionary tone and public declaration but also because it addressed multiple artistic and economic dimensions of the crisis confronting West German film. Announced in February 1962 at a press conference during the Oberhausen Short Film Festival, the manifesto is often cited as the starting point of New German Cinema by those who view this new wave as an epoch. The signatories of the manifesto were Bodo Blüthner, Boris von Borresholm, Christian Doermer, Bernhard Dörries, Heinz Furchner, Rob Houwer, Ferdinand Khittl, Alexander Kluge, Pitt Koch, Walter Krüttner, Dieter Lemmel, Hans Loeper, Ronald Martini, Hansjürgen Pohland, Raimund Ruehl, Edgar Reitz, Peter Schamoni, Detten Schleiermacher, Fritz Schwennicke, Haro Senft, Franz-Josef Spieker, Hans Rolf Strobel, Heinz Tichawsky, Wolfgang Urchs, Herbert Vesely, and Wolf Wirth.

Following the arguments expressed in *filmform*, the Oberhausen Manifesto primarily announced the economic death of a cinema that, according to the signatories, embodied a rejected "mental attitude." The signatories intended to mark the end of the old film and to venture forward in a revolutionary spirit toward a "young film." This young film was to emerge from the directors of short films who spoke a "new language of film" and had been recognized at international festivals with "a large number of awards." These young filmmakers, who had successfully completed the school of short film and aimed to create the "new German feature film," claimed "new freedoms." These were freedoms "from conventional industry norms," "from the influence of commercial partners," and from "the paternalism of interest groups." In order to radically transform film aesthetics and enrich films intellectually, these filmmakers sought to change the economic structure and decision-making procedures of existing film organizations. This pointed to the establishment of a new relationship between film art and the economy. The Oberhausen group believed that they had not only "concrete intellectual and formal" ideas about the production of New German Film but also "economic concepts." While they acknowledged that investing in the new film could be highly risky, they declared themselves ready "to bear economic risks" (*Das Oberhausener Manifest* 1962; my translation).

Later in 1962, following the proclamation of the Oberhausen Manifesto, Alexander Kluge reiterated the manifesto's demands on economic institutions within film's environment during a panel discussion with the Group of Young German Film on the topic of demands on film, held at *Internationale Filmwoche Mannheim 1962* (International Film Week Mannheim 1962): "Our economic view was that one cannot tinker with a film crisis, but rather that it must lead to a structural transformation of this film industry" (Eue and Gass 2012, 30; my translation). This statement underscores a crucial aspect of what the young German filmmakers were demanding from lawmakers and producers—specifically, to revise their funding strategies and provide financial support for a new film aesthetic that was beginning to take shape. Thus, the manifesto functioned primarily as an attempt to irritate the film industry into accepting and integrating the ruptures that young filmmakers aimed to impose on film. It was an effort to re-establish the structural coupling of this formally new film with the economy—at least with regard to film funding—despite the radical structural changes that were about to emerge in filmic utterance.

With Kluge being a lawyer besides his filmmaking profession, the young German filmmakers could initially create a lobby within the government that could secure funding for their early films. As Elsaesser reports, believing the existing film industry to be obsolete, the advocates of the Young German Film movement directed a program of professional and ideological demands at the Minister of the Interior, responsible for cultural representation abroad.

With Alexander Kluge leading lobbying efforts, the movement helped establish the *Kuratorium Junger Deutscher Film* (Board of Trustees for Young German Film) in 1965—a government-funded organization created to implement the manifesto's goals. According to Elsaesser, the *Kuratorium* supported seventeen films between 1965 and 1968, including early works by Kluge (*Abschied von gestern*), Hans Jürgen Pohland (*Katz und Maus* (Cat and Mouse; 1967)), Peter Fleischmann (*Jagdszenen aus Niederbayern* (Hunting Scenes from Bavaria; 1969)), and Werner Herzog (*Lebenszeichen*) (Elsaesser 1989, 21–2).

However, this success in structurally coupling rupturing films with the economic system was short-lived. The establishment of the *Kuratorium* posed a threat to existing film organizations, "whose representatives began to lobby parliament for a new form of tax concession to boost production almost as soon as the *Kuratorium* had been set up" (Elsaesser 1989, 22; emphasis added). As a result, the parliament passed the *Filmförderungsgesetz* (Film Subsidy Bill). According to this legislation, "one had to have made a film (the so-called *Referenzfilm* [reference film]) before applying to the [Film Subsidy] Board, since the Bill did not initially provide for subsidies on scripts or script outlines, as in the case of the *Kuratorium*" (Elsaesser 1989, 22–3; first emphasis in original; second emphasis added). Since many of the young filmmakers naturally lacked experience in producing longer and more expensive films, they struggled to access this funding. Kluge, of course, presented legal arguments against the wording of the *Filmförderungsgesetz*, but these had no effect in bringing about any changes to it (Kluge 1983, 76 ff.).

One alternative solution for securing funding for their films was for New German filmmakers to work for television (Ast 2013, 81–2). Additionally, in line with their effort to structurally couple their films with the economy and sources of production funding, a group of young German filmmakers established their own distribution company, called *Filmverlag der Autoren* (Film Publisher of the Authors), in the early 1970s. According to Meyer, these filmmakers—including "Hark Bohm, Uwe Brandner, Rainer Werner Fassbinder, Veith von Fürstenberg, Hans W. Geissendörfer, Peter Lilienthal, Hans Noever, Thomas Schamoni, Volker Vogeler, and Wim Wenders"—were inspired by *Verlag der Autoren* (Publisher of the Authors) and took the historic example of United Artists as a model. Their objective was to take control of the production, rights management, and distribution of their own films (Meyer 2011). The goal of the *Filmverlag* was "creating a cartel specifically to counter the filmmaker's fear of market goals and to ensure continuity among its members, enabling them to produce at least four films" (Kluge 1983, 353; my translation).

These historical excursions reveal how challenging it was for New German filmmakers to couple their films with the economic system and secure funding for their productions. At the same time, New German Films also struggled to resonate with national audiences. Their communication was rejected by many viewers within West Germany, leaving the other end of their structural coupling with the economy—through the box office—weak. This was despite their strong international reception, as their artistic qualities were praised outside West Germany. As Ast reports, in 1966 alone, Volker Schlöndorff with *Junger Törless*, Ulrich Schamoni with *Es* (It; 1955), Jean-Marie Straub with *Nicht Versöhnt*, and Alexander Kluge with *Abschied von gestern* celebrated their international successes—Schlöndorff, Schamoni, and Straub in Cannes, and Kluge in Venice (Ast 2013, 48).

According to Elsaesser, this difference between the national and international reception of New German Films was partly due to the more developed film cultures in other national societies than West Germany, where established criteria and expectations made it easier to embrace diverse cinematic expressions. As Elsaesser points out, these markets also had a recurring demand for cultural products labeled as "new"—such as emerging directors, movements, national cinemas, or artistic revivals (Elsaesser 1989, 290).

To ensure its communications were accepted by viewers—who belonged to its environment—New German Cinema needed to create resonance among them, which it tried to achieve through the magazine *Filmkritik*. *Filmkritik* began publication in 1957, five years before the Oberhausen Manifesto was declared, paralleling the development of venturing films and preceding the screening of *Jonas* by two years. The magazine initially focused on critiquing the artistic quality of films produced in West Germany, aiming to resonate with film producers, filmmakers, and audiences alike—a mission also pursued by various pamphlets and manifestos that circulated during that period.

Filmkritik "launched its series *Tribüne des Jungen Deutschen Films* [Tribune of Young German Film] in June 1966, featuring regular, in-depth interviews with young filmmakers [...]. [...] In these interviews, conducted with young filmmakers during the period under study [between 1962 and 1967], the dominant themes are the interrelations between society and the individual, as well as the approach to reality" (Ast 2013, 211; my translation; emphasis added). Following the example of the French magazine *Cahiers du Cinema*, which began publication in 1951 and accompanied the *Nouvelle Vague*, *Filmkritik* likewise aimed to facilitate the resonance of New German Cinema with the audience, thereby aiding their understanding and acceptance of its communication.

Although *Filmkritik* was not the first critical film magazine published in West Germany during the 1950s—the others being *film 56* and *filmforum* (Gass 2016, 49)—it played a significant role in challenging the existing film tradition and drawing public attention to the new forms and aesthetic features of New German Cinema, seeking to influence and reshape audience tastes. Published until 1984, *Filmkritik* "modernized the standards of critical engagement with cinema, raising public awareness of the historical functions and aesthetic possibilities, international stylistic tendencies, and the political relevance of film" (Aurich and Wedel 2024, 5).

The significance of the communications put forward by film magazines and manifestos—both belonging to the environment of filmic communication—lies in the fact that film had reached a crisis point in its autopoiesis and felt compelled to sound the alarm within its internal environment through rupture. However economically risky this rupturing tendency was, it could not be compensated. Therefore, the film system, as a subsystem of art, resorted to manifestos to resonate with producers and to magazines to resonate with audiences, attempting to re-establish its structural coupling with the economic system on both fronts, which could be endangered by revolutionizing the film's structure.

Finally, and most importantly, New German Cinema resonated with the political contradictions and conflicts of its time through its other-reference—namely, its information level—while simultaneously rupturing the established structure of filmic utterance stemming from the *Heimatfilm*. In 1960s West Germany, protesting students and other citizens, frustrated by the political system's rejection of their expectations, opposed not only the system's political decisions concerning the suppression of protests but also the type of filmic communication it endorsed ideologically and—for that matter—economically through the funding programs it had developed—for example, by passing the *Filmförderungsgesetz*. The films supported by this political system aimed to construct a coherent and reductionist narrative of the Nazi past and the Second World War. This narrative was in favor of the policies adopted during the Economic Miracle and the remilitarization of the West German army in the 1950s. These developments were made possible by the judicial system's failure to prosecute opportunists who had profited under the Nazi regime and could now contribute to the thriving economy, as well as officers and other functionaries from the Nazi era who remained in their positions without consequence. To draw these protesting youths back into cinemas, it was necessary not only to update the topic of filmic communication but also to formally contradict its traditional utterance in a way that resonated with the contemporary conflicts between the protestors' demands and the political system's decisions.

In this regard, it is helpful to review Elsaesser's account of audience film taste during the 1960s and 1970s, as it was shaped by the political conflicts within West German society. According to him, the most influential context for film viewing in West Germany in this period was the Student Movement, which developed a media consciousness alongside its political activism. Between 1967 and 1974, cinema shifted from being a source of entertainment to a platform for education and political engagement. As Elsaesser observes, independent cinema responded to this demand before state television began addressing current affairs more seriously in the later 1970s. The politicization of an entire generation around 1968, in Elsaesser's view, led audiences back into cinemas, now with radically different expectations than those tied to traditional filmgoing. They no longer sought nostalgic classics or state-funded film retrospectives; instead, they desired a space for political expression and resistance—an "anti-cinema" opposing the mainstream media. Given these expectations, film became a tool for collective self-expression, not dependent on conventional German cinematic traditions. Elsaesser believes that the protest movement's media awareness briefly transformed cinema into a recognized public forum for symbolic political action. Many of those most interested in political film were also active participants in the intense protests occurring in Berlin and beyond (Elsaesser 1989, 155).

The Feminist New Wave

New German Cinema stands out as a prominent new wave not only because it underwent one of the most complex evolutionary processes among cinematic new waves worldwide but also because protest movements from various countries and continents found resonance within West German society during its emergence. Another significant distinguishing feature of this new wave is the inclusion of a Feminist New Wave, which developed its own formal strategies and even launched a dedicated critical magazine, *Frauen und Film*. A comprehensive analysis of the Feminist New Wave would require a separate study. The section devoted to it here is intentionally concise, aiming solely to examine its unique evolutionary dynamics and its difference from the nonfeminist new wave.

Before examining the feminist films themselves, it is useful to review the state of *neue Frauenbewegung* (New Women's Movement) in West Germany during the 1960s and 1970s. This movement, which emerged in the 1960s, was called "new" because it was critical of *alte Frauenbewegung* (Old Women's Movement)—the feminist movement of bourgeois women in the Weimar Republic—for its limited demands focused solely on legal equality between men and women.[11] As with other contradictions that gave rise to waves of protest and artistic innovation, the zero hour of the *neue Frauenbewegung* cannot be precisely identified. Historical accounts often trace its origins to 1968, coinciding with the socialist Student Movement in West Germany and the emergence of a discourse on equality that extended beyond class to include gender (Lenz 2008, 26–7).

During the course of the Student Movement, women came to realize that they were not treated as equals to their male counterparts. According to Knight, "although they were actively involved in the movement, women in West Germany [...] were merely expected to support their male fellow students. This included typing flyers, childcare, and making coffee—that is, they were valued primarily in their role as assistants to men" (1995, 67; my translation). As Knight reports, Helke Sander, one of the most prominent directors of the Feminist New Wave, gave a speech at the 1968 *SDS* congress in which she called attention to the absence of women's interests within the Student Movement and insisted that these interests be integrated into its agenda (Knight 1995, 67). This demand was dismissed by the male *SDS* members, which led to a dramatic incident: "Angered by the indifference with which Sander's speech was received by her male comrades, Sigrid Rüger, another female delegate, threw three tomatoes at the chairmen, hitting the *SDS* theorist Hans-Jürgen Krahl" (Knight 1995, 67–8; my translation; emphasis added). According to Knight's interpretation, Sander's speech at the *SDS* congress may be seen as the starting point of the *neue Frauenbewegung* in West Germany (1995, 68).

The most striking manifestation of the *neue Frauenbewegung* occurred in 1971, when women across West Germany—not only socialist female students—protested §218 of the Criminal Code, which criminalized abortion (Lenz 2008, 27). These protests, inspired by feminist demonstrations in France that same year, sparked widespread debate and acts of solidarity, culminating in the first *Bundesfrauenkongress* (Federal Women's Congress) held in Frankfurt in 1972.[12] While socialist discourse initially dominated the Women's Movement, Lenz argues that from 1976 onward—when the law permitting abortion under medical supervision was finally enacted—the movement became increasingly pluralistic and fragmented (Lenz 2008, 28 ff.).

Despite achieving a significant legal victory, women in West Germany during the 1960s and 1970s continued to face gender-based discrimination in their daily lives. Male family members and colleagues still subjected them to unequal treatment. They were not taken as seriously in the workplace and did not receive the same pay as their male counterparts. Moreover, in public discourse surrounding critical reflections on the current state of West German society following the war and National Socialism, the specific hardships women had and still were enduring were entirely overlooked.

The feminist movement, as the articulation of contradiction against the patriarchal social structure and legal system, was accompanied by a Feminist New Wave.[13] This wave had a distinct character from the earlier, nonfeminist wave that had emerged in West Germany in terms of form and topic. According to Knight, the women who directed these films were generally aligned with the feminist movement and aimed to inform women about their rights. As a result, their early works often took on a pedagogical or documentary form (Knight 1995, 70). These included films that exposed how patriarchal power structures were already being instilled in children in daycare settings (such as *Kinder sind keine Rinder* (Children Are Not Cattle; 1969)); films that addressed women's bodily autonomy, abortion rights, and opposition to Paragraph 218 of the Criminal Code (e.g., *Macht die Pille frei?* (Does the Pill Liberate Women?; 1973), *Kinder für dieses System—Paragraph 218* (Children for This System—Paragraph 218; 1973), and *§ 218 und was wir dagegen haben* (Paragraph 218 and What We Have Against It; 1977)); and others that aimed to raise awareness about workplace discrimination and domestic violence against women (Knight 1995, 70 ff.).

Comparing the early films of the Feminist New Wave with those that emerged later in the 1970s and during the 1980s reveals a clear shift from documentary to fiction. While the earlier documentary films—some of which were mentioned above—aimed to raise awareness of broader social issues, feminist fiction films focused more on female protagonists, seeking to explore their personal struggles and psychological states throughout the narrative. This approach allowed for a more empathetic reception of the films. It also had formal consequences, such as greater use of close-ups instead of medium and long shots (Knight 1995, 72). Moreover, as some feminist filmmakers have noted, fiction films had the potential to reach a wider audience and influence how viewers perceived their own situation as women in society (Knight 1995, 73). Examples of feminist fiction films that prioritize the narrative and its female protagonist include *Schwestern oder Die Balance des Glücks* (Sisters, or the Balance of Happiness; 1979); *Die bleierne Zeit* (Marianne and Juliane; 1981), which thematizes the relationship between Gudrun Ensslin, a leading figure of the *RAF*, and her journalist sister, Christiane; and *Rosa Luxemburg* (1986)—all directed by Margarethe von Trotta.

Given the self-defined mission of feminist directors to align their filmic communication with the feminist movement in West Germany, their films exhibited significant formal differences from nonfeminist new-wave directors. At the level of filmic utterance, these films deliberately avoided the rupturing strategies employed by the nonfeminist new wave, along with the accompanying reflection typical of such strategies. Rather than attempting to alert the film system to a potential termination of its autopoiesis, thereby demonstrating a rupturing reaction to an old film tradition, these films totally ignored the tradition of *Heimatfilm* and focused, instead, on embedding themselves within an ongoing chain of feminist communication already active in society—through protests, petition campaigns, women's gatherings, group discussions, and feminist conferences. In other words, their emphasis was mainly on their other-reference—the information they intended to convey to their audience—rather than on introducing revolutionary formal ruptures. As a result, their form remained as coherent and seamless as possible, intentionally avoiding formal devices such as extra-diegetic inserts, jump cuts, successive redundant shots, or the autonomy of sound from image—with some films by Helke Sander, mentioned previously, as rare exceptions.

From this perspective, the evolution of feminist films can be conceptualized as a venture leading to departure, without rupturing formal selections. It was a venture to introduce new topics related to women's rights into filmic communication as variety, initially through the documentary form. Later fiction films, having adopted this proposed thematic variety, stabilized it within the structure of narrative cinema. These works—exemplified by Trotta's films mentioned above—embedded feminist topics within plot-driven frameworks, thereby making their utterance more compelling to a broader audience and contributing to the wider acceptance of feminist filmic communication.

By centering their stories on a female figure, films of the Feminist New Wave in West Germany present a more complex and realistic portrayal of women in their narratives than the typified submissive female figures in venturing films or the sexualized and shallow portrayals found in some rupturing films. The magazine *Frauen und Film*, founded by feminist filmmakers and film critics, criticizes the female characters in the works of Wenders, Kluge, and Fassbinder for being stereotypical—depicted as emotional and irrational, or as sadomasochistic figures—and for rarely interacting with one another (Riecke 1998, 73).

A comparison between Fassbinder's film *Die Ehe der Maria Braun* and Helma Sanders-Brahms's *Deutschland, bleiche Mutter* (Germany, Pale Mother; 1980) brings this critique into sharper focus. Both films center on the lives of their female protagonists. The diegesis in Fassbinder's film is set in post-Second World War Germany, while Sanders-Brahms's narrative follows its protagonist from the Nazi era through to the postwar period of the so-called Economic Miracle. Fassbinder's main character, Maria Braun, embodies the stereotypical postwar opportunist and seductress, lacking any psychological depth, who uses her sexuality to extract whatever she can from

Allied occupiers and influential German industrialists—ranging from a pack of cigarettes to substantial fortunes. In contrast, the portrayal of the postwar woman in Sanders-Brahms's film acknowledges the dark and complex war and postwar traumata endured by German women. This film's protagonist is not the typified desirable opportunist woman of the postwar era, as depicted by Fassbinder, but a woman who loses her beauty and health and must endure the tyranny of her war-traumatized husband. Expelled from her home during the bombings, she suffers through cold and hunger without shelter, is raped, and yet remains resilient, sustained by her devotion to her child.

Die Ehe der Maria Braun aims to prevent the audience from developing any sympathy for the female character, presenting her instead with deliberate distance. The film accomplishes this at the level of *mise-en-scène* through acting: Maria Braun shows no emotion when seeking intimacy with men, and her actions are driven solely by profit. In an unapathetic manner, Fassbinder eliminates this female character once she has fulfilled her function in the plot—namely, securing her husband's release from prison. In the film's final scene, the house where the couple have reunited and are making love explodes due to a gas leak from the stove. The mother in *Deutschland, bleiche Mutter*, by contrast, survives by her will for the sake of her child, even after being disfigured by facial paralysis, losing her teeth, and having endured severe oppression by her husband. Unlike Fassbinder, Sanders-Brahms does not shy away from confronting the camera with the harsh reality of a postwar woman's life. Her female character is not cold in her performance, nor is she a one-dimensional object of desire—playable only by a glamorous actress like Hanna Schygulla in Fassbinder's film. Rather, she is capable of suffering, of enduring physical impairment, and of continuing to live despite all this, after an attempted suicide.

Finally, it is important to examine the difference in how Feminist new-wave filmmakers sought to create resonance with their audience, compared to their nonfeminist contemporaries. Some of the feminist films were made for specific audiences—for example, they were intended to be shown in women's shelters, self-help groups, and various women's collectives (Knight 1995, 73). In this way, the films were brought to the audience, rather than the audience being brought to the screenings. This approach was one means of ensuring the acceptance of the films' communication. Another strategy involved feminist filmmakers, particularly those working in documentary, traveling around the country with their films and participating in discussions after the screenings (Knight 1995, 72). This allowed them to engage directly with the audience, ensuring that the film's communication was understood as intended and that similar filmic communications would be comprehended and accepted in the future as well.

To ensure the understanding and acceptance of their films by audiences beyond their direct reach, feminist filmmakers also founded their own film magazine, *Frauen und Film*—a feminist counterpart to the nonfeminist magazine *Filmkritik*. *Frauen und Film* aimed not only to advocate for feminist films but also to help women identify the patriarchal hierarchies embedded in the communication of other films (Knight 1995, 76). In other words, the magazine was committed to shaping its readers' overall perception of cinema, not just their view of Feminist New Wave films.

2.2

New Hollywood

The previous chapter formed the backbone of this book's central arguments and inquiries. The selection of New German Cinema as the primary case study was, as demonstrated, due to the complexity of contradictions and conflicts within West German society, as well as the internal intricacy of New German Cinema itself—with its three phases of evolution, the manifestos and film magazines that accompanied it, and the Feminist New Wave that emerged alongside the non-feminist one. This chapter, along with the next—on New Iranian Cinema—will therefore be more concise. The primary function of these chapters is to test the generalizability of the findings derived from the Luhmannian analysis of New German Cinema. They seek to answer the following questions: Did other cinematic new waves, which—as I observe—also arose concurrently with major social conflicts or protests, exhibit the same threefold evolutionary path identified in New German Cinema? That is, did they manifest venturing and rupturing tendencies as variation, and future-oriented departures that served as selection and re-stabilization? Do similar dynamics of irritation and resonance such as those observed between the social contradictions and conflicts in West Germany and the evolution of New German Cinema also appear in other new waves?

To explore these questions in this chapter, I will undertake a similar, albeit more brief, analysis of the contradictions that emerged in US society during the 1960s and the concurrent evolution of filmic communication, referred to in film-historical literature as New Hollywood.

Contradiction and Conflict in US Society, between the 1950s and 1970s

Due to its geographical location and political positioning during and immediately after the Second World War, American society had established itself by the late 1940s as a politically and militarily powerful, and economically advanced society. The United States had not only contributed to the fight against National Socialism and Fascism in Europe but its economy had also suffered less damage from the war compared to European countries. In the 1940s, "the American elite and the majority of citizens" associated the prosperous economic and political state of their society with terms such as "'American leadership,' 'democracy,' 'market economy,' and 'peaceful change'" (Heideking 2003, 342; my translation). Thus, in the postwar era, the United States was perceived as a place of safety, freedom, and the realization of dreams, while European cities lay in ruins. In addition to the physical devastation of war, the German and Italian societies were also morally and politically shattered and economically bankrupt.

However, in the 1950s, the American public did not feel as culturally fulfilled as it was economically and politically. As Gair explains, US culture during these years was perceived by many Americans as "a culture of consumption that invited conformity alongside restrictive sexual mores that indicated intolerance of transgression—[…] many 'ordinary' Americans found these values repressive" (2008, 10). This cultural dissatisfaction coincided with the era of McCarthyism—the so-called Red Scare—during which Senator Joseph R. McCarthy made false accusations against alleged communists in the State Department, and strict laws were enacted in Congress to closely monitor both the entry of communists into the country and the activities of communist organizations within US society (Schrecker 1998, 240 ff.). According to left-leaning American academics, this was a time when core American values such as freedom of speech were no longer upheld (Michaels 2017, 7).

On the other hand, "the continued racist discrimination against Black Americans in the context of the Cold War created a credibility gap for the US as the leading power of the 'Free World'" (Depkat 2016, 268). Compounding this was the intervention of the US military, as part of its Cold War strategy, in the conflict between North and South Vietnam. In 1955, it entered a war that would last twenty years and claim the lives of more than 58,000 Americans (O'Neill 2025). It also cost the lives of 2,000,000 Vietnamese civilians, 1,100,000 North Vietnamese and Viet Cong fighters, and between 200,000 and 250,000 South Vietnamese soldiers (Spector 2022). This war marked not only a military defeat but above all a moral one for American society—symbolized in 1968 by the Mỹ Lai Massacre of unarmed civilians.

The 1960s became a decade of moral decline and social protest not only because of the US government's policies mentioned above but also due to four other shocking events during that period. These included the assassination of President John F. Kennedy in 1963, the 1965 assassination of Malcolm X, and the 1968 assassinations of Dr. Martin Luther King Jr. and presidential candidate Robert Kennedy (Podair and Dochuk 2018, 61). These killings were seen not merely as attacks on individuals but as assaults on the very ideas they embodied: expanded civil rights and racial equality, the fight against organized crime, and an end to the Vietnam War. The 1970s, in turn, were marked by the Watergate scandal, which represented a further moral erosion of the political system in the United States (Podair and Dochuk 2018, 72). Through this scandal, it was revealed that the five intruders who broke into the Watergate complex—the headquarters of the Democratic Party—during the 1972 presidential campaign and attempted to install wiretaps had direct ties to Richard Nixon's administration.

The series of repressive events inside and outside the United States between the 1950s and 1970s stood in stark contrast to what the younger generation of pacifist Americans morally expected from the political system. In their view, the United States had moved rapidly "from material abundance to moral crisis" (Dippel 1996, 103; my translation). As a result, dissatisfied citizens communicated their unmet expectations back to the political system through a wave of demonstrations. These protests began with the Civil Rights Movement of the 1950s and the anti-war movements of the 1960s, but their aims quickly broadened as they aligned with other contemporary equality movements—including the women's rights movement and movements advocating for the equal rights of Native Americans and Hispanic communities (Heideking 2003, 407–8).

Parallel to these protest movements were the so-called sexual revolution and the hippie movement—two countercultures that, although they did not take the form of demonstrations, stood in radical opposition to the conservative moral values of US society and to the war-driven policies pursued by the political system against communist countries around the world, from Vietnam to Nicaragua.

The sexual revolution is commonly understood as being closely linked to the widespread availability of oral contraceptives, which liberated women's sexuality. According to Smith, the sexual revolution was associated with "the new morality and the Playboy Philosophy, communes and cohabitation, free love and easy sex, wife swapping and swinging, coming out of the closet and living out of wedlock, x-rated films and full-frontal foldouts" (1990, 416). The sexual revolution was followed by the gay and lesbian liberation movements later in the 1960s and the 1970s (Allyn 2016, 145 ff.; 246 ff.).

The hippie movement, on the other hand, extended beyond mere sexual freedom. According to Rorabaugh, hippies rejected the dominant traditional American culture, along with its values and social norms. Drawing inspiration from earlier countercultures—particularly the Beat writers Jack Kerouac and Allen Ginsberg—the central aim of the hippie movement was self-emancipation from the broader mainstream culture (Rorabaugh 2015, 15). Among the mainstream postwar values against which hippies revolted,

Rorabaugh lists monogamy, the centrality of the family, religiousness, patriotism rooted in the Second World War, and the inclination toward material abundance (Rorabaugh 2015, 15 ff.). In contrast to these values, the hippie movement was spiritual but not religious. Its spirituality was grounded in the use of psychedelic drugs and Eastern philosophies. It also embraced polyamory, internationalism, ecological awareness, and pacifism (Issitt 2009). Within 1960s and 1970s US society, hippies collectively practiced their revolutionary lifestyle at music festivals centered on psychedelic and rock music.

These protest movements and revolutionary lifestyles were accompanied by a new wave of cinema known as the Hollywood Renaissance, or New Hollywood. Much like New German Cinema, the significance and evolutional trajectory of New Hollywood is best understood by examining the dominant structure of filmic utterance from which it emerged.

Hollywood's Crisis in the 1950s

In the 1950s, filmic communication in the United States was significantly more diverse in form, genre, and narrative than in West Germany. This was due in part to its long-standing history and international influence. Furthermore, because Hollywood cinema operated entirely within the framework of the private economy and received no state funding—unlike film production in West Germany during the same period—it evolved into a profitable industry capable of generating a wide range of products tailored to different audiences. Throughout the 1950s, these filmic products encompassed multiple genres, including film noir (which had remained popular since the 1940s), Westerns, melodramas, comedies, musicals, and historical epics (Bordwell and Thompson 2002, 341 ff.).

Given the diversity of popular genres in 1950s United States, it is impossible to identify a single structural or thematic characteristic against which New Hollywood films positioned themselves. What is evident, however, is these genres' lack of reference to the prevailing social contradictions in the United States, as well as their adherence to the continuity system—characterized by the centrality of narrative and diegesis, and the unnoticeability of film-technical implementations. These films also strictly complied with the self-censorship enforced by the Motion Picture Producers and Distributors of America (MPPDA). The Production Code—also known as the Hays Code—introduced in the 1930s, remained the program by which the MPPDA regulated filmic utterance. The code prohibited, among other things, the glorification of crime, promotion of drug use, disrespect toward religious authorities, blasphemy, negative portrayals of marriage and family, and explicit depictions of sexuality or nudity (*The Motion Picture Production Code* 1956).

According to Bordwell and Thompson, Hollywood still appeared "healthy" on the surface in the early 1960s—meaning it was seemingly producing profitable films (2002, 512). However, the industry had already been undergoing a significant decline since the 1940s. As King reports, while weekly cinema attendance in the United States stood at approximately 90 million in 1946, it fell to 60 million by 1950, 40 million by 1960, and dropped further to just 17 million in the early 1970s (2002, 24).

Film historians have proposed several reasons responsible for this loss. One of them is the Paramount Decree issued by the US Justice Department in 1948. This decision, made based on the antitrust law of the United States, dismantled the existing cartel system maintained by the eight major film production companies—namely "the Big Five (Paramount, Warner Brothers, Loew's/MGM, 20th Century-Fox, and RKO), and the Little Three (Universal, Columbia, and United Artists)" (Bordwell and Thompson 2002, 327). Under this cartel system, cinema operators were obligated to purchase the entire output of these companies, a practice known as block booking. "This meant that cinema owners had to take the whole of a company's programme in order to get the box-office hits" (Hehr 2003, 9).

With the dissolution of this cartel system, production companies were compelled to market each of their films individually. As a result, every film now had to be capable of recouping at least its production costs on the market. Due to this financial uncertainty, production companies became increasingly risk-averse, hesitant to experiment with new aesthetic configurations or to collaborate with young, unknown directors. Instead, they stuck to filmic formulas that had already proven their commercial viability.

Moreover, television became increasingly popular among American citizens in the 1950s and emerged as a serious competitor to the film industry. "Americans owned 32 million sets in 1954, and by the end of the decade, 90 percent of homes had television" (Bordwell and Thompson 2002, 328). Major Hollywood studios, which had shifted their focus primarily to *A* films—high-budget films with longer runtimes, stronger marketing efforts and greater box office expectations—following the Paramount Decree, now faced the challenge of competing with television to retain audiences in film theaters.

At the same time, it was becoming increasingly difficult to draw audiences back to film theaters due to lifestyle changes that came about in the 1950s. As Bordwell and Thompson observe, post-Second World War economic prosperity enabled many families to purchase homes and cars, leading to a population shift away from city centers. Although people now had the means to travel by car, suburban families were less inclined to venture into downtown theaters and were more likely to stay home and watch television for entertainment. These demographic shifts contributed significantly to the decline in cinema attendance from the late 1940s onward (Bordwell and Thompson 2002, 328).

According to Bordwell and Thompson, for all these reasons—and also because, in the 1950s and early 1960s, audiences had access to multiple affordable forms of entertainment—filmgoers became increasingly selective about going to the cinema. They were "less inclined to buy tickets unless the film was something special, an event" (Bordwell and Thompson 2002, 335). As a response, "the film industry tried coming back with elaborate and correspondingly expensive large-scale productions that television could not offer" (Hehr 2003, 9). These included historical epics such as *Spartacus* (1960), *Lawrence of Arabia* (1962), *Cleopatra* (1963), and *Doctor Zhivago* (1965). The production of such films was highly risky: while they had the potential to yield significant profits if successful, they also carried the possibility of major financial losses if they underperformed at the box office.

Since film production companies no longer had access to the block-booking system to easily produce and sell *B* films with smaller budgets and moderate profits, which were typically shown between major releases and helped offset potential losses, such losses became more threatening than they had been prior to the Paramount Decree. Producers were now forced to speculate on audience taste, and these speculations often ended in failure. For example, as Holtz points out, *Cleopatra*, which was expected to align with audience preferences as an epic, extravagant production, failed dramatically. Additionally, following the success of *The Sound of Music* (1965), Fox produced "a number of outrageously expensive musicals, all of which flopped disastrously" (Holtz 2009, 65).

Film producers employed several other strategies to compete with television and win back their audience, including the introduction of technicolor and widescreen formats, which provided a stark contrast to the small, low-resolution, black-and-white television screens of the 1950s (Bordwell and Thompson 2002, 328–9). However, none of these measures were able to sustain or increase the number of filmgoers for sure and to re-stabilize the success of filmic communication in Hollywood in the 1950s and 1960s.

Evolution of Film Art in American Society, 1960s and 1970s

Venturing Films of New Hollywood

Besides the reasons previously discussed for the decline in Hollywood film profits during the 1950s and early 1960s, there is another factor that has been largely overlooked by film historians. According to Holtz, this financial crisis lay, among other things, in the fact that "the showy historical epics that wallowed in escapist spectacle seemed increasingly out of place in an America that was facing major political turmoil" (2009, 65). Hehr characterizes the filmgoers who rejected Hollywood's cinematic tradition in the 1960s as "an audience with intellectual, political and cultural interests" who were dissatisfied with the social developments in the United States during the 1950s and 1960s, as discussed in the previous section. As a result, they were also "not interested in the world view propagated in formulaic genre films and the values they promoted" (Hehr 2003, 11).

Both Hehr and Holtz refer to audience expectations in relation to film, which, in turn, form part of the environment of filmic communication. It was, in part, through these audiences—with their specific socio-political and moral concerns—that Hollywood cinema resonated with the political contradictions of its time and introduced a group of films in the 1960s that marked the early phases of New Hollywood cinema. While social contradictions shaped audience expectations of the political systems, these expectations also resonated with Hollywood productions through the film art's structural coupling with the economic system. When audience expectations, rooted in political concerns, were not met by films, this resulted in lower box office revenues.

Because filmic communication has no direct access to its environment—including the mental states of its audience members—it can only persist by varying its information and utterance, hoping that one of these attempts will succeed and allow further communication to build upon it. Due to its strong structural coupling with the private economy, the Hollywood film industry remained focused solely on drawing audiences back into theaters, constantly speculating about what might appeal to the public's cinematic preferences. As noted above, these initial efforts failed: producers would invest in historical epics following the grand success of a single historical film, only to lose their capital. They would produce musicals after one particular musical achieved high sales; yet, the subsequent releases would fail to recover their production budgets. Eventually, a specific set of formal and narrative choices emerged that appeared to enable the acceptance of filmic communication. These choices continued to be reproduced and were defined as the Hollywood Renaissance, marked by their venturing qualities.

Bordwell and Thompson report on the financial profits generated by these alternative venturing films—which they believe were primarily targeted at college students—as follows:

> *Bonnie and Clyde* (1967) cost \$3 million and returned \$24 million domestic rental income to Warner Bros., while *Midnight Cowboy* (1969) cost \$3 million and yielded \$20 million to United Artists. The winner in the low-budget sweepstakes was the independent release *The Graduate* (1967). It cost \$3 million and returned \$49 million to its small distributor, Embassy Pictures. This scale of profits made the sophisticated young adult film very attractive to studio decision makers. Soon an entire cycle of *youthpics* tried to capitalize on campus activism and counterculture lifestyles.
>
> (2002, 513; emphasis in original)

The films mentioned by Bordwell and Thompson, along with a broader group of others, marked a wave that stood out against the backdrop of the popular and conventional productions that preceded them in the 1950s and 1960s. The most significant venture that distinguished these films as a wave—rather than merely another new genre among the many already in existence—lay in the alternatives they introduced at the levels of *mise-en-scène* and narrative. These films depicted adultery and sex outside of marriage, drug use, and nudity. They also featured protagonists who were bandits, robbers, and drug dealers. Such images and narrative roles were absent from television, which allowed cinema to regain its appeal.

The film industry's newfound liberty to introduce these changes was made possible by the abolition of the Production Code and its replacement with a rating system. To cite Bordwell and Thompson:

> In 1966, the MPAA stopped issuing certificates. Instead, films that failed to conform to its guidelines were labeled "Suggested for Mature Audiences." Backing down from this toothless policy, the MPAA companies created a rating system coded by letter: G (general: recommended for all ages), M (mature: recommended for viewers over sixteen), R (restricted: viewers under sixteen to be accompanied by parent or guardian), and X (no one under sixteen admitted).
>
> (2002, 515)

This freedom was granted to film by the legal system—belonging to the environment of filmic communication—which, to support the economic system structurally coupled with film, recognized that permitting such liberties would help ensure the survival of the film industry's autopoiesis. To bring about these freedoms, the legal system's existing laws and regulations regarding film censorship, which constituted the program of the legal system concerning filmic communication, resonated with the economic system's needs. As a result, the legal system updated its program in favor of the film industry.

The new sovereignty that venturing New Hollywood films gained at the level of *mise-en-scène* could not have succeeded in bringing viewers back to film theaters if it had not been for the information they conveyed. On the narrative level, these films ventured to establish the new road movie genre, enabling a break with the conventional storytelling styles of 1950s and 1960s Hollywood. They also reconfigured the beginnings and endings of filmic narratives, as well as the character design within those narratives. Traditional gender roles were reversed, while outlaws and criminals were introduced as protagonists. Furthermore, and most significantly, these films thematized contemporary communication topics relevant to American citizens concerned with the trajectories of the political system and moral norms. These included the hippie movement and lifestyle, sexual freedom, homosexuality, the equal rights movement, the Vietnam War, and the society's increasingly capitalist structures. To strengthen their connection with contemporary communications that contradicted established social structures, these films also incorporated the rock and psychedelic music of the era—popular among hippies and protesting youth—at the extradiegetic level.

In the section on venturing films in West Germany, we saw how venture was demonstrated in films that are not regarded as part of the new wave by existing literature. These ventures served primarily as a very conservative first step toward updating the topic of filmic communication, while largely preserving its established structure. Venturing New Hollywood films, in contrast, exhibit a completely different quality. Similar to German films, venturing New Hollywood films too maintained the dominant structure of filmic utterance in Hollywood cinema—which adhered to storytelling within the confines of the continuity system—but they radically altered the *mise-en-scène* and narrative of films. Since these radical changes did not target the film's communication medium as manifested in its form and utterance—consisting of camera work, sound design, and editing—I still regard these films as venturing, not rupturing, works.

The Road Movie and Its Narrative Structure

Similar to the hippie movement, road movies were also culturally influenced by the Beat poets of the 1950s and 1960s. This is primarily because the road is "the key image of the Beat narrative" (Mills 2006, 37). A genre established by venturing New Hollywood films, "road movies feature characters on the move, often outsiders who cross geographic borders but also transgress moral boundaries" (Laderman 2007, 417). In both the poetry of the Beat Generation during the 1950s and the New Hollywood road movies of the 1960s and 1970s, being on the road symbolizes not only freedom from but also rebellion against social conventions.

Compared to Hollywood films of the 1950s, road movie narratives are less event-driven. It is the continuity of the journey—rather than the causal interplay of characters' motivations and actions—that provides coherence to the story. I consider the narrative structure of road movies, rather than their formal structure—which still complies with Hollywood's continuity system—to be a venture, as it diverges significantly from that of other conventional Hollywood genres of the 1950s and 1960s. These genres closely adhered to the Aristotelian three-act structure at the narrative level, which outlines the following steps in storytelling: "First Act (Beginning): 1. Introduce your star character(s); 2. Face him with a problem or crisis; 3. Introduce his antagonist (the bad guy); 4. Set up the *or-else* factor, or dreadful alternative. Second Act (Middle): Intensify your hero's problem with complications. Third Act (End): Resolve his problems, affirmatively or tragically" (cited in (Schatz 1983, 48); emphasis in original). Hollywood road movies did introduce their main characters in the first act, but these characters faced either no significant crises or only minor problems or antagonists. Typically, the road movie omits the second and third acts, where conflicts—however minor—would otherwise be intensified and resolved. Instead, these films often end abruptly with the main character's death, or they remain open-ended—meaning that the plot concludes while the story continues (Christen 2002, 27 ff.).

The motif of a man traveling alone across American landscapes is common to both road movies and the Western genre. However, a key difference between these genres lies in the direction and purpose of the journey, as well as in the nature of the character who undertakes it: in Westerns, the cowboy ventures into the "untamed" West to bring with him the law and order of the "civilized" East, whereas the protagonists of road movies tend to flee from "civilization," the way it is defined and practiced in their contemporary urban lives. Moreover, unlike cowboys, these characters are not aligned with law and order but are often anarchic criminals or social rebels. In *Bonnie and Clyde* (1967) and *Thunderbolt and Lightfoot* (1974), they are bandits;

in *The Graduate* (1967), an adulterate youth; in *Midnight Cowboy* (1969), a gay couple, conmen, and ultimately murderers outcast from the pretentious and capitalist city life; in *Easy Rider* (1969), drug dealers; in *Zabriskie Point* (1970), young rebels; and in *Vanishing Point* (1971), a driver who exceeds the speed limit and injures police officers.

Introducing the narrative structure of some of these New Hollywood road movies helps concretize my observations regarding their plot, characterization, and ending. The earliest film regarded by film historians as part of the Hollywood Renaissance is *The Graduate*. Although the film still follows the three-act structure and is not a road movie in the strict sense, it features extended driving sequences in which Benjamin travels between cities in search of Elaine, as well as an open ending—suggesting a precursor to the road movies that would follow.

The Graduate's plot centers on Benjamin, a recent college graduate who feels aimless about his future. He is seduced at the beginning of the film by Mrs. Robinson, an older woman and the wife of his father's business partner. While Benjamin initially tries to avoid her, a secret affair eventually develops between them. Complications emerge when he falls in love with her daughter, Elaine, resulting in a tense and awkward love triangle. After Elaine discovers the affair, she distances herself, but Benjamin becomes determined to win her back. In the film's final scene, Elaine and Benjamin jump onto a moving bus as they flee from her arranged wedding. The film offers no indication of their destination or what lies ahead, thus presenting an example of an open ending.

One of the first official road movies to achieve significant box office success during Hollywood's crisis was *Bonnie and Clyde*, which was released in the same year as *The Graduate*. In this film, the bandit couple—after whom the film is named—drives across the United States robbing banks, stealing cars, and constantly fleeing from the police. Along the way, their gang grows to include Clyde's brother Buck, his wife Blanche, and the gas station attendant C. W. Moss. As the film progresses, the group's robberies grow increasingly ambitious and violent, although only the wealthy are robbed, harmed, or killed by the bandit group, while financially disadvantaged citizens are consistently left unharmed.

The film does not make it clear what the couple intends to do with the stolen money. Clyde dreams of a quiet and orderly life with Bonnie, which would presumably require money. However, this desire emerges only after a significant number of their robberies and the acquisition of wealth, rather than serving as the original motive for their crimes. In this light, their actions appear as a form of pure anarchist rebellion against the established moral and economic structures of a society from which both Bonnie and

Clyde—as free spirits—feel excluded. The journey becomes an opportunity for the development of Bonnie and Clyde's relationship and the increasing complexity of their crimes. It ultimately ends with their sudden deaths occurring at the peak of their love relationship.

Thunderbolt and Lightfoot is a later Hollywood road movie that also centers on a bandit duo—this time, two men—who spend the entire film on the run and meet a tragic end. The plot follows two criminals who meet while fleeing from their respective crime scenes. The younger of the two, Lightfoot, persuades Thunderbolt to join forces for a bank robbery. After recovering the money that Thunderbolt had hidden from an earlier heist, Lightfoot ultimately gets killed. Thunderbolt continues the journey in his brand-new Cadillac, with his deceased companion seated beside him. The film merges the tragic death of one protagonist with the open ending of the other's ride.

Similar to *Thunderbolt and Lightfoot*, *Midnight Cowboy* also ends with one male protagonist dead and the other alive, both on a bus to Miami. Although not strictly a road movie, the film centers on Joe's journey from Texas, where he works as a dishwasher, to New York, where he hopes to become a male prostitute, and finally to Miami. Instead of earning money in New York, Joe comes to recognize his homosexual tendencies and ultimately accepts the seemingly homosexual affections of the conman Rico, who dies of the flu at the end.

Easy Rider is another significant Hollywood road movie featuring two male criminals. Billy and Wyatt travel with the money they earned from heroin smuggling in Mexico. They ride their motorcycles from Los Angeles to Louisiana to attend Mardi Gras in New Orleans. They journey by day and smoke marijuana at night. Along the way, they encounter a range of people and hitchhikers—from a traditional, religious farming family in Arizona to a hippie commune, a lawyer named George Hanson, and two sex workers in a New Orleans brothel. Each stop and encounter forms an episode in the film, with the journey itself supplying the narrative's cohesive continuity. By traveling from west to east—in the opposite direction of the cowboy in the Western genre, as Engell (1992, 263–4) observes—Billy and Wyatt offer viewers a glimpse of the contemporary United States: its landscapes as well as its contrasting community cultures, from religious, traditional farming families to countercultural hippie communes. In the end, Wyatt and Billy are shot by a truck passenger, simply because he does not like them.

A further example of New Hollywood road movies is *Two-Lane Blacktop* (1971). As in previous cases, the story follows two young men. They participate in car races with their self-modified vehicle and live off the money they earn from these competitions. The film's nameless characters—one the driver, the other the mechanic—encounter a girl and the driver of a Pontiac

GTO, a man from their fathers' generation. Although he knows little about cars, the GTO driver proposes a race from New Mexico to Washington, DC. This race serves as the central plot of the road movie.

In addition to the race, there is a secondary narrative thread that builds tension in the otherwise uneventful film. The three men are not only competing for victory on the road but also vying for the attention of the girl, who is at times drawn to one man and then the other, but ultimately distances herself from all of them. These rivalries between the main characters and the middle-aged GTO driver over a woman and over speed symbolically represent an Oedipal relationship between two generations of American men: the fathers' generation, which fails to understand the rebellious ideals of youth, and the sons' generation, which clings to the dream of freedom and nonconformity. Even their cars reflect these generational conflicts: the middle-aged man drives a classic American vehicle, which ultimately loses the race to the self-modified car of the young men, representing the self-defined values and lifestyle of contemporary youth. In the end, the GTO driver is forced to concede and yield the road to the men of the new generation.

Two-Lane Blacktop is notably sparse in terms of events, which allows the actors to adopt a cold and expressionless performance style. Or perhaps acting expertise was never the main focus for the lead roles, as their mere presence in the film was originally expected to ensure its success. After all, they were "stars of youth culture: James Taylor, a popular singer-songwriter, and Dennis Wilson, the drummer of the Beach Boys" (Hugo 1995, 259; my translation).

Among the notable New Hollywood road movies is also *Vanishing Point*. The film's main character, Kowalski, attempts to break a speed record by driving a Dodge Challenger from Denver to San Francisco within fifteen hours. In doing so, he inevitably exceeds the speed limit and is pursued by the police until the end of the film. The host of a radio station named *Super Soul*, who intercepts police radio communications about Kowalski, tries to warn and protect him through his broadcasts. Meanwhile, police investigations into Kowalski's background reveal that he is a Vietnam War veteran and a former successful police officer and private detective. Thanks to *Super Soul*'s radio program, Kowalski becomes a widely recognized hero within just a few hours, and citizens gather at a police roadblock along his route, hoping to witness his fate. Kowalski drives straight into the barricade and his car explodes—a kamikaze act likely driven by his war trauma. This film, too, is largely uneventful in terms of plot, with the journey serving primarily as a means for exploring Kowalski's past and the underlying causes of his will to defy all the rules that restrain him.

Zabriskie Point, a road movie from the 1970s, places greater emphasis on establishing its characters compared to the other road movies mentioned, before they set off on their respective journeys. On one side is the young woman Daria, who is driving to Phoenix to meet with her boss; on the other is a student named Mark, who, after a violent confrontation between students and the police on campus, steals an airplane and flies aimlessly into the desert. The two meet in the desert and accompany one another on a brief journey before parting ways: Daria continues her drive to Phoenix, while Mark returns to the airport from which he stole the plane, where he is ultimately shot dead by the police.

Road movie protagonists are, as noted before, often men and women who violate established moral and legal norms in the diegesis, thereby contradicting the protagonist roles of Hollywood films from the 1950s and early 1960s. As Christen points out regarding *Bonnie and Clyde*, "The central characters in the film are negative heroes or antiheroes. While this is not unique in Hollywood cinema, it was extremely unusual in the context of the conservative 1950s and 1960s" (2008, 58–9; my translation). These antiheroes are not despised by viewers, as they commit their small and large crimes not out of inherent malice, but in rebellion against a corrupt power structure. Bonnie and Clyde, for example, are gangsters, but they never rob poor people of their possessions, introducing a Robin Hood-like motif into the narrative. Within the diegesis, Bonnie and Clyde are highly respected by economically disadvantaged individuals, upon whom they show mercy. This respect is portrayed in the latter half of the film in a scene where the wounded couple is cared for by a group of homeless people.

The male bandit couple in *Thunderbolt and Lightfoot* also elicits the sympathy of viewers because they are portrayed as vulnerable characters. In one scene, they open up to each other and share stories of their troubled childhoods. While they do rob a bank, it is not they who injure or kill people in the process but rather the two malicious men who had assisted Thunderbolt in his previous bank robbery. They are, therefore, "good criminals," and their actions can be seen as excusable in light of their traumatic past.

The same holds true for Joe and Rico in *Midnight Cowboy*, who, at a certain point, reveal the traumatic experiences they endured during childhood and show so much love and caring compassion toward each other that they cannot be hated by the viewers for their conmanship and the murder they commit. Similarly, Wyatt and Billy in *Easy Rider* are nonpolarized characters. While they deal drugs, they do not endanger anyone in the process. Instead, through their carefree and joyful daytime rides and their nighttime marijuana smoking, they embody the free and peaceful lifestyle idealized by the Flower Power and hippie movements of the 1960s.

The next notable difference between character design in the narrative of Hollywood road movies and Hollywood films of the 1950s lies in their portrayals of male and female roles. Although women do not occupy central positions in road movie narratives, they display at least a partial increase in subjectivity compared to female characters in 1950s Hollywood cinema. For instance, women in road movies do not passively wait to be chosen by the male protagonist; instead, they openly and actively express their sexual desires—as exemplified in *Bonnie and Clyde*, *Zabriskie Point*, and *Two-Lane Blacktop*. More striking than the transformed female figures, however, is the way male characters behave toward these women within the road movie diegesis. Specifically, they appear insecure in heterosexual relationships with independent women. This points to a troubled male sexuality and, in some cases, even suggests homosexual tendencies among the men.

In *Bonnie and Clyde*, for example, Bonnie is ready from the outset to accept Clyde as her romantic partner. While he is clearly impressed by her beauty and courage, Clyde is unable to initiate a sexual relationship with Bonnie. Throughout the film, the two find multiple opportunities to be alone and express affection. However, it does not work for Clyde, and he repeatedly has to stop. The reason appears to be his lack of confidence with women. After the couple finally has sex in a meadow—the sex scene is not shown directly but only implied—Clyde (C) asks Bonnie (B) in an uncertain tone:

> C—Hey, how do you feel? I mean, you feel the way you're supposed to feel when you … after you … ?
> B—Hey, you did just perfect.

This uncertainty of a professional gangster regarding his relationship with a woman transforms him into a small, innocent boy, entirely unlike the macho central figures of gangster films known from Hollywood film history.

The same relationship between the male and female figures is observable in *Zabriskie Point*. Even though Mark is attracted to Daria, he is not immediately ready for a sexual relationship as Daria desires it, despite being the one who initially attracted Daria's attention with the low flight of his airplane. He remains distant toward Daria for a long time, who gives him much physical affection. Hence, the following conversation takes place between Mark (M) and Daria (D) during their walk in the desert:

> M—It was nice of you to come with a guy that doesn't turn on.
> D—I'm pretty tolerant.

The male characters in *Two-Lane Blacktop* and *Midnight Cowboy*, as well, are less interested in women than the traditional American society or the Hollywood cinema of the 1950s would expect. In the former film, the girl quickly manages to have sex with the mechanic. However, with the driver, it takes much longer until he accepts a sexual relationship, even though the girl has been inclined toward him from the very beginning. In *Midnight Cowboy*, this lack of interest in women is ultimately explained by Joe discovering his homosexual tendencies in New York, after performing oral sex with a young man and later being invited by Rico to move in with him. Rico is apparently gay, as he finds the women at the artist party, who touch him, repulsive. This seems to be the reason why he takes Joe in. Last but not least, Wyatt in *Easy Rider* is also not interested in women, despite a woman from the hippie community showing interest in him and even bathing naked with him.

This "deconstructed masculinity"—as Mills (2006, 148) refers to it—of the New Hollywood road movie figures has been interpreted from a feminist perspective. It is argued that the male characters in road movies are hysterical men. Since hysteria was traditionally attributed to women, these men do not express their hysteria in a feminine manner through an emotional eruption, but instead by leaving their homes and embarking on a journey. According to Aitken and Lukinbeal:

> Male hysteria is a disassociation from hegemonic masculinity, and its allegory, the road movie, is a spatial performance of the disenfranchised spirit. In road movies we see the flight of the phallus through motorized escape: castrated from hegemonic masculinity, mobile masculinity is the "other" to the extent that it is the rival with the father. Tim Corrigan suggests that hysteria in the road movie points to a crisis in male subjectivity and a genre that emphasizes the demise of the family unit. The myth of the road movie combines the hysterical and the disassociated into a paradigm that celebrates a search for self through spatial angst and unstable family geographies.
>
> (1997, 354)

This hysteria is sometimes grounded in the diegesis, as seen in *Vanishing Point*, where police officers discover that Kowalsky is a war veteran, and viewers infer that he may have been traumatized as a result. In other cases, it is left to the male members of the audience to search for its origins by identifying with the male protagonist through their own lived experience of being a man in 1960s US society, where women are emancipated and patriarchal masculinity is manifested in excessive capitalism, the assassination of pacifist political figures, and war-mongering foreign policies.

Finally, vehicles acquire a character of their own in road movie narratives, functioning as one of the main figures. This motorized character is referenced and fetishized as an object of desire through camera work, *mise-en-scène*, and diegetic dialogue. The male protagonists of New Hollywood road movies, who show limited interest in women, instead display a striking obsession with their means of transportation. In this way, New Hollywood road movies underscore "the 'masculine fascination with the thing that goes'" and foreground "the vehicle as a prop of desire" (Mills 2006, 114).

An exemplary instance of the fetishization of cars is *Two-Lane Blacktop*. In this film, the technical characteristics of race cars serve as the central topic of conversation—whether when the young men are questioned about their car before a race, at gas stations, or during the boasting between them and the GTO driver, each claiming that his car is faster and more powerful. For example, a dialogue unfolds between the young driver (D) and the gas station attendants (A1 and A2), who are fascinated by the modifications made to the car, while the vehicle nearly fills the frame (Figure 30):

A1—Chevy Block?
D—Yeah!
A1—Sure looks like an awful lot of work.
A2—396?
D—454
A2—No shit?
A1—What kind of transmission?
D—Four-speed
A1—You build the header?

Figure 30 Screenshot from *Two-Lane Blacktop*. The fetishization of vehicles in road movies.

D—Yeah!
A2—How fast will she run?
D—It depends on who's around.

In this example, a dialogue unfolds between men who love cars and are familiar with every technical detail. The use of the feminine pronoun *she* to refer to the car further signals that it represents their object of desire. In *Two-Lane Blacktop*, this fetishistic obsession with the self-modified vehicle is frequently portrayed as surpassing the allure of the young and attractive girl.

In *Easy Rider*, the motorcycles of Billy and Wyatt are not explicitly discussed in dialogue, yet they are fetishized through cinematography. At the beginning of their journey across the United States, a one-minute sequence presents close-up shots of Wyatt's California-style chopper, its surface adorned with the American flag. The camera's smooth pan over the motorcycle's "body" and its detailed focus mirror formal techniques familiar from Hollywood cinema that are typically used to fetishize and sexualize the female body.

In *Zabriskie Point*, the focus extends beyond driving to include flying as well. The film devotes considerable time to showcasing Mark's flight sequences in a Cessna 210, as well as Daria's drive in her 1950s car, captured from a variety of angles. The flirtation between Mark and Daria unfolds through the machines themselves, most notably when Mark flies his plane low over Daria's car along a desert road. Ultimately, the two paint the airplane with psychedelic and sexually parodic colors and patterns, including the depiction of two large female breasts on the plane's wings (Figure 31).

Figure 31 Screenshot from *Zabriskie Point*. The fetishization of vehicles in road movies.

Finally, a comparison between New Hollywood road movies and those of New German Cinema is necessary. While road movies signaled the departure of New German Cinema toward artistic and economic success, they were the most significant venturing genre in New Hollywood. This distinction is a notable outcome of a systems-theoretical analysis that examines the evolution of new waves of film within their specific contexts, rather than treating them as fixed categories. Elements of a particular film genre may function as venturing within the framework of one film structure, shaped by its specific memory function, and as a contribution to departure within another. In a third context, however, these same elements may not contribute to any new wave of cinema at all, as they do not respond in a wave-like manner to the established film structure in that setting.

Cinema's Alignment with Contemporary Communication Topics

Although the majority of venturing New Hollywood films—also referred to as the Hollywood Renaissance in film-historical literature—are road movies, this does not apply to all of them. As discussed at the beginning of this chapter, the most significant characteristic of these films, which gave them the quality of a wave rather than merely another experiment with viewers' tastes, was their resonance with the communication occurring among, and the lifestyle practiced by, their potential audiences—audiences who were critical of political developments and the moral stagnation within US society. The topics and lifestyles in question have already been outlined. Let us now examine how venturing New Hollywood films succeeded in aligning their information with the ongoing communications present in the daily lives of their audiences.

The topics shared between venturing New Hollywood films and the lived experiences of their audiences can be inferred from the choices these films made at the levels of cinematography, dialogue, and music. Essentially, several of these films underscore that they are making a statement about American society through cinematography and dialogue. Take *Easy Rider* as an example: George, the last hitchhiker to accompany Billy and Wyatt, tells the two motorcyclists, "You know, this used to be a hell of a good country. I can't understand what's gone wrong with it." He voices this criticism after experiencing the hostile stares of the locals earlier that evening, when they entered a restaurant—locals who despise this small group of young men solely because of their different appearance and free lifestyle. Furthermore, Wyatt calls himself Captain America, and the flag of the United States is printed on his helmet, his jacket, and his motorcycle (Figure 32). This is perhaps because

Figure 32 Screenshot from *Easy Rider*. Thematizing US society via cinematography.

the character was intended to represent the entire American youth at the time the film was made: rebellious, free, and future-oriented.

Easy Rider also aligns itself with the lifestyle of its target audience through its extradiegetic music. In Hollywood films of the 1950s, extradiegetic music served to underscore the plot and was never present for its own sake. *Easy Rider* reverses this convention by accompanying Billy and Wyatt's long, uneventful rides with contemporary rock music that dominates the scenes. Here, it seems as though the choices in cinematography were made to align with the extradiegetic music, rather than the other way around. Steppenwolf's *The Pusher*—a song about drug dealers—opens the film, following the scene in which viewers witness the successful drug deal carried out by Wyatt and Billy in Mexico. The film then continues with the two riding their motorcycles, accompanied by Steppenwolf's *Born to Be Wild*. Later in the film, several other songs can be heard that were popular among rebellious American citizens at the time of its release, including *The Weight* (The Band), *Wasn't Born to Follow* (Gerry Goffin and Carole King), *If You Want to Be a Bird* (The Holy Modal Rounders), *Don't Bogart Me* (Fraternity of Man), *If 6 Was 9* (Jimi Hendrix), *Kyrie Eleison / Mardi Gras* (Electric Prunes), and *It's Alright Ma* (Roger McGuinn).

The Graduate, too, emphasizes through the medium of filmic communication—beside its narrative—that its topic is the lives of American youth by highlighting both the American flag and contemporary folk-rock music popular among the youth. When Benjamin arrives at Berkeley to find Elaine, he is shown on campus from a bird's-eye perspective, with the American flag waving in the foreground and dominating the frame, while Benjamin's figure appears much smaller than the flag (Figure 33). This shot composition shows Benjamin as dominated by the flag and implies this young man's powerlessness in the context of the traditional American society. Musically, the film opens with Simon & Garfunkel's *Hello Darkness My Old Friend*. Later in the film, Benjamin's drive in search of Elaine is accompanied by Simon & Garfunkel's *Mrs. Robinson*—a song the duo composed specifically for Nichols' film.

Another statement about contemporary American society through the demonstrative portrayal of the American flag is made in *Zabriskie Point*, where Daria's boss, a real estate executive, appears in a wide shot in his office, located in a skyscraper in downtown Los Angeles. Through the large window behind him, another high-rise building—suggesting that the setting is a business district—and a waving American flag are visible (Figure 34). This shot positions Daria's boss as a symbol of capitalism in the United States. When, at the end of the film, Daria imagines the explosion of her boss's mansion in Arizona, where he is having a business meeting, she is in fact imagining the destruction of the entire American capitalist system.

Finally, *Nashville* (1975)—released later than the other films mentioned above—ends with a wide shot from the stage where Hal Philip Walker, a presidential candidate, is about to hold a fundraising gala. The back wall of the stage is covered by a massive American flag, indicating that this is the space where contemporary American culture and politics are to be staged (Figure 35). The acts and performances that take place on this stage of American pop culture and politics include country and gospel music performed by talentless musicians, as well as shooting and assassination—each referencing the political and cultural atmosphere of the United States in the 1970s.

The above analyses demonstrate the deliberate staging of the American flag through cinematography as a symbolic means of creating a critical relationship within the film between the flag and the condition of American society, as conveyed by the actions or visual compositions present in that film. In the films discussed, this condition is portrayed as a society whose dreams of freedom and peace are repressed by conservative citizens (*Easy Rider*), a society marked by confused yet morally upright youth (*The Graduate*), one in which capitalist interests align with state repression of protesting students (*Zabriskie Point*), and one characterized by a degraded pop culture and a political system that resorts to assassination (*Nashville*). This message resonated with the concerns of those audience members who were critical of contradictions between their expectations and the state of American society during the 1960s and 1970s.

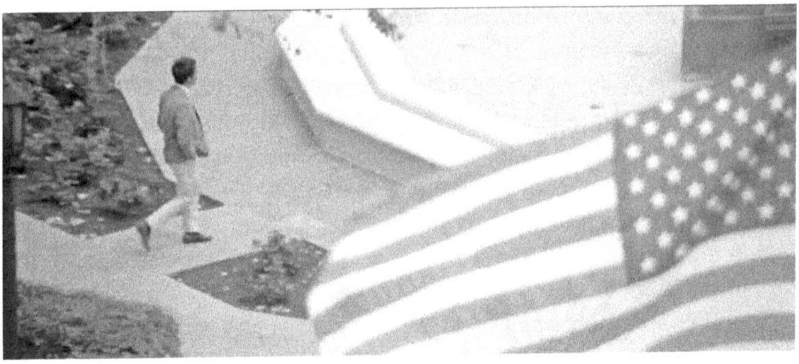

Figure 33 Screenshot from *The Graduate*. Thematizing US society via cinematography.

Figure 34 Screenshot from *Zabriskie Point*. Thematizing US society via cinematography.

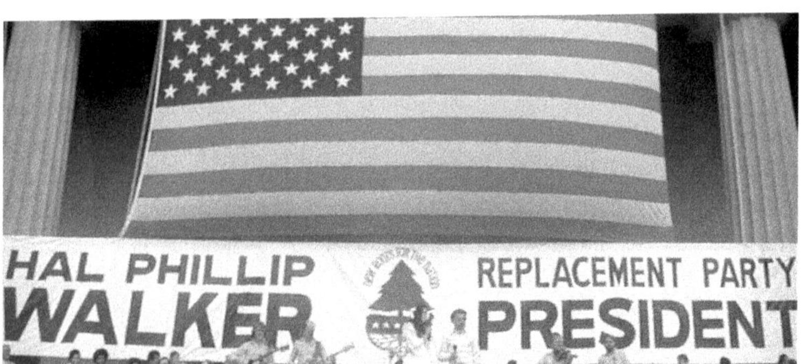

Figure 35 Screenshot from *Nashville*. Thematizing US society via cinematography.

Critical references to the contemporary events unfolding in the American political scene, both domestically and internationally, are more deliberately made in the narratives of films such as *M*A*S*H* (1970) and *The Conversation* (1974). The narrative of *M*A*S*H* centers on the medical personnel stationed at a Mobile Army Surgical Hospital (MASH) during the Korean War (1950–3). Yet, it can easily be interpreted as a critical parody of the US Army's involvement in the Vietnam War. The film portrays several American army doctors who show excessive interest in women, alcohol, money, and entertainment, demonstrating no regard for rank or military discipline. Nonetheless, despite the obscenity and negligence of the doctors and officers, the station functions with apparent efficiency: all surgeries are successful, and the doctors' and medical aides' lack of rigor leads to no serious consequences.

The plot of *The Conversation* follows Harry Caul, a surveillance expert based in San Francisco. Caul is commissioned to record a conversation between a young couple in a crowded public space. As he attempts to decipher the recording, he becomes increasingly disturbed by what he believes the couple is discussing, namely, a potential murder. The film builds tension as he comes to realize that even he, the observer, is not immune to being observed, and that the couple he has been surveilling—who may have murdered his client—are, in turn, surveilling him. In a desperate attempt to locate the bug in his apartment, he destroys everything inside it, but to no avail. The film's narrative resonated strongly in the context of the Watergate Scandal and contributed to its success at the box office.

Finally, references to the contemporary lifestyle of protesting American citizens—intended to contradict the dominant cultural norms and political decisions in US society—were made by venturing New Hollywood films through cinematography, where nudity, open sexual relationships, and drug use were deliberately depicted. Two prominent examples are *Easy Rider* and *Zabriskie Point*. Billy and Wyatt smuggle cocaine from Mexico to Los Angeles and smoke marijuana every night—either around their own campfire or with members of a hippie community they encounter along the way. The film not only depicts the protagonists selling and consuming drugs but also attempts to represent their mental states under drug influence through certain formal strategies that were unconventional for the contemporary memory of filmic communication.

The first formal choice employed for this purpose is the use of rapid cuts that flash between nighttime and daytime scenes as the riders wake and begin a new day. In these moments, the film employs shot transitions "in which images of the current and the subsequent scene are interwoven in a flash-like manner" (Christen 2008, 61; my translation). These transitions—referred to by Bordwell and Thompson (2002, 518) as "choppy transition"—can suggest the mental state of a person after smoking marijuana, in which their vision and perception of time and space become distorted.

Another notable example is the penultimate sequence of *Easy Rider*. In a scene at the end of this sequence, Wyatt and Billy visit the French cemetery during the Mardi Gras festival with two sex workers and consume LSD. The drug's effects are portrayed through a collage of disjointed and extremely brief shots. Distorted images of the four figures in the cemetery are rapidly intercut with shots of various recognizable and unrecognizable objects. On the auditory level, psychedelic music merges with the voices of the two men and women as they utter what resembles a prayer, or express their immediate sensations and fears under the influence of LSD. As Mills observes, the image resolution of this sequence is significantly lower than that of the preceding and following ones, as the cemetery scene was filmed with a 16mm camera and partially utilized fisheye lenses (Mills 2006, 123).

Despite *Easy Rider*, which opts for a different lens and camera than those used in the rest of the film and employs a specific form of editing to imply drug influence, *Zabriskie Point* achieves this effect through the *mise-en-scène*. Here, simultaneously with the love-making scene between Mark and Daria—after they have smoked marijuana—dancing figures appear in the same desert where the couple is located. As they dance, the figures gradually remove their clothing and engage in erotic movements reminiscent of contact improvisation, ultimately depicting a surreal sex orgy in the desert. This visual sequence reflects Daria and Mark's state of mind while having sex under the influence of marijuana (Figure 36). In doing so, the film also transgresses the boundaries of the level of intimacy that other New Hollywood films of the era dared to display. Whereas sex and nudity in other contemporary New Hollywood films were either edited out—as in

Figure 36 Screenshot from *Zabriskie Point*. Displaying eroticism under the influence of marijuana.

Bonnie and Clyde and *Two-Lane Blacktop*—or concealed beneath or behind props on set or in shadow—as was the case in, for example, *The Graduate*, *Midnight Cowboy*, and *Thunderbolt and Lightfoot*—they are presented openly in *Zabriskie Point*.

Fleeting Moments of Formal Rebellion

In the previous chapter on New German Cinema, numerous instances of certain formal choices were introduced that contribute to the film's reflection or interrupt its first-order observation. These formal choices dominated a large group of films and were therefore identified as a rupturing tendency. They marked moments in which elements selected from the media of camera work, sound design, or editing were not in service of the film's narrative, as was the case in the established structure of *Heimatfilm*. These elements were selected with the purpose of disrupting the seamless flow of the plot—which constitutes the information of filmic communication—and drawing the viewers' attention to themselves and their unexpectedness.

Although similar formal choices are also evident in venturing New Hollywood films, they do not constitute a rupture in this new wave for two reasons. First, they are neither prominent enough within individual films nor sufficiently prevalent across the era to signify a rupture in the conventional structure of filmic utterance. Second, they are mostly justified by the plot or adopt a humorous or experimental character rather than a rupturing tendency. Nevertheless, they are a notable feature of venturing New Hollywood films and merit closer examination.

A unique combination of zoom and editing, which draws the viewers' attention to itself rather than to the action within the diegesis, appears at the beginning of *Easy Rider*, where Wyatt discards his broken watch. Instead of simply presenting the act of throwing the watch to the ground in a full shot, this seemingly minor event is fragmented into several distinct shots: in a medium shot, Wyatt looks at his watch. A cut follows to a close-up of his face as he carefully observes the watch and realizes it has stopped. This is succeeded by a rapid zoom-out and zoom-in on his face as he throws the watch to the ground. A cut to him and Billy includes a quick zoom-out that briefly frames them in a full shot. Another cut returns to a close-up of Wyatt's face, followed by an eyeline match to the watch now lying on the ground. The two men then ride off. This interplay of zoom and editing contributes nothing to the plot. Instead, it functions as a pure play with possible forms inherent in the medium of filmic communication.

Another compelling example of such formal divergences from Hollywood film's dominant structure appears in *Midnight Cowboy*. The film begins with

Joe's coworkers at a provincial restaurant in Texas asking one another where Joe is, while, through parallel editing, Joe is shown at home, getting ready and preparing for his journey to New York. In one shot, Joe's boss, standing behind a pile of dirty dishes, looks directly into the camera and lectures Joe about punctuality at work. This cuts to Joe, who also looks directly into the camera and replies that from now on, they will have to handle the dishwashing themselves (Figure 37). The direct addresses to the camera in two successive shots both catch the viewers off guard—creating the sensation of being personally addressed—and simultaneously produce the impression of a shot/reverse shot in which two characters appear to be conversing in the same location, even though Joe and his boss are actually in two separate settings. This combination of camera work and editing playfully interrupts

Figure 37 Screenshots from *Midnight Cowboy*. Playful reflection via camera work and editing.

the viewers' first-order observation of the film and humorously demonstrates through reflection how the shot/reverse shot technique functions.

Zabriskie Point's final sequence delivers another example of formal choices that interrupt the viewers' seamless engagement with the narrative. I argue that the formal choices made in this sequence are not so much intended as a contradiction to the conventional film structure in Hollywood per se but are instead diegetically contextualized and reveal the character's frustrated state of mind. In this sequence Daria, having just driven away from the house in Arizona, where her boss had met with his business partners, hears the news of Mark's death on the radio and steps out of the car. In the distance, she witnesses the explosion of her boss's house. The explosion is repeated across thirteen cuts, shown from various camera angles—a redundancy not allowed in the continuity system of conventional Hollywood films. The camera then swiftly pans to the right. The frame, once filled with fire and smoke, now reveals a white table, two white chairs, and a white sun umbrella set against the blue sky. Another explosion occurs in this location—which, seemingly a beach, had not been previously introduced diegetically—and the aforementioned objects are blown into the air. This explosion transitions into a psychedelic scene. As an extradiegetic soundtrack by Pink Floyd plays, the scattered objects fall from the sky in slow motion. This shot is cut to the explosions of a wardrobe, a television set, a refrigerator, and a bookshelf—symbols of consumer culture and contemporary media—all presented out of diegetic context beneath the open sky. This psychedelic sequence is abruptly ended when it cuts to Daria's smiling and serene face, accompanied by a silent soundscape. She gets back into her car and drives on.

Two-Lane Blacktop, in turn, has a humorous and rebellious ending that also serves as an instance of filmic reflection. In the film's final sequence, the driver is shown in a claustrophobic close-up inside his car, just before the final race begins. With the referee's starting signal, the race commences. The driver speeds off and is depicted from behind in slow motion. After a few seconds, however, the image freezes, and the film reel on which the film was recorded catches fire. The fire destroys the last frame shown on the screen, bringing the film to an end. This formal decision to conclude the film draws attention to the film's dissemination medium, which belongs to the environment of filmic communication. *Two-Lane Blacktop* thus ends through a technical malfunction in the film projector—but which film projector?!

Finally, *M*A*S*H* ends with humorous reflexivity at the levels of sound design and cinematography. In the final sequence, the diegetic loudspeaker at the Mobile Army Surgical Hospital, which throughout the film has been announcing the program of the station's cinema, suddenly begins to provide information about the current film in which it is involved:

> Attention! Tonight's film has been *M*A*S*H*. Follow the zany antics of our combat surgeons as they cut and stitch their way along the front lines. Operating as bombs, … operating as bombs and bullets burst around them, snatching laughs and love between amputations and penicillin.

Following this reflexive cue from the film, the loudspeaker announces the names of the film's actors, while shots from the now-concluded film in which the named actors appeared are replayed on the screen.

Hollywood's Departure into the Blockbuster Era

As demonstrated thus far, New Hollywood followed a fundamentally different evolution trajectory than New German Cinema. Not only is there no significant tendency in New Hollywood to radically rupture the conventional structure of filmic utterance during the financial film crisis of the 1950s and 1960s but its venture and departure also seem to have unfolded concurrently and independently. This explains why opinions among New Hollywood film historians diverge considerably regarding which films and periods should be included in the classification of New Hollywood and which should not. For Bordwell and Thompson, venturing films were merely "youth pics," and they are not recognized as evolutionary contributions to New Hollywood (2002, 515). Hehr, in turn, describes the differing views concerning New Hollywood cinema as follows:

> Some seventies publications see New Hollywood as the so-called youth wave that started after the success of *The Graduate* and *Easy Rider*, then died off again after 1971. According to this theory, it was about a new generation of film-makers affected by left-wing alternative culture who wanted to revolutionize American mainstream cinema and were rapidly defeated by the limits of the system. Later publications identify New Hollywood as the great age of "auteur films." The hard core here are usually Robert Altman, Stanley Kubrick, John Cassavetes, Arthur Penn, Mike Nichols, Francis Ford Coppola and Martin Scorsese, and occasionally Sam Peckinpah, Paul Mazursky and Michael Ritchie. This view implies that the movement peaked between 1969 and 1975, when most of these film-makers were going through their most creative and successful phase. Other writers give the impression that it is all about a

> change of generation brought about by the surge forward of the "Film Brats." These usually include Coppola and Scorsese, and then Brian De Palma, Peter Bogdanovich, George Lucas, Steven Spielberg, William Friedkin, Paul Schrader and John Milius.
>
> (2003, 7; emphasis in original)

Viewed from this book's systems-theoretical perspective, the reason for the differing views that Hehr refers to lies in the fact that some historians regard the venturing films as part of the new wave, while others consider films of departure—as will be discussed in this section—as central. According to these historians, the two cannot be merged into a unified new wave for a clear reason: New Hollywood films that ventured to introduce narrative innovations and address contemporary communication topics contradicting moral norms and political decisions in US society remained merely a variation of filmic communication. The films departing toward the future and sustainably overcoming the financial crisis did not adopt many of the identities introduced by venturing films, nor did they restabilize these into a new structure.

Rather, the path to departure in New Hollywood involved further enriching the existing formal structure and the three-act narrative, adding to their complexity. Hence, departure films of New Hollywood were based on a variation that only presented a more complex version of the already established formal and narrative structures, rather than selecting and restabilizing the critical narratives of venturing films or the eventless continuity of the road movie. Beginning in the 1970s, these films were able to rescue Hollywood from the stagnation it had experienced for about a decade and reestablish the film system's autopoiesis through their widespread popularity, which signaled the audience's acceptance of their communication. They are often referred to as New Hollywood blockbusters due to their immense box office success.

Below, I will introduce some of the variations that were introduced, selected, and stabilized by departure films of New Hollywood. I will also highlight the few elements that departure films adopted from the variations introduced by venturing Hollywood films.

Depiction of Violence in Film

A segment of New Hollywood films contributing to the new wave's departure began once again to experiment with large, costly productions in the 1970s. The most significant *mise-en-scène* feature that these films added to the open portrayal of sex and nudity—as introduced by venturing films—was the uncensored depiction of violence. With the Production Code disbanded in 1968, and with sex, violence, horror scenes, and spectacular disasters still absent from television, these films introduced such scenes and the narratives embodying them as variation, "leaving the delta of Good Family Entertainment to TV largely" (Alloway 1997, 168).

Engell believes the display of violence to be the most important development introduced by New Hollywood films. According to him,

> This development begins with disaster films such as *Earthquake* and *The Towering Inferno*, continues with Spielberg's *Jaws*, and culminates in a kind of apex with Coppola's *Apocalypse Now*. The endurance of violence, as well as the eruption into it, constitutes Scorsese's central theme in *Taxi Driver*, and remains present in *After Midnight*, although in a somewhat more detached manner. In New Hollywood films, the emotional and narrative peaks are no longer found in love scenes, but in scenes of violence. In this respect, cinema continues to differ significantly from television.
>
> (1992, 266–7; my translation; emphasis in original)

The films that Engell refers to as New Hollywood are those that, according to the analyses in this book, contributed to the departure of New Hollywood. To the instances of violence mentioned by him, I can add the horror scenes exemplified by films such as *Night of the Living Dead* (1968) and *The Exorcist* (1973). Both films achieved significant box office success, as did the films mentioned by Engell. This indicates that the depiction of horror and violence appealed to audiences and that future Hollywood productions would likely resonate with them as well.

Increased Narrative Complexity

Films of departure in New Hollywood featured a more complex narrative structure than their predecessors, and this likely contributed to the acceptance of their communication and their economic success. This narrative complexity includes, above all, a heightened sophistication of film characters. In contrast to successful Hollywood films of the 1950s, in which characters often exhibited abrupt shifts in behavior and decision-making without any portrayal of the mental processes leading to these changes, departure films take time within the narrative to introduce the characters' developmental trajectory. Comparing the development of the leading male characters in *The Sound of Music* and *Taxi Driver* (1976) serves as an illustrative example.

In *The Sound of Music*, there is a scene in which the Captain returns from Vienna with the Baroness, whom he intends to marry soon, to his large mansion. While showing her the expansive garden and lake, they come upon Maria, the governess, and the Captain's seven children singing in a rowboat, wearing play clothes Maria had sewn for them from old drapes. When Maria, excited to see the Captain and the Baroness, causes the boat to capsize, the children are sent to their rooms to change out of their wet clothes, and the Captain orders Maria to leave immediately, claiming she has brought chaos to his previously disciplined household. Upon returning to the house, the Captain hears singing and discovers that his children are performing a song Maria taught them for the Baroness. Moved by the nostalgia of a song he also knows, he joins in, singing along with the children. Meanwhile, Maria ascends the stairs to pack and leave, but the Captain calls out to her from the foot of the staircase and pleads with her to stay, because she has brought music back into the household. This abrupt shift in tone—his unbreakable discipline, his fury at Maria and demand that she leave, followed within seconds by tenderness, apology, and a plea for her to stay—is just one example of the film's failure to portray the characters' development to the audience.

Character development takes a very different, more minute course in *Taxi Driver*. In this film, Travis Bickle's character is developed through a combination of his internal monologue, his interactions with others, and his increasingly erratic behavior. Initially, Travis appears as a lonely, disillusioned Vietnam War veteran who takes a job as a taxi driver in New York City. An isolated and alienated figure within the urban landscape, he becomes progressively more disturbed by the city's filth and corruption, which he perceives as symbolic of a broader moral decay. The narrative allows viewers to witness Travis's gradual transformation from a detached observer to an active participant in a violent fantasy of redemption. His internal struggles are revealed through his voiceovers, which convey his confusion, anger, and distorted sense of justice. The climactic turning point in his character development occurs when Travis takes matters into his own hands, ultimately resorting to violence in an attempt to "cleanse" the city and rescue the young sex worker, Iris. In *Taxi Driver*, the audience is given more insight into why Travis feels the way he does and through which process, in the end, he acts as he does. By introducing this complexity into the filmic narrative, *Taxi Driver* tells a more convincing and engaging story than a conventional Hollywood film from the 1960s, such as *The Sound of Music*, could offer.

The narrative complexity of other Hollywood films of departure was indebted to literary adaptation, which provided screenwriters with a well-structured and complex narrative foundation. Successful departure films such as *The Godfather* (1972) and *The Godfather Part II* (1974), *The Exorcist*, *One Flew over the Cuckoo's Nest* (1975), and *Apocalypse Now* (1979) were adaptations of *The Godfather* by Mario Puzo, *The Exorcist* by William Peter Blatty, *One Flew over the Cuckoo's Nest* by Ken Kesey, and *Heart of Darkness* by Joseph Conrad.

The Expansion of Film's Material Medium

The extended narrative complexity of New Hollywood films of departure was accompanied by parallel technical developments in film production, which enhanced the films' visual and auditory appeal by enriching its material medium. These advancements had already begun during the 1950s and achieved refinement in the departure cinema of New Hollywood. One such development occurred in the area of recording and printing color films. According to Monaco, "long known among cinematographers for its sense of artificiality, escapism, and lightweight genres, color suddenly became perceived in the mid 1960s among Hollywood cinematographers as a key for opening up an enormously enriched sense of cinematic naturalism" (2003, 69). In the area of color processing, Kodak made significant advancements around this time. As Monaco observes, "in conjunction with its advancements in negative (or 'camera') film during the 1960s, Kodak made parallel progress in its color positive (or 'print') films. Kodak's improvement of these films meant greater sharpness of line in the picture and accounted for truer and more balanced colors in prints that were struck for release in film theaters" (2003, 68). One of the New Hollywood blockbusters that utilized this updated technology along with the Panavision system—which enabled the recording of widescreen films on 35mm film stock with anamorphic lenses—was *2001: A Space Odyssey* (1968). The wide film images thus produced, along with their enhanced color quality and sharpness, were far more appealing than the size and quality offered by the television screen.

Besides sharper and brighter colors, departure films of New Hollywood also implemented new sound technologies to record and play sharper, more realistic audio, enhancing the immersive first-order observation of the film. According to Monaco, "the advancement of ADR, looping, and Foley techniques, all of which increased the effectiveness of adding sound to scenes in postproduction, meshed exceptionally well with Hollywood's new preference for location filming during the 1960s" (2003, 106). The ADR and looping techniques were employed to replace dialogue that was either poorly delivered on set or disrupted by ambient noise in outdoor locations, using recordings made in a studio. The Foley technique enabled the creation of sound effects that appeared realistic but could not be captured on set, allowing them to be synchronized with the recorded image—such as footsteps or the swish of a sword. Thanks to these techniques, New Hollywood blockbusters were able to achieve sonic perfection and regulate the intensity of ambient sounds captured on set, while simultaneously enhancing the film's sense of naturalness through the use of sound effects.

A good example of sounds added to the film in postproduction that enhance its sense of reality is Coppola's first feature film, *The Rain People* (1969). As Beck points out, "the tension can be sensed right from the beginning of the film when the stinger chord that introduces the first image is replaced with the realistic sound of garbage men plying their trade along a rain-dappled suburban street" (2016, 88). Although this scene's sounds make the impression of having been recorded at the set, this has not been the case in reality. Rather, they were recorded separately and added to the film in post-production. Recording the sounds of the garbage truck and the men handling garbage cans in the studio enables the director to synchronize these seemingly realistic noises with the rhythm of the pans and cuts in the scene. The film does not make the impression of being a realistic documentary, but rather only uses "codes of realism in relation to sound" (2016, 89). The result is what Beck calls *audio vérité*. According to him, "the effect of audio vérité is to create a sense of realism between the sounds and images that evokes a documentary sensibility. While this realism is evident throughout the film, it is fabricated from disparate sonic elements" (2016, 89).

Seen from the Luhmannian perspective, these technical developments enriched the material medium of film, which belongs to the environment of filmic communication just as much as the human body belongs to the environment of communication occurring between two individuals. With the medium of filmic communication consisting of cinematic techniques at the levels of camera, sound, and editing, advancements in film recording, color printing, sound recording, and editing served to enhance the quality of the forms ultimately produced by the film, but they did not expand the medium of filmic communication. For example, certain identities within the medium of camera work—such as dolly shots, close-ups, medium shots, American shots, zoom-ins and zoom-outs, pans and tilts, and depth of field—were already present in the 1940s and 1950s. However, color enhancements allowed for greater emphasis on the *mise-en-scène*, making the objects or human figures subjected to these techniques appear more vividly on screen. The same applies to sound and its relation to the visual elements in editing: while on- and off-screen sounds, as well as diegetic and non-diegetic ones, remained identities attached to meaning in the departure film—just as they were in the era before New Hollywood—the quality of their recording and editing was transformed in the New Hollywood blockbusters of the early 1970s, enhancing the film's first-order observation and, as a result, its popularity.

The Neo-Genres

Already in the early 1970s, Hollywood cinema had demonstrated that it had successfully overcome the crisis it faced in the early 1960s thanks to the films of departure. It achieved this by employing the strategies discussed above—namely, by maintaining the structure of filmic utterance centered on the continuity system while enhancing narrative complexity, visual and sonic quality, and the diversity of its *mise-en-scène*, including scenes not permitted on television.

Having secured its autopoiesis, New Hollywood cinema took the risk of reviving its classical genres that had been popular in the 1940s and 1950s—namely, slapstick, the Western, and film noir—and testing whether they would appeal to contemporary audience tastes through revision and updating. These returns and revivals led to the emergence of *neo*-genres such as neo-noir and neo-Western.

At the same time, the film industry had learned from the success of earlier venture films at the time of crisis that productions failing to resonate with contemporary communication were destined for rejection at the box office. Consequently, the neo-genre films revised their themes to more closely align with ongoing critical communication within the United States of the 1970s, focusing on equal rights in the society and the not-always-peaceful role played by its political system on the international stage. By updating their information, these films became "overt parodies, 'corrected' genre pictures, or exaggerated camp versions of Hollywood's traditional mythology" (Ray 1985, 257). In Luhmann's terms, the neo-genres were reflexive in that their films critically commented older ones from the genres that lay at their core.

Christen enumerates several neo-noir films of New Hollywood as follows: *The Long Goodbye* (1973), *Chinatown* (1974), *The Parallax View* (1974), *Night Moves* (1975), *Three Days of the Condor* (1975), *The Drowning Pool* (1975), and *The Late Show* (1977) (Christen 2008, 65). An adaptation of the novel of the same name by Raymond Chandler, *The Long Goodbye* is considered a central neo-noir film by Christen (2008, 65). It offers a critical, parodic, and revisionist take on the film noir genre, particularly by recontextualizing its key tropes and characters for the disillusioned atmosphere of the 1970s. The detective in this film, Philip Marlowe, is a far cry from the tough, cynical, hyper-competent detectives of classic noir (like the Philip Marlowe in *The Big Sleep* played by Humphrey Bogart).

Instead, this Marlowe is mumbling, passive, and often out of sync with his environment. He wanders through the plot rather than driving it. This undermines the genre's reliance on the detective as a stabilizing moral force. Altman transports Raymond Chandler's 1950s detective into 1970s Los Angeles without updating his values or mannerisms. The dissonance between Marlowe's outdated code of honor and the amoral, self-absorbed culture around him becomes a form of parody and critique. The film suggests that the moral certainties of classic noir no longer hold in a post-Watergate, post-Vietnam America.

Neo-Westerns, in turn, criticized the frontier theory that lay at the base of the Western genre, uncovering and denouncing its racist roots. According to Frederick Jackson Turner's frontier thesis, presented in 1893 in his paper *The Significance of the Frontier in American History*, the westward expansion of American settlers from the East Coast played a central role in shaping American identity. This movement aimed to "civilize" lands inhabited by Indigenous peoples and Spanish colonists, and it marked both a physical and psychological frontier. Turner argues that this process created something distinctly American—not a continuation of European traditions but a new, unique cultural product (Turner 1893).

Holtz comments on the neo-Western genre and how it criticizes the frontier thesis as follows:

> With its roots in the frontier mythology, ergo the conflict between a supposedly savage and primitive people and a morally and intellectually superior civilization, the Vietnam War became the overriding allegory of the genre. [...] Rather than eschewing the genre for its old-fashioned character, lots of directors modified the Western, often inverting its classical guise and creating perceived anti-Westerns that were critical of the established conventions regarding historical distortions, ideological inclinations, and narrative strategies.
>
> (2009, 126)

The Wild Bunch (1969) is a seminal neo-Western that critiques and revises the classical Western genre by exposing its underlying myths, glorified violence, and outdated moral codes. The film's plot follows a group of aging outlaws in 1913 who, realizing that their time is coming to an end, attempt one final heist. Led by Pike Bishop, the gang botches a robbery in Texas and flees to Mexico, where they become entangled in the Mexican Revolution. They make a deal to steal weapons for a corrupt general, but after witnessing his brutal regime, the gang faces a moral reckoning. In the end, they choose to confront the general in a final, suicidal showdown, sacrificing themselves for the emancipation of Hispanic folks who, in the frontier narrative, were considered savage and uncivilized.

Whereas traditional Westerns often depicted clear moral binaries—heroes versus villains, civilization versus savagery, lawmen versus outlaws—*The Wild Bunch* rejects such simplicity. Its protagonists are outlaws who engage in bloody and graphically depicted shootouts at both the beginning and the end of the film. In the initial shootout, they are clearly "bad" characters who kill innocent people in the course of a bank robbery. However, their characters undergo a drastic transformation when they witness the poverty and adversity suffered by the Mexican people under a dictatorship. This observation shifts them toward self-sacrifice in the name of justice and freedom. In the final shootout, they are no longer villainous bank robbers but freedom fighters. By bravely engaging in a liberating cause in a foreign country as Americans, they present a counterexample to the American soldiers who, in the name of fighting communism, were killing innocent people in the Vietnam War.

Why Was There No Rupture in New Hollywood?

The analyses in this chapter demonstrated that a significant wave of rupturing films—a key feature of New German Cinema—was absent from New Hollywood. Due to this absence, theoreticians such as King argue that New Hollywood produced no "art" cinema. According to him:

> The Hollywood Renaissance witnessed a number of stylistic innovations. This is most apparent when comparison is made with the dominant tendencies of the commercial mainstream, rather than the European "art" cinema. These did not amount to anything like a whole-sale abandonment of the "classical" style, even in the more radical or interesting products of the period. Large parts of films such as *Bonnie and Clyde*, *Easy Rider* and *Taxi Driver* conform to familiar conventions such as those of continuity editing and narrative motivation, providing a ground against which elements of innovation can be measured.
>
> (2002, 44; emphasis added)

Viewed in light of Luhmann's systems theory, Hollywood never felt the necessity to sound the alarm on the crisis it was experiencing in the early 1960s—as its filmic communications were repeatedly rejected by the audience—by radically contradicting the dominant structure of filmic utterance. This particular course of filmic evolution in the United States can be traced back to two characteristics of filmic communication in this society. First, the United States already had an established tradition of experimental cinema in the 1940s, which thrived and evolved parallel to Hollywood. This cinema—with key figures such as Maya Deren, Oskar Fischinger, John and James Whitney, Slavko Vorkapich, and Paul Burnford—had its own audience and its own financial means.[1] If Hollywood films were to rupture the established structure of the continuity system and thereby disrupt the narrative flow too drastically, they would cross into the realm of experimental cinema, and they would have little chance of effectively introducing a variation into the communication of mainstream Hollywood cinema.

There were individual directors in Hollywood though, such as Woody Allen, who were more willing to interrupt the established structure of the continuity system from time to time. For example, in his first film, *What's Up, Tiger Lily?* (1966), Allen creates a cinematic collage by taking the Japanese detective film *Kokusai Himitsu Keisatsu: Kagi No Kagi* (International Secret Police: Key of Keys; 1965), completely erasing its audio track, and editing in self-written, satirical dialogue that bears no relation to the original script or narrative. This film marks a complete separation between the sound and image, as was also the case in *Jonas*. Furthermore, at the end of *What's Up, Tiger Lily?*, Woody Allen is seen lying on a couch, biting into an apple while a woman performs a striptease in front of him. Simultaneously, a text scrolls upward on the right side of the frame. It begins by offering trivial information about the film's production, but then directly addresses the viewers, stating that anyone still reading the text instead of watching the woman should either consult their psychotherapist or visit a good eye doctor. This statement is followed by a sequence of letters that progressively decrease in size, resembling those on a Snellen chart. The scene's irrelevance to the film's invented plot and diegesis, combined with its exhibitionism—both Allen and the woman look directly into the camera while the woman undresses and the viewers are directly addressed through text—would be characteristic of the tendency toward rupture if it occurred within the context of other rupturing films in 1960s Hollywood.

In a subsequent Woody Allen film, *Annie Hall* (1977), subtitles become autonomous and function independently of the soundtrack. In the scene where Alvy and Annie drink wine and converse on the terrace after a tennis match, the subtitles do not replicate the dialogue heard on the soundtrack. Instead, they reveal additional information about the characters' conflicting emotions regarding what they are saying. In this scene, the film not only presents a narrative as information by making the interaction and conversation between Alvy and Annie visible and audible, but its reflection—expressed through the subtitle's autonomy from the dialogue, thereby observing the difference between filmic utterance and one of its media—also invites the audience to consider the meaning of subtitles as an identity of filmic communication and what the subversion of this identity in the scene means.

Filmic reflection also appears in another scene from *Annie Hall*, in which Alvy, while waiting in line at a film theater, overhears a man giving flawed interpretations of Marshall McLuhan's media theory to a female companion. Frustrated, Alvy steps out of the queue and speaks directly to the camera, complaining about the nonsense the man has been saying. The man approaches the camera as well, defending his freedom of speech while addressing the audience. To add a layer of filmic reflection to the interruption of the film's first-order observation thus caused, Allen walks toward a banner and pulls McLuhan himself from behind it to testify that the man has no idea about his theory, which McLuhan does. It is as if the filming suddenly pauses to allow a real-life figure to appear in front of a camera that continues rolling, but is no longer capturing scripted, planned scenes. In doing so, the film thematizes the difference between its utterance and its production circumstances within the environment of filmic communication.

The second reason behind the absence of rupturing tendencies in New Hollywood can be traced, as the observations in this chapter have shown, to the strong structural coupling between Hollywood cinema and the economic system. In the structural coupling of film art and the economy in West Germany, it was predominantly art that sensed the crisis. As a result, it resorted to rupturing the formal, artistic structure of filmic utterance in order to sound the alarm about a potential diminishment of film's autopoiesis. In contrast, in Hollywood, the crisis was primarily felt by the economy.

Intending to break away from identities maintained by their contemporary filmic communication, thereby radically rupturing the structure of film, New German filmmakers understood that such a break would simultaneously harm film art's structural coupling with the economy. This was the reason they declared a manifesto, both alluding to the artistic and financial crisis of film and promising to overcome this crisis by producing economically successful films. They then exercised their jurisdictional powers through Alexander Kluge to secure state funding for filmic forms that were too radically different from conventional forms to attract investment. These filmmakers, belonging to both feminist and non-feminist new waves, persisted with their exceptional formal choices for nearly a decade, despite their precarious financial situation, because, above all, they were mediating the resonance of society's contradictions and conflicts with film art.

In contrast, Hollywood filmmakers never had to exert comparable effort to secure funding for their films, as Hollywood cinema was coupled with a private economy solely focused on drawing viewers back to theaters, thereby rescuing film's economic existence. The economic system treats film as a commodity. When this commodity failed to align with audience preferences, Hollywood producers responded by allowing a range of diverse variations, speculating on which of them might ensure the success of filmic communication, so that they would select and stabilize it.

As systems in the environment of film art, the economic and legal systems in the United States worked together to facilitate variation by disbanding the Production Code, lifting censorship, and investing in advanced technical innovations that improved sound and image quality. These developments enabled the production of more engaging and entertaining visuals and sounds. They also granted venturing films the formal freedom to align their narratives with the critical communications and lifestyles of their audiences through depicting intimacy, drug use, and rebellion against traditional norms.

Because the economy played the central role in rescuing the autopoiesis of film in Hollywood, the art system did not perceive a crisis threatening its own autopoiesis. Consequently, it saw no need to raise the alarm by rupturing conventional structures of filmic communication. Instead, Hollywood underwent two smooth and parallel lines of change: one composed of venturing films that did not contribute to the full evolution of the new wave, as their variations were not selected and stabilized; the other consisting of films that successfully selected more complex narratives as a variation on the Hollywood cinema of the 1950s, thus advancing the departure of the mainstream film system in the United States toward a secure autopoiesis.

In summary, while it was primarily the art system within the structural coupling of art and economy in New German Cinema that sought to produce "other films" by rupturing the established structure of filmic utterance, the economic system in the same coupling in New Hollywood aimed to produce "better films"—that is, to manufacture filmic products with the same structure as before, but with improved formal quality and updated information.

It is conceivable, however, that the art system in the United States during the 1950s and 1960s resonated much more strongly with social contradictions and sounded the alarm in a different area than film, namely in painting and through pop art. This raises the question: was pop art the rupture through which the American art system challenged its established structures in this period? Providing an answer to this question falls beyond the scope of this book.

2.3

New Iranian Cinema

Compared to New Hollywood, there is even less consensus among researchers of New Iranian Cinema—who are also fewer in number than those studying other new waves introduced here—regarding its emergence and decline, or the films considered part of the new wave. While Naficy (2011) primarily designates a group of aesthetically diverse films produced before the 1979 revolution as the new wave, Bose (2021) divides the Iranian New Wave into three smaller waves, spanning from the 1960s to the 2000s. For others like Issa and Whitaker (1999), Afsahi (2005), Sadeghi and Rad (2014), and Talebinejad (2018), the Iranian New Wave is instead regarded as the cumulative body of work by certain directors who began their filmmaking careers before the 1979 revolution and continued producing films well beyond it, in some cases even into the 2000s.

In this chapter, as in the previous two, a new light is cast on New Iranian Cinema—one that moves away from canon formation and the delineation of epochs, focusing instead on examining Iranian New Wave Cinema to see whether the tendencies of venture, rupture, and departure, which emerged from a Luhmannian analysis of the development of New German Films, can also be recognized in its evolution parallel to social contradictions and conflicts.

Contradiction and Conflict in Iranian Society, 1960s and 1970s

Similar to the preceding national societies, Iranian society was also grappling with contradictions and conflicts in the 1960s and 1970s, during which the Iranian New Wave emerged. However, in the case of Iran, these conflicts escalated into a revolution that replaced the existing political system—a monarchy—with a new one, namely an "Islamic Republic." The roots of these conflicts lay in the Second World War era, when Soviet and British forces invaded and occupied Iran, violating its neutrality in order to use it as a supply route to Russia during the war. The Iranian monarch of the time, Riẕā

Pahlavī, was forced into exile in 1941 by British and Soviet forces, who feared that "the shah would cooperate with Nazi Germany to rid himself of their tutelage" (*Mohammad Reza Shah Pahlavi* 2025). Riẕā Pahlavī abdicated the throne in favor of his son, Muḥammad Riẕā Pahlavī, and was initially exiled to Mauritius. He later moved to Johannesburg, where he died in 1944.

Riẕā Pahlavī was regarded as a powerful tyrant within Iranian society. He was ruthless toward his critics and persistent in introducing European lifestyles and technology to Iranian society in the name of "modernizing" the country. His son, by contrast, inherited the throne from a much more vulnerable position, under the condition that he would cooperate seamlessly with the Allies. According to Abrahamian:

> In return for keeping control of the armed forces, Muhammad Reza Shah agreed to cooperate fully with the Allies. [...] He [Bullard, the British representative] wrote that the Allies had agreed to give the young shah a "trial (period) subject to good behavior, which would include the granting of extensive reforms, the restoration to the nation of the property illegally acquired by his father, and the exclusion of all his brothers from Persia."
>
> (2008, 98)

With the onset of the Cold War, the Soviets' direct influence on Iranian politics began to wane. Instead, the Soviet Union shifted its focus to widespread cultural and ideological efforts among Iranian citizens, including support for the first official Marxist group in Iran, *Ḥizb-i Tūdah* (the Party of the Masses), which was founded in 1941. Meanwhile, Muḥammad Riẕā Pahlavī, the young monarch, became increasingly dependent on the Americans for all major decisions he made, primarily for two reasons. First, he feared that the Allies might remove him—just as they had removed his powerful father—if he failed to protect their interests in Iran. Second, he was hopeful that "the rising power of the United States would give his country some respite from the long-standing imperial ambitions of Britain and Russia" (Alvandi 2014, 7).

Particularly during the first two decades of the Cold War, Pahlavī consistently sought the approval of American diplomats who were in Tehran. On one occasion, he falsely claimed that his American-backed prime minister, Aḥmad Qavām, was corrupt in order to gain their consent for Qavām's dismissal. However, they refused to grant it, and Pahlavī was forced to yield to their decision (Milani 2011, 128).

The involvement of American and British diplomats in the internal affairs of the country became problematic in 1953. This shift occurred after the highly popular and respected prime minister at the time, Muḥammad Muṣaddiq, nationalized Iran's oil industry in 1951 and dissolved the parliament in August 1953 due to his power conflicts with Pahlavī. The tensions had arisen because Pahlavī was interfering in parliamentary decisions, which lay beyond his legal authority. After dissolving the parliament, Muṣaddiq initiated a referendum to legitimize his decision to reduce Pahlavī's political role to that of a constitutional monarch. Pahlavī, in turn, feared that Muṣaddiq would use his authority to abolish the monarchy altogether and attempt to establish a republic instead.

With the support of the American CIA (Central Intelligence Agency) and the British SIS (Secret Intelligence Service), Pahlavī orchestrated a *coup d'état* against Muṣaddiq's government, placed him under house arrest, and initiated a new course of governance that extended even further beyond the constitutional limits imposed on his power (Gasiorowski 2004). From this point on, Pahlavī personally influenced every decision made in the parliament, and opposition organizations—most notably *Ḥizb-i Tūdah* and smaller left-leaning groups—were subjected to intensified surveillance and censorship, as they were also perceived as threats. Intellectual Iranian citizens who held Muṣaddiq in high regard and had hoped he would ultimately replace the dictatorial monarchy with a more democratic political system saw their political expectations shattered by the *coup*. They attributed their disappointment both to Pahlavī and to the foreign powers that had orchestrated the *coup* on his behalf.

The Iranian public's political, economic, and cultural expectations were rejected one more time through the so-called *Inqilāb-i Sifīd* (White Revolution), which Pahlavī launched in 1967 under pressure from the American president, John F. Kennedy. Intended as a program of socioeconomic reform, *Inqilāb-i Sifīd* focused primarily on land reform, redistributing property owned by large landowners to sharecroppers and small-scale cultivators (Pesaran 2014). As a result, nearly 90 percent of Iranian sharecroppers became landowners, although most lacked the knowledge or capital to cultivate their land effectively (Hooglund 1982, 73). Consequently, many former farmers migrated to major cities in search of employment in the rapidly growing industries. Unable to afford housing, they settled in slums on the urban periphery. These slum-dwellers, marked by poverty, vulnerability to criminality, and drug addiction, soon became a visible symbol of the stark class divide between workers and the middle class. The left-leaning opposition groups, supported mainly by students, voiced their protest against this growing inequality in any way they could.

Inqilāb-i Sifīd faced opposition from another front as well, particularly from the Shiite clergy and their followers. The clergy held substantial land through *vaqf* (charitable trusts), a position that had long aligned them with the landed aristocracy. The reform not only stripped them of this privilege, which they had held for over a century, but also granted women the right to vote. In addition, women and men who had received a secondary education diploma were now permitted to fulfill their two-year mandatory military service—compulsory for both sexes—by serving as teachers in impoverished rural areas through participation in the so-called *Sipāh-i Dānish* (Literacy Corps). As Floor reports, some Shiite clergy and their supporters found both developments for women unacceptable and considered them contrary to the laws of Islam (Floor 1980, 509; 519). Protesting primarily these changes regarding land ownership and women's rights, and supported by the conservative Shiite population, Rūḥallāh Khumiynī, a charismatic Shiite cleric, began mobilizing public resistance against Pahlavī and his *Inqilāb-i Sifīd*, which was once again attributed to the American government that had demanded and encouraged it.

Given the unmet political expectations of leftist and Shiite groups, as well as the financial corruption of Muḥammad Riẕā Pahlavī and his family—which, as Milani (2011, 233 ff.) describes, was not unknown to the public—a wave of escalating street protests and strikes began in 1978, culminating in the 1979 revolution that overthrew the monarchy. As Nikazmerad recounts, key events began on January 9, 1978, when police fired into a crowd in Qom, killing several protesters and sparking widespread outrage. This was followed by the February 18–19 riots in Tabriz, marking a turning point in the protest movement. As the year progressed, numerous demonstrations, strikes, and riots erupted across the country, particularly after major incidents such as the massacre of protesters on *Jum'ah-yi Sīyāh* (Black Friday; September 8, 1978). On this day, as Nikazmerad reports, the security forces opened fire on a large crowd of protesters in Tehran's Zhaleh Square, killing and injuring hundreds. The opposition continued to gain momentum through large-scale strikes, including a crippling oil workers' strike that began in September and continued into late 1978, halting the country's oil exports and severely damaging the economy (Nikazmerad 1980). The forceful suppression of the protests triggered conflicts between the demonstrators and the political system, ultimately resulting in the overthrow of the monarchy. On January 16, 1979, Muḥammad Riẕā Pahlavī left Iran with his family. On February 1 of the same year, Rūḥallāh Khumiynī returned to Iran from his exile in France and established the new political system.

New Iranian Cinema first emerged in the 1960s, around the time Pahlavī introduced the *Inqilāb-i Sifīd*. It accompanied the contradictions and conflicts within Iranian society that culminated in the 1979 revolution, experienced a period of stagnation during the Iran-Iraq war, and continued to flourish afterward.

Evolution of Film Art in Iranian Society, between the 1960s and 1980s

Filmfarsi

According to Naficy (2011, 197 ff.; 261 ff.), two film genres primarily dominated the Iranian film market in the early 1960s: the so-called *stewpot* and the *tough-guy* film genres. With *Ganj-i Qārūn* (Qārūn's Treasure; 1965) as its archetype, the stewpot genre was named so because of the "celebrated sequence in which two male buddies avidly devour lamb-and-potato stew, *abgusht*, the traditional lower-class meal, while singing a happy, humorous, and danceable tune" (Naficy 2011, 197). Figure 38 displays a screenshot from this scene. Stewpot films delivered melodramatic love stories shaped by polarized and stereotypical characters, romance-specific twists of fate, strokes of luck, music and dance scenes, and a happy ending.

Figure 38 Screenshot from *Ganj-i Qārūn*. The scene that gave the stewpot genre its name.

Ganj-i Qārūn follows Qārūn, a wealthy man burdened by regret after abandoning his wife and son decades earlier. Though surrounded by luxury, he feels spiritually empty and attempts suicide in Isfahan, only to be rescued by two humble men—'Alī Bīgham (Carefree 'Alī) and Ḥasan Jighjighah (Ḥasan the Rattler)—who take him into their modest home. Their warmth and tradition-filled life stand in contrast to Qārūn's isolation. Unaware that 'Alī is his son, Qārūn gradually bonds with them. Masquerading as Ismāl Bīkallah (Ismāl the Brainless), Qārūn begins to share in their streetwise joy, even joining in their songs that express a philosophy of contentment and spontaneity. Meanwhile, Shīrīn, a wealthy young woman, fakes an engagement to Qārūn's fictional son to escape an arranged marriage, only to cross paths with Qārūn and his companions. This leads to a farcical plan where 'Alī impersonates the son, triggering a chain of comedic and romantic encounters. Eventually, Qārūn's former wife, Zīnat, regains her identity, and Qārūn confesses his past mistakes, seeking forgiveness. In a climactic emotional scene, Qārūn reveals himself to 'Alī during a public confrontation, leading to reconciliation and mutual recognition. All pretenses fall away and family ties are restored.

Tough-guy films, on the other hand, center on the tragic life story of a solitary male character who aligns himself with justice and morality and who must seek vengeance or defend himself alone against wrongdoings and oppression perpetrated by evil individuals. These films portray an idealized version of masculinity. The protagonists of these films possess sensitive souls and are attuned to love and affection. However, they are also compelled to behave in a rough, fearless, and strong manner, which prevents them from openly expressing their emotions. As a result, when they must choose between love and the achievement of their goal, they always opt for the latter. Since the tough guys are frequently drawn into conflicts against evil, these films are filled with numerous fight scenes. The women in these cinematic narratives can, in turn, assume three main roles: "female blood relations occupy the highest and the most sacred position and are regarded as pure, virtuous, and sexually off limits; wives come next in rank, sharing some of the attributes of blood relations; followed by women entertainers, who are fair game sexually" (Naficy 2011, 289).

Qiyṣar (1969), a stereotype of the tough-guy genre, follows the story of a man named Qiyṣar, who returns to his hometown to find out that his sister has committed suicide after being raped by a group of men, who have later killed his revengeful brother as well. This big loss sets Qiyṣar on a path of vengeance. Qiyṣar discovers that the man who assaulted his sister is part of a criminal gang composed of three brothers. Although he is deeply in love with his fiancée, who has been waiting for his return to get married, his need for revenge forces him to suppress his emotions and adopt a tough, ruthless exterior. He becomes embroiled in violent confrontations as he hunts down two of the perpetrators. In the final confrontation, Qiyṣar faces Manṣūr, the man who wronged his sister, and is fatally wounded.

The combination of stewpot and tough-guy films, along with the comedic melodramas produced as early as the 1940s and popular until the late 1960s, is referred to as *filmfarsi* (Farsi-language films) in critical film-historical literature. The exact origin of this term remains unclear. According to Naficy, Amīr Hūshang Kāvūsī, a French-educated film critic, coined the term *filmfarsi* in 1953 to describe this overarching genre of Iranian films. Kāvūsī criticized these films as "formless, structureless, and storyless," claiming that the only element they retained from Iranian culture was their Farsi language (Naficy 2011, 149). Naficy also mentions another critic who offered a more precise definition of *filmfarsi*, characterizing it as popular Iranian cinema produced between 1948 and 1978 that was "a mixture of melodrama and popular tales" (Naficy 2011, 149). *Filmfarsi* narratives often revolved around the struggle between good and evil, highlighting contrasts such as wealth versus poverty, honorable behavior versus dishonor, and rural traditions versus urban modernity (Naficy 2011, 149).

Similar to many popular film genres throughout the global history of cinema, the primary goal of *filmfarsi* was to present a cohesive narrative that, for its filmic utterance, relied on the continuity system. Melodramatic Iranian films (such as *Sulṭān-i qalb-hā* (King of Hearts; 1968)) and stewpot films in 1950s and 1960s Iran followed a romance-based plot structure, in which luck and chance played pivotal roles in driving both the characters' conflicts and their resolutions. Consequently, these films did not require a complex storyline shaped by the characters' desires and flaws. Similarly, in the narratives of tough-guy films that were popular in the same decades, the protagonists' actions were not driven by free will and individual decision but by the social norms of morality and masculinity that they embodied.

In line with these properties, characterization in the *filmfarsi* narrative was typified and dichotomous, lacking psychological complexity. The distinctions between good and evil were clear-cut, and gender roles were predetermined, aligning with traditional social customs rather than challenging them. Moreover, many *filmfarsi*s lacked a strong textual foundation. As Naficy reports, the production of many of these films "would begin without a completed screenplay, with one that was directly copied from another film, or with a few notes that the director had jotted down on a piece of paper. Such an ad hoc manner of developing screenplays also factored into the repetitive structures and narrative lacunae and confusion of the films" (2011, 217).

Filmfarsi's *mise-en-scène* was characterized by the staging of film stars of the time, such as Fardīn, Nāṣir Malik Muṭīʿī, Liylā Furūhar, Pūrī Banāyī, and Shahnāz Tihrānī. Formally, extradiegetic music was consistently employed to underscore the emotional tone of the scenes—whether in melancholic moments of lovers parting, during fight sequences, chase and escape scenes, or at the point of a happy ending. In tough-guy films, speedy zoom-ins were frequently utilized to convey the shock experienced by characters upon receiving distressing news. Additionally, many fight scenes were extensively edited in order to capture both the action and the reactions of bystanders from multiple angles. Finally, nearly all *filmfarsis* were dubbed in studio by professional voice actors, since the stars of these films, while visually appealing, had received no professional acting education and had not trained their voices for cinematic performance. The fact that the dialogues were not recorded on set was evident in the cinematography and sound-image editing. The actors' lip movements did not sync with their voices, and the tone and emotion of the speech failed to align with their facial expressions and gestures. Additionally, in scenes featuring singing, the voice of a professional singer was heard instead of that of the professional voice actor who otherwise dubbed the film character.

While *filmfarsis* with these narrative and formal characteristics remained popular and did not experience a financial crisis—unlike the crises that occurred with popular films in the United States and West Germany—counter-currents began to emerge in Iranian cinema, paralleling the growing contradictions experienced by dissatisfied citizens. These new films were marked by their ventures toward an alternative storytelling approach.

Venturing Films of New Iranian Cinema

The evolution of New Iranian Cinema, like the new waves discussed previously, began with a group of films' venture toward updating their communication topics and aligning them with contemporary discourse on the contradictions observed within Iranian society. These contradictions were mainly voiced by protesting students in their public gatherings and pamphlets. They referred to the gap between the expectations of dissatisfied citizens regarding political freedom of speech and economic and gender equality on the one hand, and the decisions of the political system regarding censorship beside the dominant economic and bureaucratic corruption on the other (Matin-asgari 2002, 26 ff.). These students also criticized Britain and the United States for their imperialist support of the monarchy and efforts against the democratization process of Iranian society through the 1953 *coup*, which had long-term consequences in Iran (Teague 2024).

These films were venturing because it was uncertain whether viewers would accept their narrative structure, which was more complex than that of the popular *filmfarsi*. Furthermore, given the censorship of any form of communication that could be associated with communism in 1960s Iranian society, it was unclear whether these films, with their critical subject matter, would be permitted for production and screening.

The topics of these venturing films, later categorized as new wave, included the lack of adequate social support for the working class; the vast financial and cultural divide between life in slums, villages, and rural areas, and the lives of middle-class and affluent citizens in major cities; dysfunction and corruption within the justice system; widespread bureaucratic corruption; and political censorship and repression of free speech. Venturing films approached these issues through various narrative strategies, including literary adaptation and the use of allegory and symbolism. The adaptation of contemporary critical works of literature contributed not only to updating these films' communication topics but also to the maturity and complexity of their narratives.

Literary Adaptations

Even more prominent than the new wave of cinema was the new literary wave in Iran, which had already begun in the 1920s with figures such as Muḥammad 'Ali Jamālzādah and Nīmā Yūshīj. In the 1960s, the formally progressive new-wave poets, novelists, and playwrights began to adopt a more critical tone in their works, addressing discrimination and corruption in the Iranian society, while simultaneously gaining greater sophistication and maturity in both narrative structure and linguistic style. Among the new-wave writers who were contemporaneous with the cinematic new wave were Buzurg 'Alavī, communist fiction writer; Ṣādiq Chūbak, writer of short fiction, drama, and novels; Aḥmad Shāmlū, poet, journalist, and translator; Hūshang Gulshīrī, fiction writer, critic, and editor; Ṣamad Bihrangī, short story writer and folklorist; Ghulāmḥusiyn Sāʿidī, communist dramatist and fiction writer; and Furūgh Farrukhzād, poet—just to name a few.[1]

To contribute to the richness of their narratives and to engage with socially critical topics, some prominent new-wave films in Iran in the 1960s and 1970s ventured to adapt the works of these writers into filmic communication. The film directors even collaborated at times directly with the authors in adapting their work for the screen. This is why, in Jahed's opinion, "cinematic, dramatic and literary discourses enriched each other" in 1960s and 1970s Iranian society (2022, 95).

The most significant literary adaptations of this period include *Gāv* (The Cow; 1969), *Ārāmish dar ḥoẕūr-i dīgarān* (Tranquility in the Presence of Others; 1972), *Tangsīr* (1973), *Dāyirah-yi mīnā* (The Cycle; 1975), and the television series *Dā'ī jān Nāpil'un* (My Uncle Napoleon; 1976). The filmmakers' commitment to conveying the novels' narrative with the greatest possible fidelity led to a highly refined implementation of the continuity system in their films, while also contributing to the complexity and diversity of film techniques and *mise-en-scène*. This required, for instance, the employment of more professional actors capable of portraying sophisticated literary characters, which stood in stark contrast to the typified, unrealistic figures common in *filmfarsi*. New camera and editing techniques also had to be adopted in order to reference the mental states of the characters—an aspect that had not previously been thematized in *filmfarsi*.

Gāv, directed by Dariush Mehrjui and widely recognized as the first film of New Iranian Cinema, was an adaptation of the short story of the same name by Ghulāmḥusiyn Sāʿidī.[2] The film tells the story of Masht Ḥasan, a villager who owns the only cow in his rural village. He shares a deep emotional bond with the animal, that is his sole property, and treats it as a companion and source of identity. When the cow unexpectedly dies during his absence, the villagers—fearing Masht Ḥasan's reaction—hide the truth and claim the animal ran away. Upon his return, Masht Ḥasan descends into psychological collapse, refusing to believe the cow is gone and gradually coming to believe that he himself is the cow. As the villagers attempt to take him to a larger town for treatment, he panics, attempts to flee, but falls into a ravine and dies. *Gāv* distinguished itself not only through its surrealist narration and its reference to the poverty of Iranian village dwellers but also through the professional acting techniques employed by its cast. ʿIzzatullāh Intiẓāmī portrays the main character, who begins as psychologically stable but gradually descends into delusion. These developments in *mise-en-scène* and narrative distinguished *Gāv* from contemporary *filmfarsi*s, which were characterized by poor acting, polarized characters, and formulaic, romance-like narrative structures.

Ārāmish dar ḥoẕūr-i dīgarān, an adaptation of another short story by Ghulāmḥusiyn Sāʿidī with the same title by Nasser Taqvai, follows a retired general who sells his house and business in the village and relocates to Tehran with his young wife to live with his two daughters. The general suffers from a psychological condition that progressively worsens after the move, as he witnesses the corrupt and disoriented lifestyle of his daughters.

He is eventually committed to a sanatorium. The film employs formal innovations—against the background of *filmfarsi* structure—to depict the general's gradual psychological disintegration, giving the narrative a surrealist dimension. One such innovation is the shot/reverse shot sequence in the scene where the general converses with his daughters' maid. In this sequence, the general is shown in shots with the camera zooming out, while the maid, who is beheading a rooster for dinner during their conversation, is depicted in shots with the camera zooming in. This sequence breaks when the general hurls a flowerpot at the maid, prompting her to flee the house in a state of panic. This visual device suggests the general's increasing detachment from concrete reality and his worsening mental condition.

Ārāmish dar ḥoẓūr-i dīgarān criticizes the seemingly Westernized yet ultimately hollow and meaningless lifestyle of Iranian city dwellers, exemplified by the general's daughters in Tehran. They are absorbed in demanding daytime jobs and spend their nights at parties, engaging in extramarital affairs and superficial intellectual discussions. This lifestyle contrasts sharply with the demeanor of the general's wife—a modest yet self-assured young woman from a village, who retains her strong sense of identity among the "modern" young people of the capital. She remains devoted to her elderly and mentally ill husband until the end and continues to live as a solitary outsider among the capital's residents after committing him to the sanitarium.

Tangsīr, based on Ṣādiq Chūbak's novel with the same title, is another venturing film set in the coastal province of Bushehr. The story follows Zār Muḥammad, a hardworking man who entrusts his life savings to four local businessmen also holding positions of power. When he requests the return of his money, they dismiss him, claiming it was lost in a bad investment. Feeling humiliated and betrayed, Zār Muḥammad embarks on a relentless quest for justice, confronting the men responsible one by one. The film's portrayal of Zār Muḥammad's transformation from a victim to a vengeful man reflects a broader narrative of individual defiance against systemic injustice, as experienced by members of the deprived social classes in Iranian society during the 1970s. The film stands out for its complex and critical narrative, professional acting, and masterful camera work in service of the continuity system, employing a range of normal and telephoto lenses to capture both calm and action scenes. Furthermore, its minimalist use of extradiegetic music, in stark contrast to the exaggeratedly dramatic or melancholic, multi-instrumental extradiegetic soundtracks typical of *filmfarsi*, is remarkable. A four-note theme played on the santur modestly yet effectively heightens the narrative's tension, without attempting to manipulate the viewers' emotions by bearing the entire emotional weight of the scenes, compensating for weak acting performances.

From Political Censorship to Allegory and Symbolism in Film

As Naficy (2011) frequently emphasizes throughout his book, state censorship of films and other artistic utterances during the reign of Muḥammad Riẓā Pahlavī was severe. Any content that could be interpreted as critical of injustice and inequality in Iran, or of the government's moral and financial corruption, was denounced as Bolshevik-influenced and consequently banned. Films portraying poverty and life in the slums were subject to censorship, as they not only hinted at the significant divide between the middle class and the wealthy on one side and slum dwellers on the other—a critique associated with Marxism—but also projected an image of Iranian life that conflicted with the one the Pahlavī monarchy sought to present to the world: that of a modern and industrialized nation. Naficy reports that *SAVAK* (*Sāzmān-i Iṭṭilāʿāt va Amnīyyat-i Kishvar*, National Security and Information Service), and *Vizārat-i Farhang va Hunar* (Ministry of Culture and Art) exercised strict control over such representations in film (2011). According to Jahed, they would either order the re-shooting of specific scenes and alterations to the plot—as in the case of *Gavazn-hā* (The Deer; 1974)—or they would ban the film entirely (2022, 40 ff.).

This type of structural coupling between the art system and politics through censorship—which was not present in West German and American societies—led to a unique tendency among venturing Iranian films to employ indirect modes of communication through allegory and symbolism in order to surpass censorship, because, after all, "allegory arises most powerfully at times of sociopolitical unrest or upheaval" (Langford 2019, 13). I consider this tendency a venture, not a rupture, because allegory and symbolism are interpretive approaches to the narrative and do not directly correspond to filmic form and structure. In other words, they constitute second-order information derived from the film's first-order content—that is, its narrative as presented.[3] Allegorical and symbolic ventures in Iranian films did not disrupt the established formal structure of *filmfarsi*, which followed the continuity system. Instead, they offered narratives that could be interpreted as a critique of political power relations and cultural norms.

In literary theory, allegory is defined as an "'extended metaphor' in which characters, actions and scenery are systematically symbolic, referring to spiritual, political, psychological confrontations" (Sage 2006, 4). Hence, a narrative is (mis)understood as allegorical when the audience couples their understanding with meanings that are familiar to them from a particular cultural context—that is, through prior exposure to a set of communications that consistently generate specific meanings. A clear example of allegorical interpretations of a film is found in some analyses of *Au hasard Balthazar* (Balthazar, at Random; 1966). According to these readings, delivered by critics familiar with Christianity, the donkey Balthazar in this film symbolizes a Christ-like figure, embodying the suffering and innocence of Jesus. From an allegorical perspective, Balthazar's journey through various owners and his eventual death symbolizes the Stations of the Cross, while his burden of carrying goods is seen as a symbol of Christ bearing the cross.

As an iconic film of the Iranian New Wave, *Ragbār* (Downpour; 1972) constructs nuanced symbolic figures and allegorical constellations. The film's plot follows a young schoolteacher, Mr. Ḥikmatī, who moves to a suburb and begins teaching at a local school. He falls in love with 'Āṭifah, the elder sister of one of his students, after meeting her for the first time in the teachers' lounge. In doing so, he enters into rivalry with Raḥīm, the local butcher, who has been financially supporting 'Āṭifah, her brother, and their elderly mother in the hope that she will one day accept his marriage proposal.

Mr. Ḥikmatī transforms not only 'Āṭifah's life through his gentle and romantic expressions of love—in stark contrast to the coarse, traditional demeanor of the butcher—but also the culture of the school itself. He accomplishes this by being kind to his students instead of punishing them for their naughtiness, and publicly expressing his affection for 'Āṭifah, thereby challenging the taboo against romantic relationships between men and women within the town's traditional, patriarchal community. Furthermore, he spends his free time renovating the school's dilapidated assembly hall with his bare hands, making it suitable for hosting performative events.

As a result of his conduct, the students—who initially viewed his love for a woman as a sign of weakness within their male-dominated cultural setting—gradually develop affection and respect for Mr. Ḥikmatī. The school principal, who is equally impressed by Mr. Ḥikmatī's character, suggests that he marry his daughter, but the teacher declines the offer. Following this rejection, and during the school celebration in the newly restored hall, it is Mr. Ḥikmatī—rather than the principal—who receives the students' enthusiasm and applause. Consumed by rage and jealousy, and fearing that Mr. Ḥikmatī might ultimately liberate the minds of the students, the principal decides that he must be dismissed and reassigned to a different post in another location.

At the school celebration, Mr. Ḥikmatī steps onto the stage after the students' enthusiastic applause and notices a mysterious man in the audience wearing unusual sunglasses, who is observing the proceedings (Figure 39). This figure symbolically stands for the *SAVAK* agents, who were omnipresent during the Pahlavī reign. These agents were frequently aligned with corrupt, pro-government individuals—symbolized here by the school principal—in order to intimidate or eliminate those who, like Mr. Ḥikmatī in this film, advocated for egalitarian and democratic ideas.

Following the school celebration, Mr. Ḥikmatī receives an official notice from the Ministry of Education regarding his transfer. As he leaves the town, it is the same man with the sunglasses who pulls the cart carrying his belongings. At this moment, ʻĀṭifah is faced with a critical decision: to leave her younger brother behind in the impoverished neighborhood and depart with Mr. Ḥikmatī, or to renounce her love for him, remain selflessly with her brother, and marry Raḥīm out of financial necessity.

Mr. Ḥikmatī—with his enlightened perspectives on education, pedagogy, and love—symbolizes the leftist Iranian students of the 1970s and their ideals of enlightening and mobilizing impoverished citizens with limited access to education in the narrative. He is depicted as an educated and well-read individual who willingly lives among the traditional and insular residents of the town, patiently working to raise their awareness despite the prevailing class divide. In doing so, he exemplifies the ideal disposition expected of a left-leaning intellectual activist in the context of 1970s Iran. His modest yet resolute confrontation with the traditional, patriarchal values that continued to dominate Iranian society—and that prevented it from rising against the monarchy to demand equality and democracy—is symbolized through his rivalry with Raḥīm the butcher, who represents these outdated norms. Ultimately, the entire narrative serves as an allegorical representation of the leftist intellectuals in 1970s Iran, their attempts to awaken and mobilize the broader public, and their suppression by *SAVAK* in collusion with corrupt, influential government functionaries.

A later film by the same director, *Gharībah va mih* (The Stranger and the Fog; 1974), likewise presents an allegorical narrative. In this film, Āyat (lit. "sign" or "miracle"), a stranger, washes ashore unconscious in a boat near a coastal village. Upon waking, he tells the villagers that he does not know who he is or why he was unconscious. He recalls only that he had been fighting a group on the other side of the sea, and that they are now pursuing him. The villagers remain deeply skeptical of Āyat and refuse to accept him as one of their own. Nonetheless, he falls in love with Raʻnā, a single mother and the most beautiful woman in the village. Her husband, once the village's most skilled fisherman, had departed one day and never returned. Since then, Raʻnā has lived in mourning, dressed in black and emotionally withdrawn.

When Āyat finally wins Raʻnā's love and they marry, the villagers begin to accept him. Soon afterward, he encounters three men dressed in black who appear during the night. They tell him that he must return with them. Āyat, who does not recognize them or understand what they want, refuses to leave

Figure 39 Screenshot from *Ragbār.* Symbolic communication via *mise-en-scène.*

his wife. The following day, a large army of black-clad men arrives from the sea and violently attacks the village. Āyat joins the villagers in defending their home and succeeds in driving the invaders away. Yet afterward, he chooses to follow them in order to learn who they are and what they want from him. In doing so, Ra'nā's second husband, like her first, sets out on a journey from which there may be no return.

The diegetic setting of *Gharībah va mih* lacks a precise geographical reference. Although the film was shot in Asalem, a village in northern Iran, there are no explicit indications within the film regarding the village itself or the nationality of its inhabitants. Other elements of the *mise-en-scène*, such as the village dwellers' costumes and makeup, reveal no information about the geographical setting either. For instance, the male villagers' hairstyles resemble the Chonmage style featured in Japanese samurai films, with shaved sides and a single bundle of hair on top (Figure 40). Furthermore, the men in the village wear Japanese conical hats, and there are no indications of distinct Iranian costumes in the film. Additionally, the rituals and behaviors of the film's characters resemble those of various cultural backgrounds. As Naficy notes, "the villagers' customs are a mixture of Iranian, Islamic, Japanese, and African, encouraging allegorical speculations" (2011, 368).

Figure 40 Screenshot from *Gharībah va mih*. Costumes and makeup from non-Iranian nationalities.

There is no consensus among film critics on the allegorical meaning of *Gharībah va mih*'s narrative, although they unanimously agree that the film conveys an allegorical message. Naficy believes that the men dressed in black could represent "political and patriarchal fears and surveillance" (2011, 344). Further interpretive possibilities emerge from questions such as: "Does Ayat represent Bahaullah, the Baha'i prophet? Is Zakaria a symbol of the Mahdi, the Shiite messiah? Do the violent strangers represent modernity's disruptive forces [...]?" (cited in (Naficy 2011, 367)) Each assumption leads to a completely different interpretation of the film's narrative. However, regardless of the allegorical meaning viewers attribute to *Gharībah va mih*, one thing remains clear: the information conveyed by the film is not merely confined to a tragic love story. If the above speculations about whom the film characters symbolize are correct, then the film must have employed allegory not only to evade political censorship but also to withstand the outrage of Shiite viewers who considered Bahais (followers of Bahā'ullāh) blasphemers.

Asrār-i ganj-i darrah-yi jinnī (The Ghost Valley's Treasure Mysteries; 1974) is another film the narrative of which can be interpreted allegorically. The film's narrative follows a villager who accidentally uncovers a cave filled with gold in the middle of his field. His wife, believing that he has lost his sanity witnessing his overwhelming joy, leaves him and moves in with her brother, taking their young son with her. As the villager begins to sell portions of the treasure in Tehran, he becomes acquainted with a gold dealer. The dealer and his wife befriend the newly wealthy villager in an attempt to locate the source of the treasure. They advise him on the purchase of modern clothing, appliances, and furniture. They also orchestrate a marriage between the villager and their maid, so that she can gain his trust and report back on the treasure's location.

The villager transports his modern, and at times absurd, purchases—including a massive French horn—on the backs of donkeys from the city to his village, accompanied by his new fiancée. However, since his home is poorly constructed and lacks infrastructure such as gas, electricity, and plumbing for the appliances, he commissions the construction of a massive tower, in which he intends to live in the near future and be able to use the modern appliances he has purchased in the capital. The tower, with two spherical extensions, is a phallic symbol (Figure 41). It collapses because of a dynamite blast set off by road workers, just as the treasure is discovered by a group of greedy individuals from both the village and the city. Those who gather in the treasure cave end up killing one another, each attempting

Figure 41 Screenshot from *Asrār-i ganj-i darrah-yi jinnī.* Symbolic communication via *mise-en-scène.*

to seize the entire treasure for themselves. Following the destruction of the treasure and the collapse of the tower, the villager is boycotted by his two wives, the gold dealer and his wife, and by the entire village community. He is left completely alone and without any possessions.

In *Asrār-i ganj-i darrah-yi jinnī*, all characters and events, along with the elements of the *mise-en-scène*, function as symbols of the political and economic conditions in 1970s Iranian society: the villager stands for Muḥammad Riẓā Pahlavī; the treasure symbolizes Iran's rich oil reservoirs, the export of which led to the country's sudden economic boom in the 1970s; the gold dealer from the city and his affiliates represent the imperialist powers seeking to exploit the country's natural resources; the modern appliances the villager obtains in the capital signify the Western-oriented modernizations artificially and inappropriately introduced by Muḥammad Riẓā Pahlavī—reforms that projected an image of modernity while remaining incompatible with the country's traditional infrastructures; the villagers represent the Iranian citizens; and the phallic tower symbolizes the Shahyad Monument, which Muḥammad Riẓā Pahlavī commissioned in Tehran as a testament to his power and to the supposed economic flourishing of the nation—achievements that he attributed to himself. These symbols are woven into an allegorical narrative that serves as a critique of Pahlavī's domestic and foreign policies.

Finally, Allegory and symbolism are employed in *Sāyah-hā-yi boland-i bād* (Tall Shadows of the Wind; 1979). This adaptation of Hūshang Gulshīrī's short story *Ma'ṣūm-i Avval* (The First Innocent) opens with a tracking shot showing the inhabitants of a village standing in a windswept desert, collectively praying and calling upon God for a liberator. They then erect a scarecrow, its face wrapped in a white cloth. This scene cuts to a minibus that breaks down on its way to the village and can no longer proceed. While the driver's assistant and the passengers disembark and continue on foot to seek help, the driver, named 'Abdullāh, sits down by a stream to rest. There, he notices pebbles being thrown into the water. Through a shot/reverse shot sequence between 'Abdullāh and the distant scarecrow, the impression arises that the scarecrow itself is tossing the stones in an attempt to draw 'Abdullāh's attention. 'Abdullāh approaches the scarecrow, draws facial features on its cloth-wrapped head, and eventually places his own hat on it. The following day, the villagers remark on how skillfully 'Abdullāh has rendered his own face onto the scarecrow. From that point forward, mysterious events begin to unfold. Among them, 'Abdullāh's fiancée becomes possessed by evil spirits. Having wounded his foot with a shovel and now confined to bed with gangrene, 'Abdullāh asks his friend Muḥammad to destroy the scarecrow, convinced that it has acquired its malevolent power through a magical, mental connection with him. This, however, does not happen, and following his death, 'Abdullāh is buried beside the scarecrow.

In an attempt to interpret the film's allegorical narrative, Naficy writes:

> The film examines how power and fear are created, sustained, and destroyed by their subjects. Traditional societies, it posits, turn to mystical forces for answers. In the process, they create political leaders, religious guides, and deities, such as the scarecrow, whom they can no longer control. *Tall Shadows of the Wind* is ambivalent about intellectuals' abilities to combat these fears and figures.
>
> (2011, 378; emphasis in original)

Given that *Sāyah-hā-yi boland-i bād* was produced in the same year as the revolution, it is left to the viewers to determine whether they want to draw parallels between the film's allegorical narrative and the ideologies and dynamics that led to the overthrow of the Pahlavī monarchy and its replacement by a new political system under religious leadership.

Rupturing Films of New Iranian Cinema: Neorealism and Self-Reference

I observe a significant rupturing tendency in New Iranian Cinema, which adopted a completely different approach to challenging the established film structure compared to the rupturing films of New German Cinema. While *filmfarsi*s, particularly their fight and dance scenes, were heavily edited, these films avoided cuts as much as possible, relying instead on slow pans and tracking shots, or on long takes with a static camera. In contrast to *filmfarsi*s, the voices—spoken by mostly nonprofessional actors—and the ambient sounds in these rupturing films were recorded on set, without studio dubbing or added sound effects. In line with the same approach, extradiegetic music was either drastically minimized or completely excluded. Rather than interrupting the viewers' continuous engagement with the narrative through reflection—as was typical of New German Cinema's approach to rupturing the conventional film structure—the majority of rupturing Iranian films distanced themselves from as many formal elements of *filmfarsi* as possible. In doing so, they defied the expectations of audiences familiar only with *filmfarsi* conventions. If the rupturing films of New German Cinema entered into a battle against the established structure of filmic utterance, the rupturing films of New Iranian Cinema annulled this structure entirely and presented a cinema that was devoid of it. I refer to this rupturing tendency within the context of 1960s and 1970s Iranian cinema as *neorealism*.

Neorealism

By neorealism, I do not mean the new wave of cinema that emerged in Italy after the Second World War, but rather the structure of filmic utterance—composed of a set of identities of filmic communication—that was introduced and stabilized through the Italian Neorealism. This structure is characterized, on the level of *mise-en-scène*, by the use of nonprofessional actors instead of trained performers, filming on original locations rather than studio sets, and avoiding makeup and costumes created specifically for the production. On the level of sound design, it involves recording sound on set and avoiding extradiegetic music or other sound effects added in postproduction. In terms of camera work, neorealist films employ minimal camera movement or zooms. They rely mostly on medium, full, and long shots instead of capturing the details through close-ups and extreme close-ups. Thereby they make sure that the camera cannot "see" more than the human eye could see. Editing within each scene is also kept to a minimum, and cuts mostly serve the transition between two sequences.

The filmic identities that are absent from the structure of neorealist films are viewed by advocates of this formal policy as hindrances to the unmediated perception of the "reality" depicted by the film, and thus as mechanisms of emotional manipulation. According to Kracauer, the neorealist films "rely largely on the suggestive power of raw material brought in by the camera," (1960, 302) rather than seeking stylistic perfection through visual and auditory effects "artificially" appended to "reality."

The neorealist fraction of rupturing New Iranian Films maintains narratives that are as minimal and uneventful as possible, incorporating long takes of a realistic *mise-en-scène* to confront viewers with the hardships and poverty experienced by citizens in less industrially developed regions of Iran, as well as with the beauty of those landscapes. The open endings of these films represent a narrative break from the happy endings typical of stewpot and melodramatic films, where resolutions are achieved, or from the tragic endings of tough-guy films, which bring the plot to a close with the protagonist's death. Examples of Iranian rupturing neorealist films include *Musāfir* (The Traveler; 1974), *Sāzdahanī* (Harmonica; 1974), *Yik ittifāq-i sādah* (A Simple Event; 1974), and *Ṭabīʿat-i bījān* (Still Life; 1976).

The narrative of *Musāfir*, directed by Abbas Kiarostami, follows a boy named Qāsim, who is deeply passionate about soccer. Rather than studying for school, he devotes all of his free time either to playing soccer in the streets of his hometown or to reading soccer magazines. Upon learning that the national team will soon be playing in the capital, Tehran, he makes every effort to gather enough money for the journey and for a ticket to the match.

By stealing money from his parents, conning naive schoolboys with a fake photo shoot using a damaged camera, and eventually selling his soccer gear to other children in the neighborhood, he gathers enough funds to make his way to Tehran to see the game. After a sleepless night on his journey by bus, he arrives in Tehran and at the stadium too early. He falls asleep on the grass outside the soccer field and misses the match for which he had taken so many risks.

All the roles in this film are performed by nonprofessional actors. Qāsim's school is a real institution, and its routine activities are portrayed on screen—including the vaccination of the students and the classroom teacher by local health officials. The film reveals to the audience the harsh living conditions of an ambitious boy who, because of poverty, is denied the basic joy of attending a soccer match. His deceptive efforts to collect the money required for a trip to the capital and to buy a ticket are met with sympathy from the viewers, owing to the innocence of his yearning. The film's open ending rejects viewers' expectations, shaped by *filmfarsi*, that a clear resolution be provided. Instead, the audience remains engaged in second-order observation of the conclusion after the film ends, imagining what might happen to the poor village boy—now a stranger in the vast, chaotic capital city without any money to return home.

Sāzdahanī was also filmed on location, featuring a cast of nonprofessional actors who were residents of the village where the film was shot. The story unfolds in a village on Iran's southern coast, where parents in a wealthy family give their pampered child, ʿAbdulū, a harmonica to persuade him to take a bitter diarrhea remedy. The poorer village children, who have never seen or played a harmonica before, are willing to do anything just to play a few notes. ʿAbdulū takes advantage of their eagerness to dominate and humiliate them. He demands offerings or entertainment in exchange for a turn with the instrument. Among the children, Amīrū yearns for the harmonica most of all. He gives ʿAbdulū money, carries him on his back, and endures repeated humiliations. Eventually, however, he rises up against ʿAbdulū, seizes the harmonica, and throws it into the sea, liberating both himself and the other children from his oppression. The film ends with a freeze-frame of Amīrū's triumphant expression in a medium shot, as he stands waist-deep in the sea, following the harmonica's destruction. This is a powerful political statement that must have resonated with critical viewers amid the charged social atmosphere of 1970s Iran. In addition to the narrative, the *mise-en-scène* clearly illustrates the dire conditions of the village and its impoverished inhabitants.

Filmed in a village in northern Iran with nonprofessional actors, *Yik ittifāq-i sādah* portrays the life of a fisherman's son who, each day after school, must collect the fish his father has caught—without authorization—from the lake and deliver them to a shop. He then takes the payment to the pub where his father regularly eats and drinks vodka at midday. By evening, when the boy returns home, he is too exhausted to study, which often puts him at odds with his teacher. This cycle is repeated several times without variation. The only difference is that the boy's mother falls ill in the meantime. After his ailing mother passes away, little changes in the rhythm of his life, except that he is now permitted to eat at the pub with his father. Toward the film's conclusion, the father wants to buy a new suit for his son to express affection and bring him some comfort after the mother's death. However, he realizes in the shop that he cannot afford it. The two leave the clothing shop and walk silently down the street, bringing the film to an open end. The minimal, yet important, changes in their daily routine reflect the gradual emergence of an emotional bond between father and son. The film conveys the devastating poverty of working-class villagers in Iran simply by following its characters through the real settings in which they live.

Ṭabīʿat-i bījān is another film by the same director and also features a nonprofessional cast. In this film, an elderly signalman works daily along the railway tracks of northern Iran, while his wife stays at home, weaving carpets to supplement their modest income and preparing meals. In the evenings, the couple eats together in silence before going to bed—a routine with few variations that, much like in *Yik ittifāq-i sādah*, is repeated several times throughout the film. One day, the signalman is informed of his upcoming retirement and is consequently required to vacate the small house where he and his wife reside. He travels to the city to plead with his superiors to reconsider the decision. However, they dismiss his request and send him back. The film concludes with a scene in which the elderly couple piles their sparse belongings onto a cart and leaves their home. The film's bleak open ending, marked by the couple's unavoidable fate, serves as a pointed critique of the Pahlavī government's failure to ensure fair labor conditions and social security for workers.

In his neorealist style, Shahid-Saless, the director of *Yik ittifāq-i sādah* and *Ṭabīʿat-i bījān*, portrays poverty and aging with unflinching realism in full and medium shots (Figures 42 and 43). In addition to poverty and hardship, the landscape emerges as another protagonist in Shahid-Saless's films. His static camera frequently lingers at filming locations for extended periods, while ambient sounds are captured to allow the atmosphere of the setting to be experienced as authentically as possible by the viewers. He consistently uses long shots in both films, even when the figures within the frame are so distant, and therefore so small, that they are barely discernible (Figure 44).

Figure 42 Screenshot from *Yik ittifāq-i sādah*. Portraying poverty in neorealist films.

Figure 43 Screenshot from *Ṭabīʿat-i bījān*. Portraying age in neorealist films.

Figure 44 Screenshot from *Ṭabīʿat-i bījān*. Long shot of nature with barely visible figures (arrow added by me).

I will conclude this section by introducing a film made a decade earlier than the neorealist works discussed above. Directed by Forugh Farrokhzad, *Khānah sīyāh ast* (The House Is Black; 1961) neither fully conforms to the formal and narrative qualities characteristic of neorealist rupturing films nor clearly exhibits the kind of reflection that will be addressed in the next section. Farrokhzad, one of the few female directors of the Iranian prerevolutionary period and a prominent poet and critic of modern Persian literature, visited Bābā Bāghī Center—a leper colony near Tabriz, Iran—for the film's production. The film presents scenes from the daily lives of residents afflicted with leprosy: how they visit the clinic for treatment, receive their daily rations of food and medicine, dance, play, apply makeup, pray, celebrate weddings, and attend school.

On the auditory level, when the diegetic voices or songs of the residents are absent, a male voiceover (that of Ebrahim Golestan) provides medical information about leprosy's progression, prevention, and treatment. At several points in the film, Farrokhzad's own voice recites her poetry on the extradiegetic sound layer. Her melancholic voice and the emotional content of her poetry grant access to the sorrowful emotions of those afflicted by the disease, as they are captured by the camera.

The independence of image and sound, as well as the autonomy of individual shots in *Khānah sīyāh ast*, achieved through the absence of a narrative, disrupts the structure of both contemporary *filmfarsi* and documentary cinema with which Iranian audiences in 1961 were already well acquainted. While these genres typically focused on entertaining storytelling or delivering factual reports on people and places, *Khānah sīyāh ast*—through its formal choices—penetrates deeply into reality to reveal, beneath its harsh exterior, the essence of a poetic existence. The film's cinematography can be seen as a precedent for Iranian rupturing films with neorealist tendencies, in that it depicts the everyday lives of real leprosy patients without embellishment. However, it lacks the eventless yet present narrative and the continuity editing that gave Iranian neorealist films their slow and smooth rhythm. Given these qualities, Farrokhzad's film can be seen more as a standalone experimental innovation than as a contribution to the evolution of the new wave.

Reflexivity and Reflection

There were very few instances of reflexivity and reflection in New Iranian Films—so few, in fact, that they cannot be regarded as evidence of the Iranian film's intent to rupture its traditional, continuity-system-based structure through these modes of self-reference. Nonetheless, these instances merit brief consideration because they disrupt the continuous, straightforward narrative structure typical of *filmfarsi*, instead choosing to reflexively quote other films or genres, or to reflect on the distinction between themselves as filmic utterance and the environment of filmic communication.

Junūb-i shahr (South of the City; 1958) may be regarded as a reflexive film, as it critiques the popular tough-guy genre of its time. The film opens with a metadiegesis that aligns with the life of an Iranian middle-class family of the period. In this metadiegetic framework, a man goes to visit his friend, Farhād, after receiving an anonymous letter informing him that his wife had once worked as a dancer in a Tehran cabaret—a profession considered morally degrading for a respectable woman in 1950s Iran. Disturbed by the letter, he wants to seek advice from his friend, hoping to determine whether he should divorce his wife.

Upon the man's arrival, Farhād is not at home. He is received by Farhād's wife, to whom he explains the cause of his distress. Farhād's wife then reveals that she too had once worked as a cabaret dancer, driven by the necessities of life. As she begins to recount her past, the narrative shifts from the metadiegesis to the diegesis, in which the woman—whose former husband had died—danced in a cabaret in the impoverished southern district of Tehran to support herself and her young son. Two tough guys, both well-known figures in the southern district, fall in love with her and compete for her affection. In the end, she marries Farhād, the one who treats her with humanity, affection, and moral integrity, and who risks his life to protect her and her son from the other tough guy.

Once the woman has fully shared her life story with the family friend, the film returns to the metadiegesis of the living room where the two are conversing. At that moment, the apartment door opens and the woman's husband enters with a child. It is only then that the family friend realizes that her husband Farhād is the same one who was once a tough guy but has transformed through marriage. Farhād is now a respectable and devoted family man who has worked hard and helped his once-impoverished family rise into the middle class. Through this revelation, the family friend comes to understand that individuals are capable of change and self-improvement, and that one should not judge them based on a precarious past. He therefore decides not to divorce his own wife.

The shifts between the diegesis—which is a tough-guy film in its own right, characterized by traditional moral values and rigid gender roles—and the metadiegesis in *Junūb-i shahr* underscore the stark contrast between tough-guy films and a naturalistic portrayal of contemporary modern Iranian life, in which men and women hold more liberal views on gender roles and engage with one another respectfully. In the film's metadiegesis, as in actual urban life in 1958 Iran, men are not depicted as roaming the streets in search of conflict; instead, many pursue white-collar, middle-class careers. This functions as a pointed commentary on how outdated and diminished the tough-guy genre already was by the time the film was released.

Junūb-i shahr fell victim to censorship, despite its seemingly apolitical storyline. According to Naficy, "the Exhibition Committee ordered the film cut, [...] because the government, as the country's biggest lobby, was protecting its own public projection of Iran as modern and prosperous" (2011, 188). Therefore, the scenes depicting poverty had to be excluded from the film. Furthermore, as Naficy reports, Ghaffari—the film's director—was compelled to defend his film before several of the country's top government authorities, because the regime was reportedly concerned that the film's stark depiction of the lower classes could be exploited by the Soviets and local communist factions. The defense, however, was unsuccessful, and the film was banned five days after its premiere (Naficy 2011, 189).

In a later film, *Shab-i Qūzī* (Night of the Hunchback; 1965), Ghaffari experiments with the reflexivity of cinema by referencing international films through cinematography. The entire story revolves around a group of actors and dancers attempting to dispose of the corpse of their deceased hunchback companion. In the film's opening sequence, an extreme close-up shows the friends of the dead actor bringing a lit cigarette close to his open eye to check whether he is still alive—a moment reminiscent of *Un Chien Andalou*, in which a razor blade slices through a woman's eye (Figure 45).

Aside from its gesture toward Dadaist cinema, this allusion serves no specific narrative function. The decision to bring a threatening object

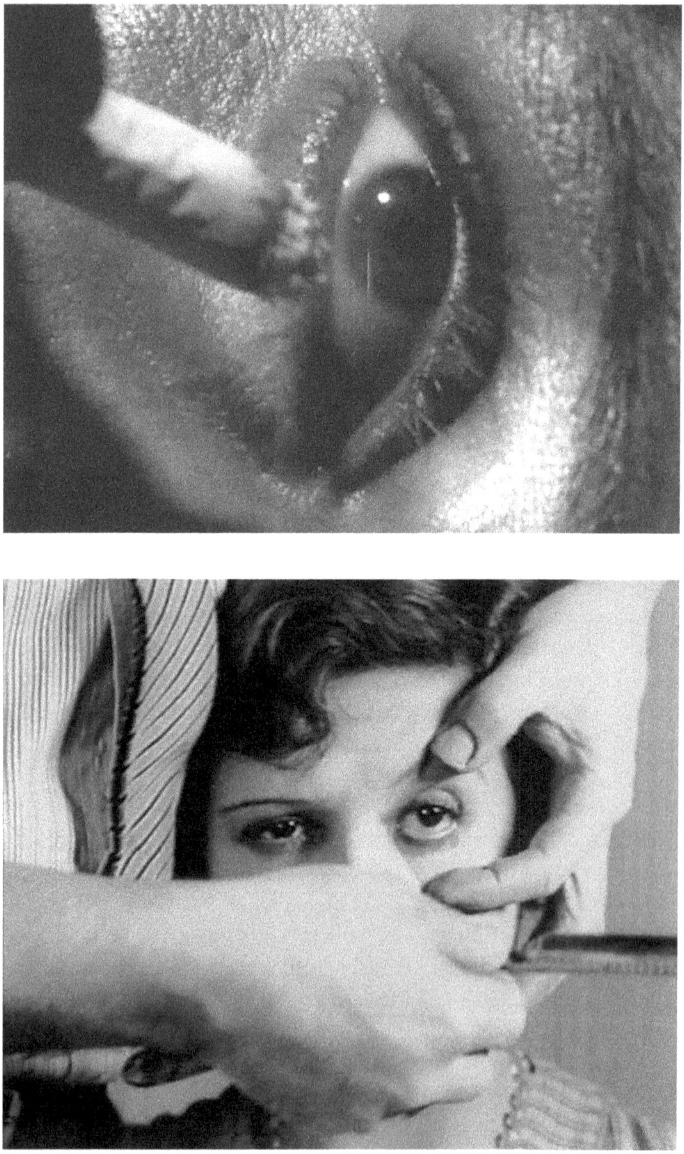

Figure 45 Screenshots from *Shab-i Qūzī* (top) and *Un Chien Andalou* (bottom). Allusion by a New Iranian Film to international cinema.

near the character's eye to check his vitality—rather than choosing from numerous other possible formal possibilities—is intended to speak to those in the audience familiar with Dadaist cinema, offering them a subtle nod of recognition. Distinguishing this formal reference requires multiple levels of second-order observation. Here, viewers not only understand the shot—through second-order observation—as an attempt by the film characters to determine whether their friend is dead but they also compare this choice in the *mise-en-scène*—independent of its narrative context—with Buñuel's film, if they know it, recognizing the formal parallels and identifying the film's tribute to an earlier cinematic work.

Similar reflexive nods of recognition appear twice in *Khisht va āyinah* (Brick and Mirror; 1964) through camera work. A number of shots in the scene where Hāshim and Tājī, the film's main characters, argue about what to do with the baby Hāshim found on the back seat of his taxi (Figure 46, bottom) correspond almost exactly to shots from *La Notte* (The Night; 1961) (Figure 46, top). Additionally, the dolly zoom on Tājī in the orphanage near the end of the film—where she stands in the corner, exhausted and disheartened after failing to locate the baby that Hāshim brought there—is a reference to Hitchcock's *Vertigo* (1958).

Khudāḥāfiẓ rafīq (Goodbye Friend; 1971), too, makes a brief, reflexive allusion to *Easy Rider*'s flash-like cuts in its opening sequence to indicate the transition from day to night. Additionally, the film's title sequence features family photos of three criminal friends who, in this story, rob a jeweler together but ultimately lose their lives as each tries to claim a larger share

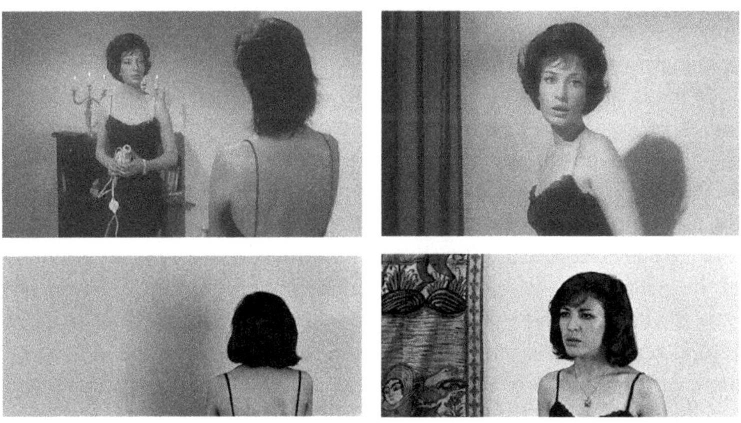

Figure 46 Screenshots from *La Notte* (top) and *Khisht va āyinah* (bottom). Allusion by a New Iranian Film to international cinema.

of the stolen jewels. Both the film's theme and its opening sequence evoke *Bonnie and Clyde*, which similarly begins with family photos of Bonnie Parker and Clyde Barrow, two real-life criminals who also meet their demise by the film's end.

Ūn shab kih bārūn ūmad (The Night It Rained; 1967) adopts a humorous approach to reflection on the distinction between filmic utterance and its environment. This satirical documentary examines the complexities of truth and media representation in 1960s Iran. It investigates a widely publicized story about a village boy who allegedly saved a train from disaster by removing his shirt, setting it on fire, and waving it in front of the oncoming train to warn the driver about flood-damaged tracks. While the boy's selfless venture is initially celebrated, the narrative becomes increasingly ambiguous as the film presents conflicting accounts from journalists, officials, and villagers. Through these divergent perspectives, the film critiques the construction of myths and the reliability of official narratives.

After *Ūn shab kih bārūn ūmad* introduces its topic by displaying newspaper clippings reporting on the village boy's heroic deed, Shirdel's—the director's—extradiegetic voice outlines the film crew's assignment to make a documentary about the boy. According to the narration, the crew is unable to meet the boy personally because he has traveled to Gorgan with his sick father to take him to the hospital. As a result, the crew decide to make a film about the village and its inhabitants instead. The voice then proceeds to describe the takes from the village that are already visible to viewers and do not require explanation. The relationship between image and sound in these descriptions is often humorous and ironic. For instance, the voice claims that the villagers are very hospitable. Simultaneously, however, the film shows only deserted village streets while barking dogs in backyards are heard, seemingly warning the crew to stay away.

What is shown and heard diegetically does not align with the narrator's notion of a warm and welcoming community. This contradiction between the narration, on the one hand, and sound and image recorded on the set, on the other, undermines the credibility of the voiceover's statements, even if the film claims to be a documentary. Instead, the viewers are encouraged to take the position of third-order observers, continually assessing the credibility of the claims made within the film. As third-order observers, viewers not only distinguish pieces of information from the filmic utterance through second-order observation, but they also have to observe the distinction between these pieces of information and examine their compatibility and credibility to find out the truth of what really happened. This role was never expected of audiences watching *filmfarsi*, documentary films, or television news and reports.

The villagers in *Ūn shab kih bārūn ūmad* are not always shown in motion by the film camera; at times, they appear in freeze frames. They seem as though they have been photographed—a filmic reflection on the medium's distinction from, and similarity to, photography. The film includes other moments of reflection: on the one hand, the voiceover outlines shooting plans and locations; on the other, profilmic techniques and tools are presented in the opening sequence—particularly the camera, the clapperboard, and even the director himself (Figure 47)—all part of the environment of filmic communication.[4] In the opening, the director's name appears on a photograph capturing him during filming. Alternating with another photograph taken just seconds later, the image (Figure 47, left) becomes animated. This humorous animation, through reflection, highlights the very process by which individual film frames, shown in rapid succession, create the illusion of movement.

Finally, *Mughul-hā* (The Mongols; 1973) is noteworthy as a film that demonstrates both reflexivity and reflection. It begins by introducing a married couple: the husband works for national television and is researching the history of cinema for a television program, while the wife is writing her dissertation on the Mongol invasion of Iran in the thirteenth century. When the husband is commissioned by the television network to construct new transmission towers in the desert near Zahedan, in southeastern Iran, to expand television broadcasting to that region, the invasion of the new medium, namely television, merges, in a surreal fashion, with the historical Mongol invasion of Iran. The Mongols in the desert, who have appeared in a surreal, parallel diegesis ever since the wife's dissertation topic was introduced are shown, at one point, carrying television antennas, symbolizing the significant threat that television, as a concurrent in the film's environment, poses to cinema (Figure 48). All visual references to television in the film are

Figure 47 Screenshots from *Ūn shab kih bārūn ūmad*. Reflection of filmic communication.

Figure 48 Screenshot from *Mughul-hā*. Reflection of filmic communication.

instances of filmic communication reflecting on its difference from another mass medium in its environment.

The narrative timeframe of the film extends from the moment the husband receives the assignment to construct the transmission towers in the desert to the moment when he and his wife are meant to be picked up by a car to travel to Zahedan. In the surrealistic diegesis, however—where the husband, through observing the Mongols' destructive actions, has come to understand how television can culturally corrupt its viewers and endanger the medium of film—no car arrives to collect the couple. Instead, it is the Mongol troop that confronts the husband in the desert. Shortly before this encounter, the husband discovers a strip of film buried beneath the desert sand and pulls it out (Figure 49). This is a reflection made through cinematography's reference to the distribution medium of film, which exists in the environment of filmic communication—an unexpected formal choice, like the film's other reflections, within the realm of the continuity system and the dominant *filmfarsi* structure.

Mughul-hā also pays tribute to the history of the moving image through a reflexive scene. This scene features a shot in which the Mongols introduce themselves in unison with the sentence "We are Mongols." The shot then cuts to an animated sequence in which a cartoon face pronounces

Figure 49 Screenshot from *Mughul-hā*. Reflection of filmic communication.

the French sentence "*Je vous aime*" (I love you), as seen in Figure 50. The animated sequence replicates a motion photography work created by Georges Demenÿ in 1891. Demenÿ produced this film for a project intended to use recorded moving images of speaking individuals, viewed through a phonoscope, to teach deaf students how to speak and lip-read—a method that required careful observation of lip movements. This reflexivity of filmic communication, achieved through the film referencing its own history, offers a cinephile tribute to film.

Alarm in the Environment of Film Art

As noted previously, one distinguishing feature of New Iranian Cinema—unlike the new waves of film in West Germany and the United States—was that the autopoiesis of cinema and the established structure of the popular *filmfarsi* were never jeopardized by declining financial returns. Thus, in the structural coupling of art and economy within the film system, the economy perceived no threat to its anticipated financial gains. Instead, it was the art system in the Iranian film industry that, in the late 1960s and early 1970s, was alerted to a decline in its artistic quality through irritation from filmmakers and critics in its environment. Venturing film art responded to this irritation

Figure 50 Screenshot from *Mughul-hā*. Reflexivity of filmic communication.

by aligning its communication topics with ongoing societal discourses criticizing poverty, injustice, and corruption. Films with a rupturing tendency, in turn, saw *filmfarsi* as the product of the traditional cultural norms and the political decisions that contradicted the expectations of dissatisfied and protesting citizens. Therefore, rupturing films resonated formally and thematically with these environmental irritations by fundamentally rejecting the established *filmfarsi* structure. They turned instead toward an extremely minimalist neorealism and experimented with reflexivity and reflection previously unfamiliar to Iranian cinema.

Similar to New German Cinema, the alarming artistic situation of Iranian cinema was thematized at a 1973 press conference held by *Kānūn-i Sīnamāgarān-i Pīshraw* (Progressive Filmmakers' Cooperative, PFC). At the event, PFC members identified a crisis in Iranian cinema and called for alternative funding models that could support a culturally and artistically ambitious Iranian cinema. They were hopeful that financial independence from the state would also grant them new narrative and thematic freedoms. Naficy presents an extensive report on this press conference, based on verified yet rare archival material. Given its historical significance, it is worth citing his report at length here:

> [The venture of new-wave filmmakers to come together and build a collective] began with the resignation in July 1973 of nineteen well-known producers, directors, cinematographers, composers, and actors

> (almost all new wave) from the National Syndicate of Film Industries, an organization to which, according to an unwritten law, every person working in cinema had to belong. The resignation itself and the manner of its announcement, at a news conference, were unprecedented. Eleven of the signatories attended the news conference in the Tehran Palace Hotel [...].[5] They claimed their resignations resulted from a desire to create a new cinema against the commercial cinema, a cinema "worthy of our culture and nationality," a culture in which even an "illiterate villager in the farthest village" in daily conversation cited poems by Sadi, Hafez, and Ferdowsi. Mehrjui claimed that the only feature of the rich Iranian culture that commercial films employed was Persian dialogue. Hajir Daryoush declared that progressive filmmakers would use every legal means possible, including private-sector financing and help from "his Excellency, Satan," to circumvent the "distribution monopoly" of the commercial sector. [...] Sayyad stated that the dissenters ultimately aimed to satisfy both the needs of consumers and their own desires to make films that "while representing our culture, national characteristics, and artistic growth, could also earn the country some foreign exchange." // This news conference and the formation a month later of the Progressive Filmmakers' Cooperative [...] officially declared the existence of a dual-track film industry—commercial and new wave. Members of the PFC stressed that the new-wave cinema did not pose a threat to the commercial cinema or to its syndicates because, while the commercial film industry put out about "ninety films annually," members of the PFC would probably only manage to make fifteen films. All they wanted to do was to provide the spectators with "the right to choose."
>
> (2011, 353–4)

It is interesting that, similar to the signees of the Oberhausen Manifesto, the PFC members also aimed to produce "valuable" films and advocated for alternative sources of funding beyond the financing structures of distribution monopolies, which supported only commercial productions. Likewise, in line with the Oberhausen filmmakers, they sought to realize their films through independent means. According to Naficy,

> To create financially successful, high-quality films "worthy of our culture and nationality," PFC members invested their own funds in their films; but, ironically, a great portion of the funding eventually came from governmental and semigovernmental agencies, such as the MCA [Ministry of Culture and Art], NIRT [National Iranian Radio and Television], Telfilm, the Ministry of the Economy, and the FIDCI [Film Industry Development Corporation of Iran]. Some PFC members did

> make films independently, with aid from the private sector. The first films produced under the aegis of the PFC were very impressive: Mehrjui's *The Cycle* [...], Shahid Saless's *Still Life* [...], and Sayyad's *Dead-End* [...].
> (2011, 354–5; emphasis in original)

The parallels between the Oberhausen Manifesto and the PFC press conference are intriguing. Both declarations were made by filmmakers intent on creating venturing and, even more determinedly, rupturing films. Both groups anticipated that their turn toward entirely new film narratives and their rupture of the established structure of filmic utterance would likely disrupt film's structural coupling with the economic system and create challenges for securing funding. As a result, both articulated their reasons for breaking away from conventional film structures at press conferences, citing the declining artistic quality of mainstream cinema and, in the case of the Oberhausen Manifesto, the financial crisis facing the contemporary film industry. In this way, they sought to persuade funding bodies, whether private or state-affiliated, that their films were worthy of financial support and could prove economically viable. In other words, given the art system's intention to commit rupture on its own structure and narrative, these filmmakers attempted to irritate the economic system in the environment of filmic communication into accepting their work by funding it.

Could it be that artistic manifestos always emerge alongside rupturing tendencies in art, in order to increase the likelihood of acceptance for the radically new identities these tendencies propose, be it acceptance by funders or by audiences? Once again, addressing this question falls outside the scope of the present book.

Revolution, War, and a Delayed Departure

The 1979 revolution was the result of escalating conflicts between the political system of the Pahlavī monarchy in Iran and those citizens who opposed its decisions. The revolution dismantled the entire political and economic structure of society and replaced it with a new one. As a result, the wave-like evolution of filmic communication, which was heavily reliant on its structural coupling with the economy, came to a standstill following the revolution. On the other hand, while venturing and rupturing films had previously introduced new information and identities—as variations on the *filmfarsi* narrative and structure—the Iranian film system in 1979 and 1980 was, due to the interruption caused by the revolution, unable to make decisions regarding the selection and stabilization of these variations. Furthermore, these variations had emerged in resonance with the contradictions and conflicts present in Iranian society prior to the revolution, whereas the revolution seemed to have erased those contradictions and conflicts by replacing the old political system with a new one. Consequently, venturing and rupturing tendencies lost their other-referential reference point in the ongoing communications of society.

In the nearly one and a half years between the revolution and Iraq's invasion of Iran in September 1980—which marked the beginning of an eight-year war—the new political system was stabilized and it began imposing new censorships on artistic communication based on ideological Islam, including in the realm of film. In addition to the previous bans on criticizing the political system, which had been enforced during the Pahlavī era, the new political system introduced further restrictions on the film's *mise-en-scène*. These included prohibitions against the portrayal of women without full body and hair coverage, solo singing or dancing by women, and the depiction of any physical contact between the two sexes. As a result, filmic communication now operated within a significantly reduced range of permissible topics and formal identities.

Although the war film genre—centered on the heroic battles of Iranian troops against the Iraqi invaders—dominated much of the 1980s and received extensive state funding, the departure of Iranian New Wave began to emerge toward the end of the war, with a delay of approximately eight years. The selection and restabilization of the variations introduced by venturing and rupturing tendencies prior to the revolution became possible primarily due to the continuity maintained by the creative forces behind these films, who remained in Iran and endured the postrevolution and war years. Without this continuity within the environment of film—specifically, the persistence of individual filmmakers—the departure of Iranian New Wave Cinema might not have occurred.

Nasser Taqvai, who had explored new filmic identities to depict the mental states of characters in his pre-1979 literary adaptation and had achieved mastery in employing the continuity system to construct complex filmic narratives, produced only a limited number of films after the revolution. In 1987, he adapted another literary work—Ernest Hemingway's novel *To Have and Have Not*—into an Iranian context with his film *Nākhudā Khurshīd* (Captain Khurshīd; 1987). The film was awarded the Bronze Leopard at the Locarno Film Festival in 1988. Set in southern Iran along the Persian Gulf, the narrative follows Captain Khurshīd, a one-handed boatman struggling to survive amid poverty and political unrest. When a group of dangerous criminals escapes from exile and offers him money to smuggle them out by sea, he reluctantly accepts, driven by desperation. As tensions rise during the perilous journey, Khurshīd finds himself torn between the demands of survival and the threat of moral collapse. Despite being outnumbered and physically limited, he engages in a brutal confrontation at sea. He succeeds in killing all the criminals but ultimately dies from the injuries he sustains during the fight, perishing aboard his boat.

Mehrjui's second postrevolution film, *Ijārah nishīn-hā* (The Tenants; 1986), employs allegory and symbolism again to critique the chaotic Iranian culture and politics of the time, as direct criticism was prohibited. The film is a satirical comedy centered on the disordered lives of residents in a dilapidated apartment building in Tehran. Each tenant represents a different social class or character type, and tensions rise as they contend with unpaid rent, building decay, and the scheming manager, Mr. Khursandī, who seeks to evict them in order to sell the property for profit. Conflicts among the tenants and a series of absurd events gradually unfold, allegorically exposing social hypocrisy and bureaucratic dysfunction in contemporary Iranian society. Ultimately, the building collapses—both literally and symbolically—marking the culmination of corruption, greed, and neglect, and leaving the tenants homeless.

In his later films, Mehrjui shifted toward philosophical themes with a reduced focus on political commentary, allowing him to move away from allegorical expression. His films *Hāmūn* (1989), *Parī* (1995), and *Liylā* (1997)—each named after its central character—reach greater formal maturity and delve, at the narrative level, into the internal struggles of these protagonists, positioned between spiritual and material existence; that is, between their personal ideals on one side, and the capitalist and traditional values of society on the other.

Kiarostami, in his turn, remained devoted to his neorealist style and refined it in films such as *Khānah-yi dūst kujāst?* (Where Is the Friend's House?; 1987), *Zīr-i dirakhtān-i ziytūn* (Through the Olive Trees; 1994), and *Bād mā rā khvāhad burd* (The Wind Will Carry Us; 1999). *Khānah-yi dūst kujāst?* synthesizes the neorealist aesthetic that Kiarostami had developed prior to the revolution with subtle symbolic elements. The film tells the story of a young boy named Aḥmad, who lives in an Iranian village and realizes he has accidentally taken his friend Muḥammad's school notebook. Fearing that Muḥammad might be expelled for failing to complete his homework again, Aḥmad sets out on a determined journey to the neighboring village to return the notebook. However, adults around him hinder his progress—either because he has not yet finished his own homework, because he is neglecting his responsibilities in helping his mother with chores, or simply because elderly relatives believe they must restrain him in order to teach him obedience. The village where the film was shot is a real location, and the nonprofessional actors featured in the film are its actual residents.

When Aḥmad finally arrives in the neighboring village, night has already fallen. He seeks assistance from an elderly carpenter who knows where Muḥammad lives. This carpenter, who makes wooden windows with colorful glass in the traditional style, is the only person in the village whose house is lit and who is willing to help Aḥmad. As they walk together to Muḥammad's home, the carpenter laments that people are replacing their beautiful, handcrafted wooden windows with drab, mass-produced metal ones and, as a result, no longer seek his work. Within the film's narrative, the old man symbolizes traditional wisdom capable of guiding individuals along a moral path—one that Aḥmad has embarked upon against all odds. This wisdom is portrayed as increasingly neglected and overshadowed by industrialized modes of life, much like the old carpenter's handcrafted wooden windows are by their industrially manufactured counterparts.

Finally, reflection in the form of filmic communication thematizing the production circumstances of film remained one of the identities to which a number of postrevolution Iranian films returned, marking its selection and stabilization. For instance, *Salām sīnamā* (Hello Cinema; 1995) presents a real mass audition that Makhmalbaf, the film's director, organized to select actors for his next project. The entire film documents interactions between Makhmalbaf—who appears on screen himself—and the applicants. They are asked to introduce themselves and explain their motivations for wanting to become film actors, after which they are given roles to perform. For example, they are asked to act as if they were shot, to cry, or to show compassion toward a fellow applicant playing the role of a lover. The applicants' behaviors, opinions, or performances are edited into sequences of short clips with asynchronous sound, forming a parody of how these individuals imagine the fulfillment of their cinematic dreams and aspirations for fame.

Salām sīnamā is a grand reflection of filmic communication in that it marks the distinction between its own filmic utterance and the casting process for a future film—a process that belongs to the environment of filmic communication. However, by 1995, reflection no longer qualified as rupture in Iranian film, having already been introduced in prerevolution cinema and counting as a familiar identity of filmic communication that had ever since been remembered by film's memory. Other postrevolution films, such as *Mashq-i shab* (Homework; 1989), which reveals the filming set; *Close-Up* (1990), featuring Makhmalbaf, a film director, appearing as himself; and

Nāṣir-al-dīn Shāh āktur-i sīnamā (Once Upon a Time, Cinema; 1992), which thematizes the introduction of cinematography in Iran during the Qājār era, select and stabilize reflection as an identity that can contribute to the departure of Iranian cinema's communication toward a sustained artistic autopoiesis.

Conclusion

The discussions and analyses in the previous chapters were driven by the initial observation that, despite significant formal and contextual differences, new-wave cinemas share one key characteristic: they all emerged alongside major contradictions and conflicts within their societal environments. A survey of global history since the advent of cinema reveals that, although not every contradiction or conflict in a social context leads to the emergence of a new wave, such waves arise as a by-product of these tensions.

The analyses in this book, grounded in Luhmann's systems theory of society, have shown that the defining feature of a new wave lies primarily in the difference between its formal and thematic choices and the conventional topics and structure of filmic utterance within its contemporary society. This difference seems to be related to protests within the film's societal environment, expressing unmet political, economic, or cultural expectations. The contradictions that are thematized by these protests may escalate into conflicts if the political, economic, or legal systems reject the expectations voiced by protesting citizens.

A detailed examination of New German Cinema, New Hollywood, and New Iranian Cinema demonstrates that filmic communication can get irritated by these tensions in its environment, and it resonates with them through its wave-like evolution. This irritation is mediated either by declining box office sales—which are sensed by the economy, structurally coupled with film art—or by individuals and institutions representing the art system, themselves affected by environmental irritation, who reject the prevailing qualities of filmic communication through publishing critiques or by withholding awards. These rejections coming from the film's environment indicate that its autopoiesis may be at risk unless it rapidly alters its structure and information. Hence, new waves of cinema appear to represent a specific mode of film art's evolution when it perceives a threat to its autopoiesis. Although society and its functional subsystems—including art, with film as a subsystem of art—are in a state of constant evolution, this development takes the form of a new wave only when the film system perceives such a threat.

According to the examination of three distinct new waves in the previous chapters, if the film system interprets environmental irritations as a threat to its autopoiesis, it responds by resonating with them. It does so by excessively and redundantly introducing new topics (at the level of other-reference) and, when necessary, adopting new formal selections (at the level of utterance) to test whether these variations can restore its artistic and economic autopoiesis. If successful, the new topics are retained for future use, while the formal variations are selected and stabilized as identities that the memory of filmic communication marks as worthy of remembering in the future. Together, these new identities construct an alternative structure to that of the previously rejected communications. In this way, new waves operate as a self-induced mutation—following Luhmann in adopting terminologies from biological theories of evolution—that increases the chances of the film system maintaining its autopoiesis beyond the crisis brought on through the rejection of its communications by producers and viewers as well as by institutions, mass media, and individuals representing the art system.

The course of this wave-like evolution is reflected in the three tendencies identified in the development of New German Cinema and later rediscovered in New Hollywood and New Iranian Cinema—tendencies which I have labeled *venture*, *rupture*, and *departure*. Venture arises in a context where dominant filmic communications largely ignore contemporary critical discourses in society, instead presenting diegeses populated by typified, polarized characters and narratives marked by reduced complexity and no contemporary reference. As the analyses in the previous chapters have demonstrated, venture emerges when the film system becomes irritated by the rejection of its communication and attempts to regain viewer engagement. It introduces variations at the level of information—thematically diverging from conventional filmic communication while still conforming to its established formal structure—and repeats this variation redundantly to test whether it can reestablish the film system's autopoiesis. Through this redundancy, venture acquires the status of an evolutionary stage within a wave, rather than being seen as a sporadic or accidental occurrence.

Venturing films in the context of West Germany, however, are not generally classified as part of New German Cinema because, despite shifting their topics from the fairytale romances of *Heimatfilm* to the Second World War and National Socialism, they retained shallow, uncritical narratives that failed to engage with the complexity of these themes as discussed by the protesting youth in West Germany.

The second tendency, rupture, was observed only in New German Cinema and New Iranian Cinema. Based on these observations, rupture—that is a different kind of variation from venture—appears to result primarily from the art system's irritation—in the structural coupling of film art and economy—in response to the threat posed to film's autopoiesis. Rupture either triggers alarm within the film system by radically contradicting the established structure of filmic utterance, as seen in New German Cinema, or completely dismantles this structure, resulting in extremely minimalist films in both form and narrative, as seen in New Iranian Cinema. Both approaches function as acts of reflection because rupturing films, beyond conveying a narrative as information, observe the stark contrast between their formal choices and the expectations shaped by audiences' prior experiences with conventional filmic structures.

Rupture, which is more targeted toward the form and structure of filmic utterance, along with those venturing films that fundamentally alter narrative structures and topics on the level of information, appears to endanger the structural coupling of art and economy in film—a relationship typically stabilized within the framework of established film industry in a given social context. In other words, the art system acknowledges that by radically modifying its structure or information, it risks undermining its structural coupling with the economic system. This is because the economy is generally reluctant to invest in new identities whose acceptance by audiences has not yet been tested or secured. For the economic system, investing in a new product is only meaningful when the product's alignment with the positive side of the economy's code payment/nonpayment is predictable.

As the analyses of New German Cinema and New Iranian Cinema have demonstrated, the anticipation of potential financial loss seems to have motivated public declarations and the publication of manifestos. The Oberhausen Manifesto and the PFC's press conference were primarily addressed to film producers and investors, aiming to build confidence in the financial viability of emerging rupturing and venturing filmic forms. In doing so, filmmakers attempted to irritate the economic system in a way that would maintain its structural coupling with a radical variation of the established film tradition and encourage investment in the production of their proposed films.

At the same time, through magazines such as *Filmkritik* and *Frauen und Film*, New German Cinema aimed to resonate with viewers. This strategy was intended to secure financial success in the post-projection phase, thereby not only sustaining the economic autopoiesis of film but also ensuring that the communications of new-wave films, which introduced self-rupturing forms and critical topics, were understood and accepted.

These manifestos and press conferences did not immediately resonate with the economic system. The analysis of rupturing films within New German Cinema has shown that many of these films had to be at least partially self-financed by the filmmakers and that a significant number failed to achieve commercial success. This further demonstrates that the production of rupturing films was motivated by artistic necessity rather than economic rationale. Had the economic system deemed these films profitable according to its own code, their promotion and potential success would likely have been pursued through advertising in mass media and on billboards—tools the economic system uses to irritate its communication partners, namely consumers, into accepting its communication, namely selling—rather than through manifestos and specialized magazines. In contrast, in the case of New Hollywood, irritating the economic system through a manifesto was not necessary, since it was primarily the economic system, rather than the art system, that was irritated by the endangered autopoiesis of film and was already speculating on how to move beyond this problem.

Departure marks the final phase in the wave-like evolution of film, in which certain variations—introduced redundantly and proven successful in reaching mass audiences or gaining recognition at film festivals and among critics—are selected and restabilized into a new structure. This new structure ensures the continued autopoiesis of filmic communication. Departure thus represents the successful resolution of the crisis perceived by the art and/or economic systems within their structural coupling in filmic communication. The analysis of New Hollywood showed that films of departure in this new wave ignored the majority of variations introduced by venturing films, instead selecting and stabilizing heightened narrative complexity and enhanced technical means of film production as viable variations. This demonstrates that departure does not always rely on the variations initially introduced by venture and rupture, but may instead depend on a different set of variations, some of which stem from the environment of filmic communication, such as advancements related to technical means of film production.

Venture, rupture, and departure, as defined in this book, are not categories that can establish fixed canons. In other words, it is impossible to label a film as definitively venturing, rupturing, or departure-oriented—a distinction I have deliberately avoided throughout the text. Instead, these are tendencies characterized by two important features, as the analyses have demonstrated.

First, they are meaningful only as differences between redundantly produced new decisions by a group of films and the already established structure and narrative of filmic communication. No formal or thematic choice can be considered venture, rupture, or departure in isolation. Venture becomes recognizable only when multiple films diverge from the narrative contents and structure of conventional films within their social context. These films introduce topics that resonate with contemporary, predominantly critical communications, while maintaining the formal scope and quality of conventional films. The same applies to rupture, which is meaningful only in opposition to or as a negation of an existing filmic structure. Finally, it is useful to speak of departure only once a wave has redundantly introduced new variations at the levels of form and narrative—variations that can be selected and restabilized as a new formal and narrative structure with an increased likelihood of sustaining autopoiesis.

Second, the tendencies venture, rupture, and departure are not mutually exclusive. The discussions in the previous chapters have shown that certain films can exhibit two or even all three tendencies simultaneously, while in others, one tendency may be more dominant. It all depends on the specific structures of filmic communication or narrative from which a film distinguishes itself. For example, venturing West German films like *Wir Wunderkinder*, or venturing New Hollywood films like *M*A*S*H*, demonstrate instances of reflexivity and reflection that could have been perceived as rupturing. But these elements are less prominent than these films' venture to introduce contemporary and critical communication topics within the established structure of filmic utterance. As another example, films of departure in New Hollywood embody both venture and departure simultaneously, without selecting or stabilizing many of the identities introduced by the preceding venturing films in the United States.

Therefore, venture, rupture, and departure do not correspond to specific formal choices; rather, they are abstract terms indicating a recurring difference between formally and thematically unexpected filmic communication, introduced as variation, and the topics and structures anticipated by the memory of filmic communication within a particular social and cinematic context. The established structure of filmic utterance, as anticipated by the memory of film prior to the introduction of venturing and rupturing variations, happened to be the continuity system in all the new waves studied here. But this may not always be the case. Therefore, venture and rupture are not necessarily variations to the continuity system but to any structure perceived as established and foreseeable within a certain social context.

Given all of the above observations, it seems to be more insightful to study the evolution of a new wave by examining how instances of venture, rupture, and departure organically emerge, build upon one another, and decline across a group of films—sometimes more prominently in some than in others—rather than by focusing on a canon or epoch perceived to encompass the entirety of a new wave. This approach is particularly important because, as demonstrated in the chapter on New German Cinema, rigid categories such as canons and epochs often overlook significant developments that contributed to the emergence of the new wave. This was the case with West German war films and the two individual films *Die Parallelstraße* and *Jonas*, the contributions of which to New German Cinema are neglected in canon-based studies because they were released prior to the declaration of the

Oberhausen Manifesto. The manifesto, in turn, is commonly regarded as the epochal starting point of New German Cinema.

The Luhmannian film theory outlined here has not only advanced the study of new waves of cinema as a universal phenomenon but has also, through concrete analyses, enabled the observation of significant formal and evolutionary differences between individual new waves: unlike the other two new waves discussed in this book, New Hollywood Cinema did not display a notable rupturing tendency. At the same time, rupture in New Iranian Cinema assumed a form that was fundamentally different from that in New German Cinema. Yet both tendencies can be identified as rupture because they represent instances of the film system's reflection on—and dismantling of—previously established filmic structures.

A further contribution of the systems-theoretical approach adopted in this book for observing the evolution of new-wave cinema is the challenge it poses to the widespread belief that such waves worldwide are defined primarily by the formal inspiration they drew from the *Nouvelle Vague*, and that this shared stylistic influence is what distinguishes them as new waves. As demonstrated in the analytical chapters, most formal decisions regarding new-wave films—such as Wim Wenders's departure road movies, New Hollywood venturing road movies, New Hollywood departure blockbusters, and the rupturing neorealism of New Iranian Films—exhibit no formal similarity to films typically associated with the French *Nouvelle Vague*, such as the use of jump cuts, the asynchrony of image and sound, or unbalanced frame compositions. A new wave can only be perceived as such in relation to the established filmic structure within the society where it emerges. Therefore, mere formal imitation of the French New Wave cannot generate a new wave in another national context if (a) it is not perceived as a reaction to the existing structure of filmic utterance, and (b) it does not occur redundantly enough to signify a wave-like evolution. Although various new waves of cinema have borrowed formal elements from one another and from other international films—such as Wim Wenders from New Hollywood road movies or Kiarostami from Italian Neorealism—these borrowings can contribute to a new wave only if they meet the aforementioned criteria.

This Book's Reflexivity and Departure

In my discussions, I have argued that the most significant contribution of venturing films to new waves of cinema lies in the alignment of their information (or other-reference) with the critical communications occurring in the film's environment. On the other hand, following Luhmann, I have argued that information is derived by each individual from the filmic utterance through assigning meaning to the distinction between the actual decisions made in the film's utterance and the potential alternatives that could have been selected instead. Consequently, the understood information is only observable when it becomes the topic of subsequent communication. Hence, any analysis of the information conveyed by a particular communication—including filmic communication—is inherently risky, as there may be no communication or consensus about what specific information a filmic utterance delivers.

Whenever I have addressed the information in filmic communication—whether discussing its alignment with critical communications in film's environment or attributing allegorical meaning to certain Iranian films by further interpreting their narrative—I have done so based on my own observations, which were mostly in line with a consensus among film scholars and historians who have written about those films. However, this is not a universal claim; anyone may interpret a film differently than I or the other scholars cited here. And that, in turn, could undermine the arguments of this book that are based on the information of filmic communication.

This book by no means claims to have analyzed or named all the films designated to New German Cinema, New Hollywood, and New Iranian Cinema by existing film historical literature, let alone considered all other films made parallel to the canonical new-wave films that might have demonstrated venturing or rupturing tendencies or contributed to the new wave's departure. This limitation stems from the restricted resources that every book project and every researcher face. I sincerely hope that future research will take into account these neglected filmic utterances from the three new waves analyzed here, as well as films from other new waves of cinema, to criticize and complement the discussions presented in this book.

Along the way of analyzing the simultaneity of new-wave cinema with contradictions and conflicts in film's societal environment, and how the wave evolves in the context of these communications, further questions were raised regarding other art forms:

1. Could the major filmic evolutions that also developed within social contexts marked by political struggle but preceded the *Nouvelle Vague*—such as the expressionist cinema of the Weimar Republic, Italian Neorealism, and New Indian Cinema—and are therefore not considered new waves in existing film-historical literature be understood as such in the terms proposed by this book? Were these filmic movements also responding to a dominant filmic structure with a constrained

thematic and formal scope—one that required reform at the levels of form and information to ensure the continued autopoiesis of filmic communication? If that is the case, can the tendencies of venture, rupture, and departure also be identified within these earlier wave-like evolutions?

2. Could similar evolutionary trajectories to that of new-wave cinema—as observed in this book—also be found in the evolution of other art forms beyond cinema? For example, in 1950s United States, could it be that it was painting, rather than film, that initiated a radical rupture of its own structure through the introduction of pop art, in an effort to resonate with the contradictions prevailing in its societal environment? If yes, did painting perceive its autopoiesis as endangered in this context, and did it sound the alarm by rupturing its own structure through pop art?
3. Viewed from this perspective, could movements such as futurism and dadaism also be understood as instances of art rupturing its conventional structures in the context of the horrors caused by the First World War—its anticipation, unfolding, and aftermath—which left Europe in devastation? Could the new wave of literature in 1920s Iran also have echoed the contradictions arising from the radical reforms introduced to Iranian society by Riẓā Pahlavī?
4. Why can no more new waves of cinema be observed in the twenty-first century, even though political and cultural contradictions and conflicts still persist in many regions of the world? Does the film art no longer perceive a threat to its autopoiesis in the context of these contradictions and conflicts? Could it be that the multitude of newly emerged electronic and internet media in this century has taken over the function that film art previously fulfilled for society? If so, what has that function been?

These questions and many more pave the way for the departure of this book's discussions into future research on the evolution of art, with new waves of cinema being only one of its instances.

Notes

Preface

1 To access these guidelines, visit the following link: https://www.loc.gov/catdir/cpso/romanization/persian.pdf.

Introduction

1 Examples of scholarly works that treat new waves of cinema as canons are found in all the books and articles cited in this book on new waves in France, West Germany, the United States, Iran, Czechoslovakia, Hong Kong, and sub-Saharan African countries.
2 For one such study, see, for example, Geimer (2018).
3 Scholarly works with both film-sociological approaches are galore. Examples in English and German include Osterland (1970), Winter (1992), Harbers (1996), Schroer (2008), Jarvie (2013), Tudor (2014), Cagle (2016), and Geimer, Heinze and Winter (2018a, b).
4 The first point of criticism regarding causation is discussed at length in Luhmann (1994/95). The second one can most prominently be found in works of empiricist philosophers such as Hume (2007).
5 The most prominent applications of Luhmann's systems theory of society in film scholarship are found in Engell (1992; 1995; 2002; 2006) and Baecker (1996b).

1.1 Introduction to Systems Theory of Society

1 See, for example, Bertalanffy (1968).
2 Some of these theories are mentioned in the notes within the section on Memory.
3 In an earlier book, *The Reality of the Mass Media*, Luhmann speculated whether mass media constitute a functional system of their own within modern society (2000b). But in his final major work, *Theory of Society*, he holds to the idea of these media primarily as tools for enhancing communication with distant addressees (Luhmann 2012b, 120 ff.). He also notes that mass media, by disseminating communication across time and space, contribute to the formation of public opinion (Luhmann 2012b, 314 ff.).

4 Luhmann also lists "religious belief" as one of the symbolically generalized communication media in an earlier work (1995, 161).
5 Luhmann (2012b, 111 ff.) brings more examples of the structural coupling of different functional systems.
6 These theories have been outlined in Halbwachs (1992), Assmann and Assmann (1994), and Assmann (2011).
7 The gap between the public's expectations and the political system's performance as the context in which revolutions occur has been thematized by Gurr (1970).

1.2 Film as a Subsystem of Art

1 These are also the techniques that Bordwell and Thompson explore when they write about cinematography (2013, 160 ff.).
2 These are the techniques that Kracauer explores as "areas and elements" of film sound (1960, 102 ff.).
3 Diegesis refers to the narrated world or space in which the story takes place. The term was first used by Aristotle in his *Poetics*—where he contrasted *diegesis* (narration) with *mimesis* (imitation)—and then adapted by theorists of filmic and literary narrative, such as Souriau (1951), Metz (1991) and Genette (1983). Filmic diegesis is actively created by the viewer as part of the information that he distinguishes from the film form. Plot, in formalist narratology, is the order in which the events constituting a story are narrated (Liveley 2019, 112 ff.). Characterization in turn relates to the development of the characters as "paradigms of traits" and the roles assigned to them in a narrative (Chatman 1980, 126 ff.). Finally, voice determines the narrating instance. It can for example be a first-person voice or an omniscient narrator, an extradiegetic or an intradiegetic one (Genette 1983, 212 ff.).
4 Narrative, as the information of a fiction film, functions as a communication medium in its own right and reveals additional information of a different nature. The information conveyed by the narrative is a *story*. From this perspective, the film narrative is classified as a third-order communication medium, as it is derived from the communication medium of film, which itself serves as a second-order medium, similar to the communication media of all other art forms, as previously noted. This book will not explore the complexities of understanding the communication of fiction films or the intricate layers of communication media involved.
5 Prominent theories of filmic communication include Eco (1976), Pasolini (1976), Metz (1991), and Mitry (2000) among many more.
6 For the film's impression of reality in systems-theoretical terms, see also Baecker (1996b).

7 Compare the conscious first-order observation of film to Coleridge's idea of the "willing suspension of disbelief" that can happen by reading poetry (2014, 208).

8 Compare the idea of film as the observation of another observer that is now being observed by the viewer as second-order observer to Cavell's concept of film as "the world viewed" in Cavell (1979). Cavell engages with the idea of the camera as the observer (in the optical sense of the word) of film scenes. According to him, when the camera declares its existence as an observer and when the viewers realize that they are observing another observer's observations, the camera thereby becomes able to communicate, because through its declaration "it must give at least the illusion of saying something" (1979, 128–9).

2.1 New German Cinema

1 Steil (2018) engages extensively with the Marshall Plan and its political and economic dimensions at the dawn of the Cold War.

2 de Jong (2022) closely introduces these individuals and firms and how they profited from National Socialism.

3 For the critique of the *Notstandsgesetze*, see Schneider (1986).

4 For the history of the *RAF*'s formation, see Hoffmann (1997). For a concise introduction to the operations of all three generations of the *RAF*, see Kellerhoff (2020). For a detailed documentation of the *RAF*'s activities in 1977, see Peters (2017).

5 Acousmatic sound refers to a diegetic sound that is heard while its source remains unseen. I consider it an identity of filmic communication constructed through the interplay of camera work/cinematography, sound design, and editing. For the definition of acousmatic sound and the meanings attached to it in filmic communication, see Chion (1994, 71 ff.).

6 For the literary genre romance and its characteristics, see Frye (1957, 186 ff.).

7 Is the film trying to imply that the annihilation of the Jews during the Nazi era was not a systematic crime committed with the complicity of the majority of German citizens but rather the work of psychopathic individuals?

8 For examples of the censorship imposed on sex and violence scenes in Hollywood films by the PCA, see Leff and Simmons (2001).

9 For the sound design in *Jonas*, see also Keitz (1997, 240).

10 In 1963, two years after the film's release, Wilfried Berghahn wrote an interpretation of *Die Parallelstraße*'s information in the magazine *Filmkritik*. According to him: "Today, only a Kandinsky of film can help us, proclaims Dörries; a man who has 'the courage to direct the camera directly, without any detour through some kind of plot, onto the world around us.' // The

perfect film in this sense is probably *Die Parallelstraße*. Ferdinand Khittl and Bodo Blüthner fulfill what Dörries demands. They flew around the world and pointed their camera at anything photographable that happened to be in their path. But to ensure that no one gets the idea that the images created could have any meaning other than being film footage, they have five anonymous test subjects (camera from above, so we do not need to see any faces!), who, in a sense, stand in for all the diligent critics who continually try to decipher connections of meaning using preconceived theories, demonstrating extensively that nothing, absolutely nothing, can be read from them. The true film is, after all, indecipherable and mysterious, as you can see! It may be, say Khittl and Blüthner, who contributed the strongly dark 'lyricism,' that the shots contain ultimate existential truths for the one who creates them. However, you, who are not the creators of this imagination, will never comprehend them" (1963, 162; my translation).

11 For the *alte Frauenbewegung*, see Frevert (1989, 168 ff.).

12 Knight (1995, 68–9) argues that Alice Schwarzer, a German journalist who was in Paris at the time and active in the feminist movement in France, "imported" the idea of protests against the ban on abortion to West Germany.

13 Films associated with the Feminist New Wave in West Germany are often referred to as *Frauenfilm* (Women's Film) in film-historical literature. Gertrud Koch rightly criticizes this label, arguing that "feminist film aesthetics" cannot be reduced to "female aesthetics," because "the discourse on 'female aesthetics' clearly stems from a biologically-grounded definition of woman and femininity, whereas the concept of 'feminist aesthetics' is a political one. It assumes that woman and femininity are socially constituted—not biologically or anthropologically determined, but rather historically shaped" (cited in (Riecke 1998, 73); my translation). In other words, these films' distinguishing feature within New German Cinema is not merely that they were directed by women but that they articulated a feminist contradiction to the patriarchal social structures of West German society through filmic forms that best served this purpose. Therefore, throughout this book, I will refer to this movement as the Feminist New Wave rather than Women's Film.

2.2 New Hollywood

1 For the American experimental cinema in the post-Second World War era, see Jacobs (1948).

2.3 New Iranian Cinema

1 It is interesting to observe that the new wave of literature in Iran emerged simultaneously with the reign of Riẓā Pahlavī (1925–41), which marked the first nationalist monarchy of Iran in the modern sense. His rule introduced radical changes aimed at the industrialization of the country and a transformation of citizens' lifestyles, including the forceful imposition of European-style clothing on both men and women. Riẓā Pahlavī did not tolerate criticism and was known to imprison or execute his critics. Could his radically imposed "reforms" and his departure from the constitution—developed between 1905 and 1911 to limit monarchical power—have motivated the emergence of the literary new wave in Iran? This, once again, is a question answering which lies beyond the scope of this book.

2 *Gāv* has been recognized as the first film of Iranian New Wave by Dabashi (2001, 27–8), Mehrabi (2006, 38), Sadr (2006, 130 ff.), Naficy (2011, 336 ff.), and Honarpisheh (2016, 136).

3 Second-order information should not be confused with second-order observation. The information conveyed through filmic communication—specifically, the narrative in fiction films—is distinguished from its utterance through the viewers' second-order observation. This initial information remains first-order information, as additional layers of meaning can be derived from it when the distinction between this information and its potential allegorical and symbolic meanings is observed. These allegorical and symbolic meanings allow for the extraction of second-order information from the film's first-order content.

4 Drawing on Souriau (1951), profilmic reality consists of any objective, real-world elements that are intentionally created, arranged, or selected to be filmed. This includes actors in makeup, purpose-built sets, real locations chosen for filming, and lighting.

5 According to Naficy, "The original signatories were Bahram Baizai, Naser Taqvai, Manuchr Anvar, Nemat Haqiqi, Hushang Baharlu, Masud Kimiai, Behrouz Vossoughi, Esfandiar Monfaredzadeh, Zakaria Hashemi, Ali Hatami, Parviz Sayyad, Dariush Mehrjui, Ezatollah Entezami, Ali Nasirian, Davud Rashidi, and Hajir Daryoush. Jalal Moqaddam, Khosrow Haritash, and others were added later" (2011, 467).

References

Abrahamian, E. (2008), *A History of Modern Iran*, Cambridge: Cambridge University Press.

Afsahi, A. (2005), *The New Wave Movie Directors*, Tehran: Hamrah Books.

Aitken, S. C. and C. L. Lukinbeal (1997), "Disassociated Masculinities and Geographies of the Road," in S. Cohan and I. R. Hark (eds.), *The Road Movie Book*, 349–70, London and New York: Routledge.

Alloway, L. (1997), "Popular Culture and Pop Art," in S. H. Madoff (ed.), *Pop Art: A Critical History*, 167–74, Berkeley: University of California Press.

Allyn, D. (2016), *Make Love, Not War: The Sexual Revolution: An Unfettered History*, London and New York: Routledge.

Alvandi, R. (2014), *Nixon, Kissinger, and the Shah: The United States and Iran in the Cold War*, New York: Oxford University Press.

Archimedes (2025), Available online: https://en.wikiquote.org/wiki/Archimedes (accessed May 26, 2025).

Arnheim, R. (1957), *Film as Art*, Berkeley and Los Angeles: University of California Press.

Assmann, J. (2011), *Cultural Memory and Early Civilization: Writing, Remembrance, and Political Imagination*, New York: Cambridge University Press.

Assmann, J. and A. Assmann (1994), "Gestern im Heute. Medien und soziales Gedächtnis," in K. Marten, S. J. Schmidt and S. Weischenberg (eds.), *Die Wirklichkeit der Medien: Eine Einführung in die Kommunikationswissenschaft*, 114–40, Opladen: Westdeutscher Verlag.

Ast, M. S. (2013), *Der alte Film ist tot. Wir glauben an den neuen: Die Genese des Jungen Deutschen Films*, Marburg: Tectum-Verlag.

Aumont, J., A. Bergala, M. Marie and M. Vernet (1994), *Aesthetics of Film*, trans. R. Neupert, Austin: University of Texas Press.

Aurich, R. and M. Wedel (2024), "Einleitung," in R. Aurich and M. Wedel (eds.), *Die »Filmkritik«: Eine Zeitschrift und die Medien*, 7–15, Munich: edition text+kritik.

Baecker, D. (1996a), "Die Adresse der Kunst," in J. Fohrmann and H. Müller (eds.), *Systemtheorie der Literatur*, 82–105, Munich: Fink.

Baecker, D. (1996b), "The Reality of Motion Pictures," *MLN*, 111 (3): 560–77.

Baecker, D. (2015), "Working the Form: George Spencer-Brown and the Mark of Distinction," in C. Martínez and P. Bischof (eds.), *The Future Is Here*, 42–7, Milan: Mousse Magazine & Publishing, Supplement Settimana Basileia.

Baraldi, C. (2021a), "Differentiation of Society (Differenzierung der Gesellschaft)," in C. Baraldi, G. Corsi and E. Esposito, *Unlocking Luhmann:*

A Keyword Introduction to Systems Theory, trans. K. Walker, 65–70, Bielefeld: Bielefeld University Press.
Baraldi, C. (2021b), "Political System (Politisches System)," in C. Baraldi, G. Corsi and E. Esposito, *Unlocking Luhmann: A Keyword Introduction to Systems Theory*, trans. K. Walker, 171–4, Bielefeld: Bielefeld University Press.
Baraldi, C. (2021c), "Symbolically Generalized Media (Symbolisch generalisierte Kommunikationsmedien)," in C. Baraldi, G. Corsi and E. Esposito, *Unlocking Luhmann: A Keyword Introduction to Systems Theory*, trans. K. Walker, 229–34, Bielefeld: Bielefeld University Press.
Baudry, J.-L. (1986), "The Apparatus: Metapsychological Approaches to the Impression of Reality in the Cinema," in P. Rosen (ed.), *Narrative, Apparatus, Ideology*, 299–318, New York: Columbia University Press.
Beck, J. (2016), *Designing Sound: Audiovisual Aesthetics in 1970s American Cinema*, New Brunswick and London: Rutgers University Press.
Berghahn, W. (1963), "Die 'Münchner Schule'. Ansichten einer Gruppe," *Filmkritik*, April: 156–62.
Bergmann, U. (1968), "Das ›Vietnam‹-Semester 1965/66," in U. Bergmann, R. Dutschke, W. Lefèvre and B. Rabehl, *Rebellion der Studenten oder Die neue Opposition*, 18–20, Reinbek bei Hamburg: Rowohlt.
Bertalanffy, L. von (1968), *General System Theory: Foundations, Development, Applications*, New York: George Braziller.
Bordwell, D. (2008), *Poetics of Cinema*, London and New York: Routledge.
Bordwell, D. and K. Thompson (2002), *Film History: An Introduction*, New York: McGraw-Hill.
Bordwell, D. and K. Thompson (2013), *Film Art: An Introduction*, New York: McGraw-Hill.
Bordwell, D., J. Staiger and K. Thompson (2005), *The Classical Hollywood Cinema: Film Style and Mode of Production to 1960*, London and New York: Routledge.
Bose, S. D. (2021), "From Kiarostami to Farhadi: 10 Essential Films from the Iranian New Wave." Available online: https://faroutmagazine.co.uk/iranian-new-wave-10-best-films-Farhādi-kiarostami/ (accessed September 1, 2022).
Cagle, C. (2016), *Sociology on Film: Postwar Hollywood's Prestige Commodity*, New Brunswick and London: Rutgers University Press.
Canudo, R. (1993), "The Birth of a Sixth Art," in R. Abel (ed.), *French Film Theory and Criticism: A History/Anthology. 1907–1939*, vol. 1, 58–66, Princeton: Princeton University Press.
Cavell, S. (1979), *The World Viewed: Reflections on the Ontology of Film*, Cambridge: Harvard University Press.
Chatman, S. (1980), *Story and Discourse: Narrative Structure in Fiction and Film*, Ithaca and London: Cornell University Press.
Chion, M. (1994), *Audio-Vision: Sound on Screen*, trans. C. Gorbman, New York: Columbia University Press.
Christen, T. (2002), *Das Ende im Spielfilm: Vom klassischen Hollywood zu Antonionis offenen Formen*, Marburg: Schüren.

Christen, T. (2008), "New Hollywood: Renaissance des amerikanischen Films," in T. Christen and R. Blanchet (eds.), *New Hollywood bis Dogma 95*, 51–74, Marburg: Schüren.

Civil Rights Act (1964), Available online: https://www.archives.gov/milestone-documents/civil-rights-act#:~:text=No%20person%20in%20the%20United,activity%20receiving%20Federal%20financial%20assistance. (accessed June 6, 2025).

Coleridge, S. T. (2014), *Biographia Literaria*, Edinburgh: Edinburgh University Press.

Corsi, G. (2021a), "Evolution," in C. Baraldi, G. Corsi and E. Esposito, *Unlocking Luhmann: A Keyword Introduction to Systems Theory*, trans. K. Walker, 91–3, Bielefeld: Bielefeld University Press.

Corsi, G. (2021b), "Legal System (Rechtssystem)," in C. Baraldi, G. Corsi and E. Esposito, *Unlocking Luhmann: A Keyword Introduction to Systems Theory*, trans. K. Walker, 125–7, Bielefeld: Bielefeld University Press.

Corsi, G. (2021c), "Structure (Struktur)," in C. Baraldi, G. Corsi and E. Esposito, *Unlocking Luhmann: A Keyword Introduction to Systems Theory*, 227–8, Bielefeld: Bielefeld University Press.

Coury, D. N. (2004), *The Return of Storytelling in Contemporary German Literature and Film: Peter Handke and Wim Wenders*, Lewiston: Mellen Press.

Dabashi, H. (2001), *Close Up: Iranian Cinema, Past, Present and Future*, London and New York: Verso.

Das Oberhausener Manifest (1962), Available online: https://kluge-alexander.de/das-oberhausener-manifest/ (accessed April 29, 2025).

de Jong, D. (2022), *Nazi Billionaires: The Dark History of Germany's Wealthiest Dynasties*, Boston and New York: Mariner Books.

Depkat, V. (2016), *Geschichte der USA*, Stuttgart: W. Kohlhammer.

Die Verfassung des Deutschen Reichs vom 11. August 1919 (Weimarer Verfassung). Available online: https://germanhistorydocs.ghi-dc.org/docpage.cfm?docpage_id=4860&language=german (accessed August 13, 2022).

Dillmann, C. (2016), "Der Pakt mit dem Publikum. Zu den Produktionsbedingungen des Adenauer-Kinos," in C. Dillmann and O. Möller (eds), *Geliebt und Verdrängt: Das Kino der jungen Bundesrepublik Deutschland von 1949 bis 1963*, 46–53, Frankfurt/Main: Deutsches Filminstitut—DIF e.V.

Dippel, H. (1996), *Geschichte der USA*, Munich: C. H. Beck.

Eco, U. (1976), "Articulations of the Cinematic Code," in B. Nichols (ed.), *Movies and Methods*, 590–607, Berkeley: University of California Press.

Elsaesser, T. (1989), *New German Cinema: A History*, New Brunswick: Rutgers University Press.

Elsaesser, T. (2012), *Rainer Werner Fassbinder*, Berlin: Bertz + Fischer.

Engell, L. (1992), *Sinn und Industrie: Einführung in die Filmgeschichte*, Frankfurt/Main: Campus Verlag.

Engell, L. (1995), *Bewegen Beschreiben: Theorie zur Filmgeschichte*, Weimar: Verlag und Datenbank für Geisteswissenschaften (VDG).

Engell, L. (2002), "Form und Medium im Film," in J. Brauns (ed.), *Form und Medium*, 155–66, Weimar: Verlag und Datenbank für Geisteswissenschaften (VDG).

Engell, L. (2006), "Filmgeschichte als Geschichte der Sinnzirkulation," in R. Winter and M. Mai (eds.), *Das Kino der Gesellschaft— die Gesellschaft des Kinos: Interdisziplinäre Positionen, Analysen und Zugänge*, 48–59, Cologne: Herbert von Halem Verlag.

Epstein, J. (2008), *Jean Epstein: Bonjour Cinéma und andere Schriften zum Kino*, ed. N. Brenez, trans. R. Eue, Wien: SYNEMA—Ges. für Film und Medien.

Esposito, E. (2002), *Soziales Vergessen: Formen und Medien des Gedächtnisses der Gesellschaft*, trans. A. Corti, Frankfurt/Main: Suhrkamp.

Esposito, E. (2021a), "Code," in C. Baraldi, G. Corsi and E. Esposito, *Unlocking Luhmann: A Keyword Introduction to Systems Theory*, trans. K. Walker, 41–4, Bielefeld: Bielefeld University Press.

Esposito, E. (2021b), "Economic System (Wirtschaftssystem)," in C. Baraldi, G. Corsi and E. Esposito, *Unlocking Luhmann: A Keyword Introduction to Systems Theory*, trans. K. Walker, 79–81, Bielefeld: Bielefeld University Press.

Eue, R. and L. H. Gass (2012), *Provokation der Wirklichkeit: Das Oberhausener Manifest und die Folgen*, Munich: edition text + kritik.

Floor, W. M. (1980), "The Revolutionary Character of the Iranian Ulama: Wishful Thinking or Reality?," *International Journal of Middle East Studies*, 12 (4): 501–24.

Frevert, U. (1989), *Women in German History: From Bourgeois Emancipation to Sexual Liberation*, Oxford and New York: Berg.

Frisch, S. (2007), *Mythos Nouvelle Vague: Wie das Kino in Frankreich neu erfunden wurde*, Marburg: Schüren.

Frye, N. (1957), *Anatomy of Criticism*, Princeton: Princeton University Press.

Fuchs, P. (2012), "Die Religion der Gesellschaft (2000)," in O. Jahraus, A. Nassehi, M. Grizelj, I. Saake, C. Kirchmaier and J. Müller (eds.), *Luhmann-Handbuch: Leben—Werk—Wirkung*, 247–53, Weimar: J.B. Metzler.

Gair, C. (2008), *The Beat Generation: A Beginner's Guide*, Oxford: Oneworld.

Gasiorowski, M. J. (2004), "The 1953 Coup d'État Against Mosaddeq," in M. J. Gasiorowski and M. Byrne (eds.), *Mohammad Mosaddeq and the 1953 Coup in Iran*, 227–60, Syracuse: Syracuse University Press.

Gass, L. H. (2016), "Resignatorische Befunde. Manifest vor Oberhausen," in C. Dillmann and O. Möller (eds.), *Geliebt und Verdrängt: Das Kino der jungen Bundesrepublik Deutschland von 1949 bis 1963*, 46–53, Frankfurt/Main: Deutsches Filminstitut—DIF e.V.

Geimer, A. (2018), "Filmsoziologie und Diskursanalyse," in A. Geimer, C. Heinze and R. Winter (eds.), *Handbuch Filmsoziologie*, 437–57, Wiesbaden: Springer VS.

Geimer, A., C. Heinze and R. Winter, eds. (2018a), *Handbuch Filmsoziologie*, Wiesbaden: Springer VS.
Geimer, A., C. Heinze and R. Winter, eds. (2018b), *Die Herausforderungen des Films: Soziologische Antworten*, Wiesbaden: Springer VS.
Genette, G. (1983), *Narrative Discourse: An Essay in Method*, trans. J. E. Lewin, Ithaca and New York: Cornell University Press.
Gilgen, P. (2013), "System–Autopoiesis–Form: An Introduction to Luhmann's Introduction to Systems Theory," in N. Luhmann, *Introduction to Systems Theory*, ed. D. Baecker, trans. P. Gilgen, viii–xvi, Cambridge and Malden: Polity Press.
Grob, N. (2004), "Film der sechziger Jahre. Abschied von den Eltern," in W. Jacobsen, A. Kaes and H. H. Prinzler (eds), *Geschichte des deutschen Films*, 207–44, Stuttgart and Weimar: J. B. Metzler.
Grundgesetz für die Bundesrepublik Deutschland (2025, March 22), Available online: https://www.gesetze-im-internet.de/gg/BJNR000010949.html (accessed May 23, 2025).
Gunning, T. (2006), "The Cinema of Attraction[s]: Early Film, Its Spectator and the Avant-Garde," in W. Strauven (ed.), *The Cinema of Attractions Reloaded*, 381–8, Amsterdam: Amsterdam University Press.
Gupta, S. K. (1974), "'New Wave' Cinema in India," *Cinéaste*, 6 (3): 23–5.
Gurr, T. R. (1970), *Why Men Rebel*, Princeton: Princeton University Press.
Halbwachs, M. (1992), *On Collective Memory*, trans. L. A. Coser, Chicago and London: The University of Chicago Press.
Hall, S. (1996), "Encoding/Decoding," in S. Hall, D. Hobson, A. Lowe and P. Willis (eds.), *Culture, Media, Language: Working Papers in Cultural Studies, 1972–79*, 128–38, London and New York: Routledge.
Hames, P. (2006), "The Czechoslovak New Wave," in L. Badley, R. Barton and S. J. Palmer (eds.), *Traditions in World Cinema*, 67–79, Edinburgh: Edinburgh University Press.
Harbers, S. (1996), *Amerikanische Gesellschaftsbilder in den Filmen David Lynchs*, Alfeld/Leine: Coppi-Verlag.
Hehr, R. (2003), *New Hollywood: Der amerikanische Film nach 1968 / The American Film after 1968*, Stuttgart and London: Edition Axel Menges.
Heideking, J. (2003), *Geschichte der USA*, Tubingen and Basel: A. Francke.
Heinzlmeier, A. (1988), *Nachkriegsfilm und Nazifilm: Anmerkungen zu einem deutschen Thema*, Frankfurt/Main: Frankfurter Bund für Volksbildung.
Hoffmann, M., ed. (1997), *Rote Armee Fraktion. Texte und Materialien zur Geschichte der RAF*, Berlin: ID-Verlag.
Holl, K. (1988), *Pazifismus in Deutschland*, Frankfurt/Main: Suhrkamp.
Holtz, M. (2009), *American Cinema in Transition: The Western in New Hollywood and Hollywood Now*, Frankfurt/Main: Peter Lang.
Honarpisheh, F. (2016), "Fragmented Allegories of National Authenticity: Art and Politics of the Iranian New Wave Cinema, 1960–79," PhD diss., Columbia University.

Hooglund, E. J. (1982), *Land and Revolution in Iran, 1960–1980*, Austin: University of Texas Press.
Hugo, C. (1995), "New Hollywood: Ökonomie und Filmstil," in A. Horwath (ed.), *The Last Great American Picture Show: New Hollywood 1967–1976*, 248–69, Vienna: Wespennest.
Hume, D. (2007), *An Enquiry Concerning Human Understanding*, New York: Oxford University Press.
Issa, R. and S. Whitaker (1999), *Life and Art: The New Iranian Cinema*, London: National Film Theatre.
Issitt, M. L. (2009), *Hippies: A Guide to an American Subculture*, Santa Barbara: ABC-CLIO.
Jacobs, L. (1948), "Experimental Cinema in America (Part Two: The Postwar Revival)," *Hollywood Quarterly*, 3 (3): 278–92.
Jahed, P. (2022), *The New Wave Cinema in Iran: A Critical Study*, New York: Bloomsbury Academic.
Jahraus, O. (2012), "Supertheorie?," in O. Jahraus, A. Nassehi, M. Grizelj, I. Saake, C. Kirchmaier and J. Müller (eds.), *Luhmann-Handbuch: Leben—Werk —Wirkung*, 432–6, Stuttgart and Weimar: J. B. Metzler.
Jarvie, I. C. (2013), *Toward a Sociology of the Cinema*, London and New York: Routledge.
Kar, L. (2001), "An Overview of Hong Kong's New Wave Cinema," in E. C. M. Yau (ed.), *At Full Speed: Hong Kong Cinema in a Borderless World*, 31–52, Minneapolis: University of Minnesota Press.
Keitz, U. von (1997), "Film als Partitur: Polyphonie und Gedächtnis in Ottomar Domnicks Jonas," in P. Goetsch and D. Scheunemann (eds.), *Text und Ton im Film*, 237–49, Tubingen: Gunter Narr Verlag.
Kellerhoff, S. F. (2020), *Eine kurze Geschichte der RAF*, Stuttgart: Klett-Cotta.
King, G. (2002), *New Hollywood Cinema: An Introduction*, New York: Columbia University Press.
Kluge, A., ed. (1983), *Bestandsaufnahme: Utopie Film*, Frankfurt/Main: Zweitausendeins.
Knight, J. (1995), *Frauen und der Neue Deutsche Film*, Marburg: Hitzeroth.
Knodt, E. M. (1995), "Foreword," in N. Luhmann, *Social Systems*, trans. J. Bednarz Jr. and D. Baecker, ix–xxxvi, Stanford: Stanford University Press.
Knörr, K. S. (2012), "Sie nahmen die Parallelstraße. Das Manifest als Endpunkt," in R. Eue and L. H. Gass (eds.), *Provokation der Wirklichkeit. Das Oberhausener Manifest und die Folgen*, 170–5, Munich: edition text + kritik.
Kolker, R. P. and P. Beicken (1993), *The Films of Wim Wenders: Cinema as Vision and Desire*, Cambridge: Cambridge University Press.
Kracauer, S. (1960), *Theory of Film: The Redemption of Physical Reality*, New York: Oxford University Press.
Krause, D. (2005), *Luhmann-Lexikon: Eine Einführung in das Gesamtwerk von Niklas Luhmann*, Stuttgart: Lucius & Lucius.

Kundnani, H. (2024), "Zionism über alles," *Dissent*, March 15. Available online: https://www.dissentmagazine.org/online_articles/zionism-uber-alles/ (accessed April 17, 2025).
Laderman, D. (2007), "Road Movies," in B. K. Grant (ed.), *Schirmer Encyclopedia of Film*, vol. 3: *Independent Film—Road Movies*, 417–21, Detroit: Schirmer Reference.
Langford, M. (2019), *Allegory in Iranian Cinema: The Aesthetics of Poetry and Resistance*, London: Bloomsbury.
Langguth, G. (1976), *Die Protestbewegung in der Bundesrepublik Deutschland 1968–1976*, Cologne: Verlag Wissenschaft und Politik.
Leff, L. J. and J. Simmons (2001), *The Dame in the Kimono: Hollywood, Censorship, and the Production Code*, Lexington: University of Kentucky Press.
Lenz, I. (2008), "Die unendliche Geschichte?—Zur Entwicklung und den Transformationen der Neuen Frauenbewegung in Deutschland," in I. Lenz (ed.), *Die Neue Frauenbewegung in Deutschland*, 21–44, Wiesbaden: VS Verlag für Sozialwissenschaften.
Liveley, G. (2019), *Narratology*, New York: Oxford University Press.
Ludewig, A. (2011), *Screening Nostalgia: 100 Years of German Heimatfilm*, Bielefeld: transcript.
Luhmann, N. (1985a), "Die Autopoiesis des Bewußtseins," *Soziale Welt*, 36 (4): 402–46.
Luhmann, N. (1985b), "Sinn als Grundbegriff der Soziologie," in J. Habermas and N. Luhmann, *Theorie der Gesellschaft oder Sozialtechnologie: Was leistet die Systemforschung?*, 25–100, Frankfurt/Main: Suhrkamp.
Luhmann, N. (1986), "Das Medium der Kunst," *Delfin*, 7: 6–15.
Luhmann, N. (1989), *Ecological Communication*, trans. J. Bednarz Jr., Chicago: The University of Chicago Press.
Luhmann, N. (1990), *Soziologische Aufklärung*, vol. 5: *Konstruktivistische Perspektiven*, Opladen: Westdeutscher Verlag.
Luhmann, N. (1993), "Die Paradoxie der Form," in D. Baecker (ed.), *Kalkül der Form*, 197–212, Frankfurt/Main: Suhrkamp.
Luhmann, N. (1994/95), "Das Risiko der Kausalität," *Zeitschrift für Wissenschaftsforschung*, (9/10): 107–19.
Luhmann, N. (1995), *Social Systems*, trans. J. Bednarz Jr., Stanford: Stanford University Press.
Luhmann, N. (2000a), *Art as a Social System*, trans. E. M. Knodt, Stanford: Stanford University Press.
Luhmann, N. (2000b), *The Reality of the Mass Media*, trans. K. Cross, Stanford: Stanford University Press.
Luhmann, N. (2006), "System as Difference," *Organization*, 13 (1): 37–57.
Luhmann, N. (2012a), *Theory of Society*, vol. 1, eds. M. Bal and H. de Vries, trans. R. Barrett, Stanford: Stanford University Press.
Luhmann, N. (2012b), *Theory of Society*, vol. 2, eds. M. Bal and H. de Vries, trans. R. Barrett, Stanford: Stanford University Press.

Luhmann, N. (2013), *Introduction to Systems Theory*, ed. D. Baecker, trans. P. Gilgen, Cambridge & Malden: Polity Press.

Lyotard, J.-F. (1984), *The Postmodern Condition: A Report on Knowledge*, trans. G. Bennington and B. Massumi, Manchester: Manchester University Press.

Marinetti, F. T. (1973), "The Founding and Manifesto of Futurism," in U. Apollonio (ed.), *Documents of 20th-Century Art: Futurist Manifestos*, trans. R. Brain, R. W. Flint, J. C. Higgitt and C. Tisdall, 19–24, New York: Viking Press.

Matin-asgari, A. (2002), *Iranian Student Opposition to the Shah*, Costa Mesa: Mazda Publishers.

Maturana, H. R. and F. J. Varela (1980), *Autopoiesis and Cognition: The Realization of the Living*, Dordrecht, Boston, and London: D. Riedel.

McLuhan, M. (1994), *Understanding Media: The Extensions of Man*, Cambridge and London: The MIT Press.

Mehrabi, M. (2006), "A Bed and Several Dreams: A Short History of Iranian Cinema," *Cinéaste*, 31 (3): 38–47.

Metz, C. (1991), *Film Language: A Semiotics of the Cinema*, trans. M. Taylor, Chicago: The University of Chicago Press.

Meyer, H.-H. (2011), "Filmverlag der Autoren," *Lexikon der Filmbegriffe*, February 8. Available online: https://filmlexikon.uni-kiel.de/index.php?action=lexikon&tag=det&id=4836 (accessed November 20, 2020).

Michaels, J. (2017), *McCarthyism: The Realities, Delusions and Politics Behind the 1950s Red Scare*, London and New York: Routledge.

Milani, A. (2011), *The Shah*, New York: Palgrave Macmillan.

Mills, K. (2006), *The Road Story and the Rebel: Moving through Film, Fiction and Television*, Carbondale: Southern Illinois University Press.

Mitry, J. (1997), *The Aesthetics and Psychology of the Cinema*, trans. C. King, Bloomington: Indiana University Press.

Mitry, J. (2000), *Semiotics and the Analysis of Film*, London: Athlone.

Moeller, R. G. (2003), *War Stories: The Search for a Usable Past in the Federal Republic of Germany*, Los Angeles: University of California Press.

Mohammad Reza Shah Pahlavi (2025), *Encyclopædia Britannica*, March 25. Available online: https://www.britannica.com/biography/Mohammad-Reza-Shah-Pahlavi (accessed May 12, 2025).

Moltke, J. von (2012), "Zur Sache Schätzchen," in N. Grob, H. H. Prinzler and E. Rentschler (eds.), *Neuer Deutscher Film*, 116–22, Stuttgart: Reclam.

Monaco, P. (2003), *History of the American Cinema*, vol. 8: *The Sixties: 1960–1969*, Berkeley: University of California Press.

The Motion Picture Production Code (1956), Available online: https://digitalcollections.oscars.org/digital/collection/p15759coll11/id/10796/ (accessed May 5, 2025).

Naficy, H. (2011), *A Social History of Iranian Cinema*, vol. 2: *The Industrializing Years, 1941–1978*, Durham and London: Duke University Press.

Naficy, H. (2012), *A Social History of Iranian Cinema*, vol. 3: *The Islamicate Period, 1978–1984*, Durham and London: Duke University Press.

Nikazmerad, N. M. (1980), "A Chronological Survey of the Iranian Revolution," *Iranian Studies*, 13 (1/4): 327–68.

O'Neill, A. (2025), "Number of Military Fatalities in All Major Wars Involving the United States from 1775 to 2024," *Statista*, July 30. Available online: https://www.statista.com/statistics/1009819/total-us-military-fatalities-in-american-wars-1775-present/ (accessed September 5, 2025).

Osterland, M. (1970), *Gesellschaftsbilder in Filmen: Eine soziologische Untersuchung des Filmangebots der Jahre 1949 bis 1964*, Stuttgart: Enke.

Pasolini, P. P. (1976), "The Cinema of Poetry," in B. Nichols (ed.), *Movies and Methods*, 542–58, Berkeley: University of California Press.

Peirce, C. S. (1960), *Collected Papers of Charles Sanders Peirce—Vol. I & II*, eds. C. Hartshorne and P. Weiss, Cambridge: The Belknap Press of Harvard University Press.

Pesaran, M. H. (2014), "Economy ix. in the Pahlavi Period," January 16. Available online: https://www.iranicaonline.org/articles/economy-ix/ (accessed May 13, 2025).

Peters, B. (2017), *1977: RAF gegen Bundesrepublik*, Munich: Droemer.

Pfaff, F. (1997), "New African Cinema," *Cinéaste*, 22 (4): 58–9.

Podair, J. and D. Dochuk (2018), *The Routledge History of the Twentieth-Century United States*, London and New York: Routledge.

Rancière, J. (2006), *Film Fables*, trans. E. Battista, Oxford and New York: Berg.

Rauscher, J. (2012), "Abschied von Gestern," in N. Grob, H. H. Prinzler and E. Rentschler (eds.), *Neuer Deutscher Film*, 107–15, Stuttgart: Reclam.

Ray, R. B. (1985), *A Certain Tendency of the Hollywood Cinema, 1930–1980*, Princeton: Princeton University Press.

Riecke, C. (1998), *Feministische Filmtheorie in der Bundesrepublik Deutschland*, Frankfurt/Main: Peter Lang.

Robertson, R. (2009), *Eisenstein on the Audiovisual: The Montage of Music, Images and Sound in Cinema*, London and New York: I. B. Tauris.

Rorabaugh, W. J. (2015), *American Hippies*, Cambridge: Cambridge University Press.

Sadeghi, A. and F. Rad (2014), "Sociological Analysis of the Formation and Evolution of New Wave of Iranian's Cinema," *The Journal of Sociology Studies*, 7 (24): 35–50.

Sadr, H. R. (2006), *Iranian Cinema: A Political History*, London and New York: I. B. Tauris.

Sage, L. (2006), "Allegory," in P. Childs and R. Fowler (eds.), *The Routledge Dictionary of Literary Terms*, 4–5, London and New York: Routledge.

Sannwald, D. (2012), "Neun Leben hat die Katze," in N. Grob, H. H. Prinzler and E. Rentschler (eds.), *Neuer Deutscher Film*, 123–9, Stuttgart: Reclam.

Sarkar Farshi, G. (2021), "Wim Wenders Roadmovie-Trilogie als Evolution der Filmsemantik. Eine Annäherung mit Niklas Luhmann," in J. Glasenapp (ed.), *Kontinuität im Wandel: Begegnungen mit dem Filmemacher Wim Wenders*, 58–72, Munich: edition text + kritik.

Saussure, F. de (2011), *Course in General Linguistics*, eds. P. Meisel and H. Saussy, trans. W. Baskin, New York: Columbia University Press.

Schatz, T. (1983), *Old Hollywood/New Hollywood: Ritual, Art, and Industry*, Ann Arbor: UMI Research Press.

Schneider, M. (1986), *Demokratie in Gefahr? Der Konflikt um die Notstandsgesetze: Sozialdemokratie, Gewerkschaften und intellektueller Protest (1958–1968)*, Bonn: Verl. Neue Gesellschaft.

Schrecker, E. (1998), *Many Are the Crimes: McCarthyism in America*, Boston, New York, Toronto, and London: Little, Brown and Company.

Schroer, M., ed. (2008), *Gesellschaft im Film*, Konstanz: UVK-Verl.-Ges.

"Siebzehntes Gesetz zur Ergänzung des Grundgesetzes vom 24. Juni 1968," (1969), in D. Sterzel (ed.), *Kritik der Notstandsgesetze: Kommentierungen; mit dem Text der Notstandsverfassung*, 210–19, Frankfurt/Main: Suhrkamp.

Smith, T. W. (1990), "A Report: The Sexual Revolution?," *The Public Opinion Quarterly*, 54 (3): 415–35.

Sobchack, V. C. (1992), *The Address of the Eye: A Phenomenology of Film Experience*, Princeton: Princeton University Press.

Souriau, É. (1951), "La structure de l'univers filmique et le vocabulaire de la filmologie," *Revue Internationale de Filmologie*, 2 (7/8): 231–40.

Spector, R. H. (2022), "Vietnam War," *Britannica*, August 24. Available online: https://www.britannica.com/event/Vietnam-War (accessed November 2, 2022).

Spencer-Brown, G. (1972), *Laws of Form*, New York: E. P. Dutton.

Steil, B. (2018), *The Marshall Plan: Dawn of the Cold War*, Oxford: Oxford University Press.

Sterzel, D., ed. (1969), *Kritik der Notstandsgesetze: Kommentierungen; mit dem Text der Notstandsverfassung*, Frankfurt/Main: Suhrkamp.

Stiglegger, M. (2016), "Aus den Gräben, aus den Trümmern … Der deutsche Kriegsfilm der 1950er Jahre," in C. Dillmann and O. Möller (eds.), *Geliebt und Verdrängt: Das Kino der jungen Bundesrepublik Deutschland von 1949 bis 1963*, 268–81, Frankfurt/Main: Deutsches Filminstitut—DIF e.V.

Talebinejad, A. (2018), *The New Wave Book: Or, How the Iranian Cinema Was Transformed*, Tehran: Cheshmeh.

Tauber, F. (2016), "Heimatfilm. Versuch der Systematisierung eines Phänomens," in C. Dillmann and O. Möller (eds.), *Geliebt und Verdrängt: Das Kino der jungen Bundesrepublik Deutschland von 1949 bis 1963*, 102–7, Frankfurt/Main: Deutsches Filminstitut—DIF e.V.

Teague, W. (2024), "Resistance/Rise: Iranian Student Activism in the Late 1970s US," *History of Education Quarterly*, 64 (4): 510–37.

Trimborn, J. (1998), *Der deutsche Heimatfilm der fünfziger Jahre: Motive, Symbole und Handlungsmuster*, Cologne: Leppin.

Truffaut, F. (2022), "A Certain Tendency in French Cinema," in P. Graham and G. Vincendeau (eds.), *The French New Wave: Critical Landmarks*, 38–59, London: Bloomsbury Publishing.

Tudor, A. (2014), *Image and Influence: Studies in the Sociology of Film*, London and New York: Routledge.

Turner, F. J. (1893), "The Significance of the Frontier in American History," *The Internet Archive*. Available online: https://archive.org/details/significanceoffr00turnuoft/mode/2up (accessed May 9, 2025).

Vogt, G. (2009), "Außenseiter? Avantgarde- und Stadtfilm—Ottomar Domnicks *Jonas* (1957) und Herbert Veselys *Das Brot der frühen Jahre* (1962)," in H. Segeberg (ed.), *Das Kino der Bundesrepublik Deutschland als Kulturindustrie (1950–1962)*, 433–69, Munich: Wilhelm Fink.

Wedel, M. (2012), "Genealogie einer Bewegung: Die DOC-59-Gruppe und die Anfänge des Neuen deutschen Films," in R. Eue and L. H. Gass (eds.), *Provokation der Wirklichkeit: Das Oberhausener Manifest und die Folgen*, 161–7, Munich: edition text + kritik.

Wehler, H.-U. (2008), *Deutsche Gesellschaftsgeschichte*, vol. 5: *Bundesrepublik und DDR, 1949–1990*, Munich: C. H. Beck.

Williams, R. (2004), *Television: Technology and Cultural Form*, London and New York: Routledge.

Winter, R. (1992), *Filmsoziologie: Eine Einführung in das Verhältnis von Film, Kultur und Gesellschaft*, Munich: Quintessenz.

Filmography

- *08/15* (1954), [Film] Dir. Paul May, West Germany: KG Divina-Film GmbH.
- *2001: A Space Odyssey* (1968), [Film] Dir. Stanley Kubrick, USA: Metro-Goldwyn-Mayer, Inc.
- *Abschied von gestern* (Yesterday Girl; 1966), [Film] Dir. Alexander Kluge, West Germany: Kairos-Film, Independent Film GmbH.
- *Achtung! Feind hört mit!* (Beware! The Enemy Is Listening!; 1940), [Film] Dir. Arthur Maria Rabenalt, Germany: Terra-Filmkunst.
- *Alice in den Städten* (Alice in the Cities; 1974), [Film] Dir. Wim Wenders, West Germany: Filmverlag der Autoren.
- *Angst essen Seele auf* (Ali: Fear Eats the Soul; 1974), [Film] Dir. Rainer Werner Fassbinder, West Germany: Tango-Film.
- *Annie Hall* (1977), [Film] Dir. Woody Allen, USA: United Artists Corp.
- *Apocalypse Now* (1979), [Film] Dir. Francis Ford Coppola, USA: Omni Zoetrope.
- *Ārāmish dar ḥoẓūr-i dīgarān* (Tranquility in the Presence of Others; 1972), [Film] Dir. Nasser Taqvai, Iran: Haft Film Organization, Telfilm.
- *Asrār-i ganj-i darrah-yi jinnī* (The Ghost Valley's Treasure Mysteries; 1974), [Film] Dir. Ebrahim Golestan, Iran: Studio Golestan.
- *Au hasard Balthazar* (Balthazar, at Random; 1966), [Film] Dir. Robert Bresson, France & Sweden: Argos Films, Parc Film, Athos Films, SF Studios, Swedish Film Institute (SFI).
- *Baal* (1970), [Film] Dir. Volker Schlöndorff, West Germany: Hallelujah-Film GmbH, Hessischer Rundfunk (HR), Bayerischer Rundfunk.
- *Bād mā rā khvāhad burd* (The Wind Will Carry Us; 1999), [Film] Dir. Abbas Kiarostami, Iran: MK2 Productions.
- *Barque sortant du port* (Boat Leaving the Port; 1895), [Film] Dir. Louis Lumière, France: Société Lumière.
- *Behinderte Zukunft* (Handicapped Future; 1971), [Film] Dir. Werner Herzog, West Germany: Werner Herzog Filmproduktion.
- *Berlin Alexanderplatz* (1980), [TV Mini Series] Dir. Rainer Werner Fassbinder, West Germany: Bavaria Atelier GmbH.
- *The Big Sleep* (1946), [Film] Dir. Howard Hawks, USA: Warner Bros.
- *Bonnie and Clyde* (1967), [Film] Dir. Arthur Penn, USA: Tatira-Hiller Productions.

- *Chinatown* (1974), [Film] Dir. Roman Polanski, USA: Long Road Productions, Inc.
- *Cleopatra* (1963), [Film] Dir. Joseph L. Mankiewicz & Rouben Mamoulian, USA: Twentieth Century-Fox Film Productions, MCL Films, Walwa Films.
- *Close-Up* (1990), [Film] Dir. Abbas Kiarostami, Iran: Institute for the Intellectual Development of Children and Adolescents.
- *The Conversation* (1974), [Film] Dir. Francis Ford Coppola, USA: The Directors Company.
- *Dā'ī jān Nāpil'un* (My Uncle Napoleon; 1976), [TV Series] Dir. Nasser Taqvai, Iran: National Iranian Television.
- *Das Cabinet des Dr. Caligari* (The Cabinet of Dr. Caligari; 1920), [Film] Dir. Robert Wiene, Germany: Decla Film-Gesellschaft.
- *Dāyirah-yi mīnā* (The Cycle; 1975), [Film] Dir. Dariush Mehrjui, Iran: Telfilm, Iranian Cinema and Film Company, Ministry of Culture and Arts, Iranian Cinematographers Cooperative Company.
- *Der Beginn aller Schrecken ist Liebe* (Love Is the Beginning of All Terror; 1984), [Film] Dir. Helke Sander, West Germany: Provobis Gesellschaft für Film und Fernsehen mbH, Helke Sander Filmproduktion, Zweites Deutsches Fernsehen (ZDF).
- *Der junge Törless* (Young Törless; 1966), [Film] Dir. Volker Schlöndorff, West Germany: Franz Seitz Filmproduktion, Nouvelles Éditions de Films S.A.
- *Der subjektive Faktor* (The Subjective Factor; 1981), [Film] Dir. Helke Sander, West Germany: Helke Sander Filmproduktion GmbH, Zweites Deutsches Fernsehen (ZDF).
- *Des Teufels General* (The Devil's General; 1955), [Film] Dir. Helmut Käutner, West Germany: Real-Film GmbH.
- *Despair—Eine Reise ins Licht* (Despair; 1978), [Film] Dir. Rainer Werner Fassbinder, West Germany: NF Geria II Film GmbH, Westdeutscher Rundfunk (WDR).
- *Deutschland, bleiche Mutter* (Germany, Pale Mother; 1980), [Film] Dir. Helma Sanders-Brahms, West Germany: Helma Sanders-Brahms Filmproduktion, Literarisches Colloquium Berlin e.V., Westdeutscher Rundfunk (WDR).
- *Deutschland im Herbst* (Germany in Autumn; 1978), [Film] Dir. Alf Brustellin, Hans Peter Cloos, Rainer Werner Fassbinder, Alexander Kluge, Maximiliane Mainka, Edgar Reitz, Katja Rupé, Volker Schlöndorff, Peter Schubert, and Bernhard Sinkel, West Germany: Project Filmproduktion im Filmverlag der Autoren GmbH, Kairos Film,

Hallelujah-Film GmbH, ABS-Filmproduktion, Tango-Film, and Edgar Reitz Filmproduktion GmbH.

- *Die allseitig reduzierte Persönlichkeit—Redupers* (The Allround Reduced Personality—ReduPers; 1977), [Film] Dir. Helke Sander, West Germany: Basis-Film Verleih GmbH, Zweites Deutsches Fernsehen (ZDF).
- *Die Artisten in der Zirkuskuppel: ratlos* (Artists Under the Big Top: Perplexed; 1968), [Film] Dir. Alexander Kluge, West Germany: Kairos-Film.
- *Die Blechtrommel* (The Tin Drum; 1979), [Film] Dir. Volker Schlöndorff, West Germany: Franz Seitz Filmproduktion, Bioskop-Film GmbH, Artemis Filmgesellschaft mbH, Hallelujah-Film GmbH, Argos Films S.A., Hessischer Rundfunk (HR), GGB Gesellschaft für Geschäftsführung und Beteiligung GmbH & Co.
- *Die bleierne Zeit* (Marianne and Juliane; 1981), [Film] Dir. Margarethe von Trotta, West Germany: Bioskop-Film GmbH, Sender Freies Berlin (SFB).
- *Die Brücke* (The Bridge; 1959), [Film] Dir. Bernhard Wicki, West Germany: Fono-Film GmbH.
- *Die dritte Generation* (The Third Generation; 1979), [Film] Dir. Rainer Werner Fassbinder, West Germany: Pro-ject Filmproduktion im Filmverlag der Autoren GmbH, Tango-Film Produktion.
- *Die Ehe der Maria Braun* (The Marriage of Maria Braun; 1979), [Film] Dir. Rainer Werner Fassbinder, West Germany: Albatros Produktion, Trio-Film GmbH, Westdeutscher Rundfunk (WDR).
- *Die Fliegenden Ärzte von Ostafrika* (The Flying Doctors of East Africa; 1970), [Film] Dir. Werner Herzog, West Germany: Werner Herzog Filmproduktion.
- *Die große Ekstase des Bildschnitzers Steiner* (The Great Ecstasy of Woodcarver Steiner; 1974), [Film] Dir. Werner Herzog, West Germany: Werner Herzog Filmproduktion.
- *Die Parallelstraße* (The Parallel Street; 1962), [Film] Dir. Ferdinand Khittl, West Germany: Gesellschaft für bildende Filme (GBF).
- *Die Sehnsucht der Veronika Voss* (Veronika Voss; 1982), [Film] Dir. Rainer Werner Fassbinder, West Germany: Süddeutscher Rundfunk (SDR), Laura Film GmbH, Trio-Film GmbH, Tango-Film, Maran Film GmbH & Co. KG, Rialto Film GmbH.
- *Die unbezähmbare Leni Peickert* (The Indomitable Leni Peickert; 1969), [Film] Dir. Alexander Kluge, West Germany: Kairos Film.
- *Die verlorene Ehre der Katharina Blum* (The Lost Honor of Katharina Blum; 1975), [Film] Dir. Volker Schlöndorff & Margarethe von

Trotta, West Germany: Bioskop-Film GmbH, Paramount-Orion Film Production GmbH, Westdeutscher Rundfunk (WDR).

- *The Drowning Pool* (1975), [Film] Dir. Stuart Rosenberg, USA: First Artists.
- *Easy Rider* (1969), [Film] Dir. Dennis Hopper, USA: The Pando Company, Inc., Raybert Productions, Inc.
- *Es* (It; 1965), [Film] Dir. Ulrich Schamoni, West Germany: Horst Manfred Adloff-Filmproduktion.
- *The Exorcist* (1973), [Film] Dir. William Friedkin, USA: Hoya Productions, Inc.
- *Falsche Bewegung* (The Wrong Move; 1975), [Film] Dir. Wim Wenders, West Germany: Westdeutscher Rundfunk (WDR), Solaris-Film- und Fernsehproduktion, Genée–Eichinger oHG.
- *Fata Morgana* (1971), [Film] Dir. Werner Herzog, West Germany: Werner Herzog Filmproduktion.
- *Fontane Effi Briest* (Effi Briest; 1974), [Film] Dir. Rainer Werner Fassbinder, West Germany: Tango-Film.
- *Ganj-i Qārūn* (Qārūn's Treasure; 1965), [Film] Dir. Siamak Yasami, Iran: Puriya Film.
- *Gāv* (The Cow; 1969), [Film] Dir. Dariush Mehrjui, Iran: Studio Misaqieh.
- *Gavazn-hā* (The Deer; 1974), [Film] Dir. Masoud Kimiai, Iran: Studio Misaqieh.
- *Gelegenheitsarbeit einer Sklavin* (Part-Time Work of a Domestic Slave; 1973), [Film] Dir. Alexander Kluge, West Germany: Kairos Film.
- *Gharībah va mih* (The Stranger and the Fog; 1974), [Film] Dir. Bahram Beyzai, Iran: Rex Cinema and Theater Company.
- *The Godfather* (1972), [Film] Dir. Francis Ford Coppola, USA: Paramount Pictures Corp., Alfran Productions, Inc.
- *The Godfather Part II* (1974), [Film] Dir. Francis Ford Coppola, USA: The Coppola Company.
- *The Graduate* (1967), [Film] Dir. Mike Nichols, USA: Lawrence Turman, Inc.
- *Grün ist die Heide* (The Heath Is Green; 1951), [Film] Dir. Hans Deppe, West Germany: Berolina-Film GmbH.
- *Hāmūn* (1989), [Film] Dir. Dariush Mehrjui, Iran: Pakhshiran.
- *Händler der vier Jahreszeiten* (The Merchant of Four Seasons; 1971), [Film] Dir. Rainer Werner Fassbinder, West Germany: Tango-Film, Zweites Deutsches Fernsehen (ZDF).

- *Herrenpartie* (Destination Death; 1964), [Film] Dir. Wolfgang Staudte, West Germany: Neue Municher Lichtspielkunst GmbH (Neue Emelka), Avala Film.
- *Herz aus Glas* (Heart of Glass; 1976), [Film] Dir. Werner Herzog, West Germany: Werner Herzog Filmproduktion.
- *Ijārah nishīn-hā* (The Tenants; 1986), [Film] Dir. Dariush Mehrjui, Iran: Pakhshiran.
- *Im Lauf der Zeit* (Kings of the Road; 1976), [Film] Dir. Wim Wenders, West Germany: Wim Wenders Produktion.
- *In Gefahr und größter Not bringt der Mittelweg den Tod* (In Danger and Deep Distress, the Middleway Spells Certain Death; 1974), [Film] Dir. Alexander Kluge & Edgar Reitz, West Germany: Kairos-Film, RK-Film.
- *Jagdszenen aus Niederbayern* (Hunting Scenes from Bavaria; 1969), [Film] Dir. Peter Fleischmann, West Germany: Houwer-Film, Film- und Fernsehproduktion (München).
- *Je vous aime* (I Love You; 1891), [Film] Dir. Georges Demenÿ, France: Georges Demenÿ.
- *Jonas* (1957), [Film] Dir. Ottomar Domnick, West Germany: Dr. Ottomar Domnick Verlag und Film.
- *Junūb-i shahr* (South of the City; 1958), [Film] Dir. Farrokh Ghaffari, Iran: Iran Nama Studio.
- *Katz und Maus* (Cat and Mouse; 1967), [Film] Dir. Hansjürgen Pohland, West Germany: modern art film gmbh.
- *Khānah sīyāh ast* (The House Is Black; 1961), [Film] Dir. Forugh Farrokhzad, Iran: Studio Golestan.
- *Khānah-yi dūst kujāst?* (Where Is the Friend's House?; 1987), [Film] Dir. Abbas Kiarostami, Iran: Institute for the Intellectual Development of Children and Adolescents.
- *Khisht va āyinah* (Brick and Mirror; 1964), [Film] Dir. Ebrahim Golestan, Iran: Studio Golestan.
- *Khudāḥāfiẓ rafīq* (Goodbye Friend; 1971), [Film] Dir. Amir Naderi, Iran: Aryana Film.
- *Kinder für dieses System—Paragraph 218* (Children for This System—Paragraph 218; 1973), [Film] Dir. Ingrid Oppermann & Gardi Deppe, West Germany: Deutsche Film- und Fernsehakademie Berlin (dffb).
- *Kinder sind keine Rinder* (Children Are Not Cattle; 1969), [Film] Dir. Helke Sander, West Germany: Deutsche Film- und Fernsehakademie Berlin GmbH (dffb).
- *Kokusai Himitsu Keisatsu: Kagi No Kagi* (International Secret Police: Key of Keys; 1965), [Film] Dir. Senkichi Taniguchi, Japan: Toho.

- *La Montagne Infidèle* (The Unfaithful Mountain; 1923), [Film] Dir. Jean Epstein, France: Pathé Frères.
- *La Notte* (The Night; 1961), [Film] Dir. Michelangelo Antonioni, Italy: Nepi Film, Sofitedip, Silver Film.
- *La Soufrière—Warten auf eine unausweichliche Katastrophe* (La Soufrière—Waiting for an Inevitable Disaster; 1977), [Film] Dir. Werner Herzog, West Germany: Werner Herzog Filmproduktion.
- *Land des Schweigens und der Dunkelheit* (Land of Silence and Darkness; 1971), [Film] Dir. Werner Herzog, West Germany: Werner Herzog Filmproduktion.
- *L'Arrivée d'un train en gare de La Ciotat* (Arrival of a Train at La Ciotat; 1896), [Film] Dir. Auguste & Louis Lumière, France: Société Lumière.
- *The Late Show* (1977), [Film] Dir. Robert Benton, USA: Lion's Gate Films.
- *Lawrence of Arabia* (1962), [Film] Dir. David Lean, USA: Horizon Pictures.
- *Le Sang d'un Poète* (The Blood of a Poet; 1932), [Film] Dir. Jean Cocteau, France: The Criterion Collection.
- *Lebenszeichen* (Signs of Life; 1968), [Film] Dir. Werner Herzog, West Germany: Werner Herzog Filmproduktion.
- *Liebe ist kälter als der Tod* (Love Is Colder Than Death; 1969), [Film] Dir. Rainer Werner Fassbinder, West Germany: Antiteater-X-Film GmbH.
- *Lili Marleen* (1980), [Film] Dir. Rainer Werner Fassbinder, West Germany: Rialto Film Preben Philipsen GmbH & Co. KG, Roxy Film GmbH & Co. KG, Bayerischer Rundfunk (BR), CIP Filmproduktionsgesellschaft mbH.
- *Liylā* (1997), [Film] Dir. Dariush Mehrjui, Iran: Farabi Cinema Foundation.
- *Lola* (1981), [Film] Dir. Rainer Werner Fassbinder, West Germany: Westdeutscher Rundfunk (WDR), Rialto Film Preben Philipsen GmbH & Co. KG, Trio-Film GmbH.
- *The Long Goodbye* (1973), [Film] Dir. Robert Altman, USA: Lion's Gate Fims, Inc.
- *M* (1931), [Film] Dir. Fritz Lang, Germany: Nero-Film AG.
- *Macht die Pille frei?* (Does the Pill Liberate Women?; 1973), [Film] Dir. Helke Sander & Sarah Schumann, West Germany: Norddeutscher Rundfunk (NDR).
- *Mahlzeiten* (Lust for Love; 1967), [Film] Dir. Edgar Reitz, West Germany: Edgar Reitz Filmproduktion GmbH.
- *M*A*S*H* (1970), [Film] Dir. Robert Altman, USA: Aspen Productions.

- *Mashq-i shab* (Homework; 1989), [Film] Dir. Abbas Kiarostami, Iran: Institute for the Intellectual Development of Children and Adolescents.
- *Midnight Cowboy* (1969), [Film] Dir. John Schlesinger, USA: Jerome Hellman Productions.
- *Mughul-hā* (The Mongols; 1973), [Film] Dir. Parviz Kimiavi, Iran: National Iranian Radio and Television (NIRT), Telfilm.
- *Musāfir* (The Traveler; 1974), [Film] Dir. Abbas Kiarostami, Iran: Institute for the Intellectual Development of Children and Adolescents.
- *Nachts, wenn der Teufel kam* (The Devil Strikes at Night; 1957), [Film] Dir. Robert Siodmak, West Germany: KG Divina-Film GmbH.
- *Nākhudā Khurshīd* (Captain Khurshīd; 1987), [Film] Dir. Nasser Taqvai, Iran: Nasser Taqvai Cultural and Art Institute, Pakhshiran, Peyman Film Group.
- *Nashville* (1975), [Film] Dir. Robert Altman, USA: ABC Entertainment, Inc.
- *Nāṣir-al-dīn Shāh āktur-i sīnamā* (Once Upon a Time, Cinema; 1992), [Film] Dir. Mohsen Makhmalbaf, Iran: Jozan Film.
- *Neun Leben hat die Katze* (The Cat Has Nine Lives; 1968), [Film] Dir. Ula Stöckl, West Germany: Filmproduktion Ula Stöckl, Thomas Mauch, Arri Film & TV.
- *Nicht Versöhnt* (Not Reconciled; 1966), [Film] Dir. Jean-Marie Straub, West Germany: Straub-Huillet.
- *Night Moves* (1975), [Film] Dir. Arthur Penn, USA: Hiller Productions, Ltd.—Layton.
- *Night of the Living Dead* (1968), [Film] Dir. George A. Romero, USA: Image Ten.
- *One Flew over the Cuckoo's Nest* (1975), [Film] Dir. Milos Forman, USA: Fantasy Films.
- *§ 218 und was wir dagegen haben* (Paragraph 218 and What We Have Against It; 1977), [Film] Dir. Sabine Eckhard, West Germany: Hochschule für Fernsehen und Film Munich (HFF).
- *The Parallax View* (1974), [Film] Dir. Alan J. Pakula, USA: Doubleday Productions, Inc., Gus Productions, Inc., Harbor Productions, Inc.
- *Parī* (1995), [Film] Dir. Dariush Mehrjui, Iran: Farabi Cinema Foundation.
- *Qiyṣar* (1969), [Film] Dir. Masoud Kimiai, Iran: Aryana Film.
- *Ragbār* (Downpour; 1972), [Film] Dir. Bahram Beyzai, Iran: Panorama Film Organization.
- *The Rain People* (1969), [Film] Dir. Francis Ford Coppola, USA: American Zoetrope.

- *Rhythmus 21* (Rhythm 21; 1921), [Film] Dir. Hans Richter, Germany: Hans Richter.
- *Rhythmus 23* (Rhythm 23; 1923), [Film] Dir. Hans Richter, Germany: Hans Richter.
- *Rosa Luxemburg* (1986), [Film] Dir. Margarethe von Trotta, West Germany: Bioskop-Film GmbH, Pro-ject Filmproduktion im Filmverlag der Autoren GmbH, Ziegler Film GmbH & Co. KG, Bärenfilm-Produktion GmbH.
- *Rosen für den Staatsanwalt* (Roses for the Prosecutor; 1959), [Film] Dir. Wolfgang Staudte, West Germany: Kurt Ulrich Film GmbH.
- *Salām sīnamā* (Hello Cinema; 1995), [Film] Dir. Mohsen Makhmalbaf, Iran: Amun, Sabz Film House, Makhmalbaf Film House.
- *Sāyah-hā-yi boland-i bād* (Tall Shadows of the Wind; 1979), [Film] Dir. Bahman Farmanara, Iran: Iran Biograph, Ministry of Culture and Arts, Telfilm.
- *Sāzdahanī* (Harmonica; 1974), [Film] Dir. Amir Naderi, Iran: Institute for the Intellectual Development of Children and Adolescents.
- *Schwarzer Kies* (Black Gravel; 1961), [Film] Dir. Helmut Käutner, West Germany: Universum-Film AG (UFA).
- *Schwarzwaldmädel* (The Black Forest Girl; 1950), [Film] Dir. Hans Deppe, West Germany: Berolina-Film GmbH.
- *Schwestern oder Die Balance des Glücks* (Sisters, or the Balance of Happiness; 1979), [Film] Dir. Margarethe von Trotta, West Germany: Bioskop-Film GmbH & Co. Produktionsteam KG, Westdeutscher Rundfunk (WDR).
- *Shab-i Qūzī* (Night of the Hunchback; 1965), [Film] Dir. Farrokh Ghaffari, Iran: Iran Nama Studio.
- *The Sound of Music* (1965), [Film] Dir. Robert Wise, USA: Argyle Enterprises, Inc., Twentieth Century-Fox Film Corp.
- *Spartacus* (1960), [Film] Dir. Stanley Kubrick, USA: Bryna Productions.
- *Sulṭān-i qalb-hā* (King of Hearts; 1968), [Film] Dir. Mohammad Ali Fardin, Iran: Studio Misaqieh.
- *Ṭabīʿat-i bījān* (Still Life; 1976), [Film] Dir. Sohrab Shahid-Saless, Iran: Progressive Filmmakers Cooperative, Telfilm.
- *Tangsīr* (1973), [Film] Dir. Amir Naderi, Iran: Payam Film Organization.
- *Taxi Driver* (1976), [Film] Dir. Martin Scorsese, USA: Bill/Phillips Productions, Italo-Judeo.
- *Three Days of the Condor* (1975), [Film] Dir. Sydney Pollack, USA: Dino De Laurentiis Corp., Wildwood Enterprises, Inc.
- *Thunderbolt and Lightfoot* (1974), [Film] Dir. Michael Cimino, USA: The Malpaso Company.

- *Two-Lane Blacktop* (1971), [Film] Dir. Monte Hellman, USA: Universal Pictures, Michael Laughlin Enterprises, Inc.
- *Un Chien Andalou* (An Andalusian Dog; 1929), [Film] Dir. Luis Buñuel, France: Ursulines Film Studio and Studio-28.
- *Ūn shab kih bārūn ūmad* (The Night It Rained; 1967), [Film] Dir. Kamran Shirdel, Iran: Ministry of Culture and Arts.
- *Vanishing Point* (1971), [Film] Dir. Richard C. Sarafian, USA: Cupid Productions.
- *Vertigo* (1958), [Film] Dir. Alfred Hitchcock, USA: Alfred J. Hitchcock Productions.
- *What's Up, Tiger Lily?* (1966), [Film] Dir. Woody Allen, USA: Benedict Pictures, Toho Co.
- *The Wild Bunch* (1969), [Film] Dir. Sam Peckinpah, USA: Phil Feldman Productions, Inc., Warner Bros.–Seven Arts, Inc.
- *Wir Wunderkinder* (Aren't We Wonderful?; 1958), [Film] Dir. Kurt Hoffmann, West Germany: Filmaufbau GmbH.
- *Yik ittifāq-i sādah* (A Simple Event; 1974), [Film] Dir. Sohrab Shahid-Saless, Iran: Central Film Office of the Iranian Ministry of Culture and Arts.
- *Zabriskie Point* (1970), [Film] Dir. Michelangelo Antonioni, USA: Metro-Goldwyn-Mayer, Inc., Trianon Productions.
- *Zīr-i dirakhtān-i ziytūn* (Through the Olive Trees; 1994), [Film] Dir. Abbas Kiarostami, Iran: Abbas Kiarostami Productions, CiBy 2000, Farabi Cinema Foundation.
- *Zur Sache Schätzchen* (Go for It, Baby; 1968), [Film] Dir. May Spils, West Germany: Peter Schamoni Filmproduktion.

Index

www.ingramcontent.com/pod-product-compliance
Ingram Content Group UK Ltd.
Pitfield, Milton Keynes, MK11 3LW, UK
UKHW020206290926
15470UKWH00001B/26

9 798765 125106